D1545723

THE NATURALISTIC
INNER-CITY NOVEL IN AMERICA

THE NATURALISTIC
INNER-CITY NOVEL IN AMERICA

ENCOUNTERS WITH THE FAT MAN

JAMES R. GILES

UNIVERSITY OF SOUTH CAROLINA PRESS

Published in Columbia, South Carolina, by the
University of South Carolina Press

Manufactured in the United States of America

99 98 97 96 95   5 4 3 2 1

Library of Congress Cataloging-in-Publication Data

Giles, James Richard, 1937–
    The naturalistic inner-city novel in America : encounters with the
fat man / James R. Giles.
      p. cm
    Includes bibliographical references and index.
    ISBN 1–57003–046–4
    1. American fiction—20th century—History and criticism.
2. Naturalism in literature. 3. Inner cities in literature.
4. Narration (Rhetoric) I. Title.
PS374.N29G55 1995
813'.50912–dc20   95–4340
                                                          CIP

To the students in my graduate seminars in American urban naturalism during the past four years

Contents

Acknowledgments

As is true for any meaningful project, this book would not have been possible without the support and advice of a number of people. Among them are:

All the teachers, in the classroom and out, who have contributed to my understanding of literary naturalism. This list would include, but not be limited to, Joseph Jones, Gordon Mills, Charles C. Walcutt, Maxwell Geismar, Warren French, John H. Conder, June Howard, Don Graham, Lee Clark Mitchell, Richard Lehan, Blanche Gelfant, Michael Davitt Bell, Earle Labor, and, of course, Donald Pizer;

Joe McElrath, Jesse Crisler, Dick Davison, Don Cook and all the Frank Norris Society people, who have been a treasured scholarly community for me over the past few years;

My department chair, James I. Miller, who provided me with a PC and a printer for this project;

Two colleagues, Rose Marie Burwell and James Mellar, who patiently taught me how to use the PC, and more important than that, have generously encouraged and supported my work throughout most of my career;

Karen Blaser, Dolores Henry, and Jonie Barshinger from the Northern Illinois University College of Liberal Arts Manuscript Services Office who simply made the writing of this book possible;

The staff of the Founders Memorial Library at Northern Illinois University, especially those in Interlibrary Loan Service;

Matt Bruccoli, whose support for this project was crucial; and Wanda H. Giles, whose life with me and editing of the manuscript have created a much better book.

THE NATURALISTIC
INNER-CITY NOVEL IN AMERICA

Introduction

In a seminal 1984 essay Richard Lehan argues for a new emphasis in studying literary naturalism. Instead of the traditional "scientific" approach to defining naturalism, Lehan advocates that the genre should be viewed from a "social/historical/cultural" perspective. He points out that scholars have traditionally used, as the starting point for their discussions of literary naturalism, Zola's argument, outlined in the 1880 essay *Le Roman experimental*, that the "best novelist was an empirical observer rather than an imaginative creator."[1] Zola's fascination with scientific theory led him to believe that "man was finally a product of his heredity and environment, that life was simply the play of temperaments in a social context, subject to human observation and description" (529). Because of the pervasive influence of Zola, the concept of determinism has commonly been assumed as a defining, if not *the* defining, characteristic of naturalism. In the 1890s Frank Norris, more than any of his contemporaries, saw himself as a kind of evangelist charged with spreading the doctrine of naturalism in America, and Norris unapologetically described himself as "the Boy Zola." It has seemed natural, then, to assume that Norris and his fellow American naturalists in the late nineteenth century were committed to following Zola's example in all ways, including emphasizing the centrality of determinism to their fiction.

Lehan believes, however, that, in France, England, *and* the United States, literary naturalism was much more the result of dramatic social and economic change than of such innovations in scientific thought as the concept of determinism. Specifically, he argues that literary naturalism "cannot be divorced from a historical process that saw the movement from a landed to an urban economy, saw the rise of the bourgeoisie and at least the appearance of republican government, and that was ultimately founded upon empirical/scientific assumptions about reality which, coupled with the new technology and power of money (new banks and credit theories), led to the

1

impulse of nationalism and the rise of empire" (530). Lehan's idea that naturalism was, in part, a response to the emergence of a thirst for empire working in conjunction with a new technological capitalism is accurate at least as far as the United States is concerned. One need only look at the more blatantly imperialist and racist writings of Norris and, despite his socialism, Jack London to see this. In fact, Norris and London inspired a fiction that can best be described as the naturalistic and imperialistic epic that has been a mainstay of twentieth-century American popular literature and culture.

Still, one must point out that, as Charles C. Walcutt and other critics have emphasized, turn-of-the-century literary naturalism often reveals a reformist impulse that runs counter to its racist, imperialist emphasis. It, in fact, anticipates, and has obvious ties with, the muckraking school of journalism, which emerged in the first decade of the twentieth century. Harvey Swados has identified the "core" of these journalists who militantly advocated the reform of corrupt U.S. capitalist society as being Ida Tarbell, Lincoln Steffens, Ray Stannard Baker, Charles Edward Russell, and Upton Sinclair.[2] He further identifies Henry Demarest Lloyd's *Wealth against Commonwealth* (1894) as a major influence on these reformers and defines their three central themes as "corruption in government, the irresponsibility of the trusts, and the exploitation of women and children" (20–21).

Norris, London, and Crane each did his own journalistic muckraking. Among other things Frank Norris, commissioned by *Everybody's Magazine*, reported on the living conditions in the strike-torn mining region surrounding Wilkes-Barre, Pennsylvania. London's commitment to socialism inspired a significant body of writing devoted to exposing economic and political corruption and oppression. Arrested for vagrancy in Niagara Falls, New York, in 1894 and subsequently spending thirty days in the Erie County Penitentiary, London, in 1907, described his experience in "the pen" for *Cosmopolitan*. Moreover, in addition to his 1903 exposé on the slum-infested East End of London, *The People of the Abyss*, he published, two years later, a collection of militant socialist essays, *War of the Classes*. As Christopher Benfey points out in his excellent recent biography of Crane, *The Double Life of Stephen Crane*, the author of *Maggie: A Girl of the Streets* (1893) not only wrote exposés of prostitution and New York City slum life for the New York *Journal* but, in fact, made news through his ambiguous role in the 1896 Dora Clark scandal.[3]

What is of special relevance to this volume, however, is Lehan's treatment of American literary naturalism as a response to the emergence of an urban culture. More obviously than any other literary genre, naturalism in

2

the United States was, in part, a literary reaction to the rise of the city. Moreover, since the 1890s U.S. practitioners of naturalism have been fascinated with the ghetto, the foreign-seeming inner city. In her influential study of American literary naturalism, *Form and History in American Literary Naturalism*, June Howard investigates the ways in which the new immigrants crowded into the inner cities of America were transformed by "native," middle-class Americans into personifications of the "Other." She points out that late-nineteenth- and early-twentieth-century popular literature in the United States reveals an obsession with a perceived threat to order and stability and that the source of this threat was assumed to be "the increasingly visible and largely immigrant industrial proletariat living in the cities."[4] For the "native" middle class the danger was intensified by a shift in the nature of immigration in the 1880s: the new American arrivals tended to come from southern and eastern Europe and seemed even more "foreign" than earlier immigrants. Thus, the slum emerged as a frightening new entity for the middle class. In a recent book Gerd Hurm emphasizes that the growth of the U.S. city in the last half of the nineteenth century was always chaotic and economically driven and points out a central paradox in the response within the United States to these intimidating new urban centers: "This expansion of the national system of cities had occurred unimpeded and almost unaccompanied by political or cultural adjustments. Cities boomed, driven by a compound of forces beyond the grip of single municipal governments. Although developments in cities, such as the growing dissatisfaction in slums, were perceived as a threat to stability, reforms on the federal, state, and local level remained inadequate."[5]

Frank Norris, Stephen Crane, and Jack London, Howard argues, shared with middle-class America a vision of the slum or ghetto, the enforced residence for these foreign newcomers, as dangerous and exotic "internal colonies": "The creature who defines humanity by negation and represents a problematical area of existence is imagined as living not outside the bounds of human society, not in the wilderness (where images of the American Indian as savage placed it), but within the very walls of the civilized city" (80). It is worth noting that, next to Zola, Frank Norris was most influenced by Rudyard Kipling. The newly emerging ghetto, with its foreign population, served Norris in much the same way that India did Kipling. For Norris the inner city was a place in which the "civilized" Anglo-Saxon might encounter exotic "lesser breeds." Thus, his protagonist McTeague, a displaced frontiersman, finds himself in a bewildering realm inhabited by Zerkows and Maria Macapas.

For Norris and, somehow less obviously, his fellow late-nineteenth-century naturalists, the inner city ceased to be primarily a physical place; it assumed, instead, the status of an idea or image of something sordid and dangerous as well as mysterious and fascinating. More or less subconsciously, it came to represent for them the world of the Other, the unacknowledged and repressed areas of middle-class sexuality and the subconscious. For Norris, Crane, and London, a trio of young male writers in nineteenth-century Victorian America, the inhabitants of the urban ghetto personified a complex set of conflicting but interrelated ideas and values. In fact, the foreign slum dweller represented to them something quite close to what Toni Morrison has recently suggested that the African American has represented, historically, for white Americans.

In *Playing in the Dark: Whiteness and the Literary Imagination* Morrison argues that white Americans have traditionally posited for themselves the illusion of stability and certainty, while transferring to African Americans a capacity for experimentation, freedom, and license. The amorphous and ever-shifting identity that white Americans ascribe to African Americans can be either a positive or a negative concept or, in fact, positive *and* negative. She believes: "Images of blackness can be evil *and* protective, rebellious *and* forgiving, fearful *and* desirable—all of the self-contradictory features of the self. Whiteness, alone, is mute, meaningless, unfathomable, pointless, frozen, veiled, curtained, dreaded, senseless, implacable. Or so our writers seem to say."[6] Similarly, for Norris, Crane, and London the established and thus respectable middle class represented the "frozen" void, while the exotic slum dweller personified the frightening uncertainty of the human potentiality for extreme and contradictory behavior.

Perhaps the most memorable appearance of the slum dweller as a personification of the sordid reality of the inner city, as well as of the human capacity for grotesque and "evil" actions, is that of the "fat man" who appears in the original 1893 version of chapter 17 of Crane's *Maggie: A Girl of the Streets*. Crane describes this character in such sordid and even gruesome detail that, especially in the context of a chapter that can only be read surrealistically, it is difficult to accept him as an actual living being. He seems, instead, to be a projection of Crane's worst fantasy of existence in the Bowery, of the unimaginably evil forces that must either corrupt or destroy everyone in their way, even such a pure flower as Maggie. Significantly, the fat man is deleted from the 1896 revision of the novel. It is as if, having gone this far in giving his dark vision of the kind of being who inhabited the Bowery a living shape, Crane immediately wished to retreat from what he

4

had done. In large part *because* of this attempted supression, the fat man, the embodiment of the submerged horrors of the ghetto, immediately begins to haunt the American naturalistic inner-city novel. Crane, Norris, and London adopted variations on two related forms of narrative perspective, the tour guide and the explorer of the exotic, to shield their narrators from too close contact with such a horror.

As the twentieth century progressed, the repressed fat man forced his way to the surface of the naturalistic ghetto novel and, while sometimes grotesque and even savage, turned out to be undeniably human, though with experiences and agendas different from those of the respectable middle class. When the naturalistic ethnic novel merged with the Marxist proletarian novel, characters who had suffered from genuinely horrible economic oppression, but were nevertheless as unmistakably human as any middle-class reader, assumed center stage in American inner-city fiction. Richard Wright's Bigger Thomas is certainly a frightening young man, but he is even more a frightened character, forced to live a life of impossible repression and self-denial. After World War II the American inner-city novel became less overtly political and depicted an increasingly bleak vision of existence. Nelson Algren, Hubert Selby, John Rechy, and Joyce Carol Oates collectively brought this fictional genre to its present maturity and sophistication. My aim in this study is to investigate the evolution of the inner-city novel, from Stephen Crane's *Maggie* to Joyce Carol Oates's 1969 novel *them*.

Before beginning this investigation, it is useful to review the most significant critical and scholarly discussions of naturalism in American fiction. Specifically, I want to look at the scholarly debate concerning two central questions about the genre—what definitively identifies a work of fiction as naturalism and how long the movement continued to be viable in the United States. For Richard Lehan naturalism was a literary response to the sweeping social, economic, and cultural revolution of the last half of the nineteenth century and, most specifically, a response to the emergence of the city and of urban technology; as the reality of life in the new America became known and familiar, naturalism ceased to be a viable literary form. To Lehan, Upton Sinclair was "perhaps the last of the pure naturalists . . . and the closest to being an American Zola" (556).

Charles C. Walcutt, whose 1956 book, *American Literary Naturalism*, still remains the most thorough study of the genre as it was understood and practiced by American writers, asserts that it enjoyed a considerably longer life span. He discusses John Steinbeck, Ernest Hemingway, John Dos Passos, and a small group of post–World War II novelists, including Nelson Algren, as being, at least to some degree, practitioners of naturalism. In his study Walcutt is especially concerned with defending naturalism against a common criticism—the argument that, because it stresses determinism, it disallows free will and hence the possibility of moral choice; thus, it presents an unnaturally limited and distorted vision of human life. In attempting to establish a definition of the genre, he initially points out that, "whereas one authority describes it as an extreme form of romanticism, another counters that it is the rigorous application of scientific method to the novel. When others say it is desperate, pessimistic determinism, they are answered by those who insist that it is an optimistic affirmation of man's freedom and progress."[7]

Walcutt then asserts that all of these conflicting views about naturalism are correct and that "the Beast . . . is indeed of a Protean slipperiness" (3). For him the protean nature of naturalism is the inevitable result of its origins and ancestry; the movement grew, he believes, out of the legacy of American transcendentalism:

> When [the] mainstream of transcendentalism divides, as it does toward the end of the nineteenth century, it produces two rivers of thought. One, the approach to Spirit through intuition, nourishes idealism, progressivism, and social radicalism. The other, the approach to Nature through science, plunges into the dark canyon of mechanistic determinism. The one is rebellious, the other pessimistic; the one ardent, the other fatal; the one acknowledges will, the other denies it. (vii–viii)

If one accepts this analysis, the naturalistic inner-city novel belongs overwhelmingly to Walcutt's second "river"; such novels in the United States are indeed "dark" and "pessimistic," and they do at least severely limit the characters' free will. It should be said, however, that Walcutt finds a way to allow a kind of free will even to this kind of fiction. He grants to even the most pessimistic examples of this school of fiction a reformist emphasis, the faith that, while the characters lack the freedom of choice, the author and reader do not and that the author can thus convince the reader of the need for social reform. It should be obvious that the original "scientific" definitions of naturalism were, from the first, inadequate to describe the complexity of the U.S. version of this genre.

In fact, prior to a review of subsequent scholarly discussions of American literary naturalism, it should be emphasized that Walcutt and later commentators are indebted in no small degree to Frank Norris for their own freedom to ascribe a protean quality to *American* literary naturalism. In his chosen role as the American Zola, Norris wrote a few essays defining Zolaesque naturalism. One of these esaays, entitled "Zola as a Romantic Writer," contains this analysis of the French novelist's aesthetic:

> To be noted of M. Zola we must leave the rank and the file, either run to the forefront of the marching world, or fall by the roadway; we must separate ourselves; we must become individual, unique. The naturalist takes no note of common people, common in so far as their interests, their lives, and the things that occur in them are common, are ordinary. Terrible things must happen to the characters of the naturalistic tale. They must be twisted from the ordinary, wrenched out of the quiet, uneventful round of every-day life, and flung into the throes of a vast and terrible drama that works itself out in unleashed passions, in blood, and in sudden death.[8]

For Norris American naturalism needed to follow the example of Zola and be a form of writing that stressed the "terrible" things that happen to individuals who do not belong to the "ordinary" mainstream of life. It should be, he believed, a distinctly "romantic" writing depicting uncommon individuals suffering extreme and unusual fates. Obviously, the newly emerging U.S. inner city represented a perfect example of an appropriate environment for this kind of writing.

As Donald Pizer points out, Norris's definition of naturalism was just as important for what it left out as for what it said: "What is particularly absorbing in this definition is that it is limited entirely to subject matter and method. It does not mention materialistic determinism or any other philosophical idea, and this differs from the philosophical orientation of Zola's discussions of naturalism and of those by modern critics of the movement."[9] The young American writer appeared to respond to Zola's fiction, and especially to *L'Assommoir*, much more than to *Le Roman experimental*. At any rate, he did not posit determinism or any other scientific or philosophical concept as the determining aspect of literary naturalism. The philosophical void left Walcutt and later scholars and critics room to explore the protean nature of naturalism.

Donald Pizer, the most perceptive and important critic of American literary naturalism since Walcutt at least, has also emphasized that in the

United States the genre has been constantly evolving, rather than static and fixed:

> American naturalism . . . has been largely a movement character-
> ized by similarities in material and method, not by philosophical co-
> herence. And perhaps this very absence of a philosophical center to
> the movement has been one of the primary reasons for its continuing
> strength in this country, unlike its decline in Europe. For writers as
> different as Dreiser and Crane, or Farrell and Faulkner, have responded
> to the exciting possibilities of a combination of romantic grandioseness,
> detailed verisimilitude, and didactic sensationalism, and yet, like
> Norris, have been able to shape these possibilities into works express-
> ing most of all their own distinctive temperaments.[10]

Again, in no small part because of the ironically liberating philosophical void at the center of American naturalism (largely the legacy of Norris),
it was always impossible to define the U.S. variety of this literary mode as
being completely defined by an external biological or environmental determinism. Throughout the twentieth century the kind of determinism manifested in American literature became increasingly more internal and
universal, and thus more frightening, than any manifestation of Darwinian
scientific theory.

In *Realism and Naturalism in Nineteenth-Century American Literature* Pizer
thus proposes "a modified definition of late nineteenth-century American
naturalism." He argues that, in its initial phase, American naturalism was
distinguished by "two tensions or contradictions" that together came "to
constitute the theme and form of the naturalistic novel." The first tension
results from a contradiction between "the subject matter of the naturalistic
novel and the concept of man which emerges from this subject matter."
While the characters in naturalistic fiction come from "the lower middle
class or the lower class" and are usually "poor," "uneducated," and "unso-
phisticated," they prove capable of "heroic or adventurous" actions that
"culminate in desperate moments and violent death." Thus, the naturalist
finds in "commonplace and unheroic" individuals and environments "the
extraordinary and excessive in human nature."[11]

Pizer's second tension relates specifically to the charge that determinism prevents moral complexity in naturalistic fiction. He argues that, while
the naturalistic writer "often describes his characters as though they are
conditioned and controlled by environment, heredity, instinct, or chance . . .

he also suggests a compensating humanistic value in his characters or their fates which affirms the significance of the individual and of his life" (11). This thesis that the naturalist's denial of free will to his or her fictional characters does not negate a belief in their essential human dignity and worth seems valid. In *Maggie: A Girl of the Streets* Stephen Crane creates a world in which a degraded environment controls and destroys human beings, but he still persists in idealizing Maggie as a rare and beautiful product of the tenements. In *McTeague* (1899), perhaps the most thoroughly deterministic of all American naturalistic novels, Frank Norris repeatedly emphasizes the stupidity and impotent will of his central character, but it is nevertheless clear that he cares a great deal for his doomed and helpless dentist.

Pizer's 1982 study *Twentieth-Century American Literary Naturalism: An Interpretation* is an invaluable analysis of what Walcutt called the protean nature of American naturalism and of the ongoing relevance of such fiction. Pizer's thesis here is that, in the twentieth century, naturalism merged with other philosophical and scientific ideas and thus retained its viability. By focusing on James T. Farrell's *Studs Lonigan* (1932–35), John Dos Passos's *U.S.A.* (1937), and John Steinbeck's *The Grapes of Wrath* (1939), Pizer demonstrates the way in which, during the 1930s, the naturalistic tradition incorporated ideas and impulses from Marxism and Freudianism to produce a new kind of fiction which seemed exactly right for the decade of the Great Depression.

Just as perceptive is his analysis of the parallels that certain novelists of the 1940s and 1950s saw between naturalism and French existentialism:

> The felt sense of many American intellectuals of the post-war period that communal life and belief were chaotic and irrational and that the only valid source of value lay in individual experience echoes both American naturalism of the 1890s and contemporary French existentialism. For these post-war American writers, the supernatural support of ethical systems was not only unproven but patently untrue; there remained only the individual seeking meaning in his own immediate experience. Thus there occurs a retreat both in existentialism and in the American naturalistic novel of the late 1940s and early 1950s from systems, codes, and structures in any form—from the army and its hierarchy of power, from the family, and from the "adoptive" mechanisms of society. And thus there is the centering of an oblique value on the seeker of the unknown in himself and life.[12]

Pizer specifically discusses Norman Mailer's *Naked and the Dead* (1948), William Styron's *Lie Down in Darkness* (1951), and Saul Bellow's *Adventures of Augie March* (1953) as examples of the ways in which naturalism was not, as usually claimed, invalidated by the emergence of existentialism but was, in fact, revitalized by it. He might even have extended his argument—it now seems clear that such postwar naturalists as Nelson Algren and Hubert Selby felt a sense of recognition with the existential concept of "the Absurd," especially as it was articulated by Céline. Pizer concludes his study with a reference to such "harbingers" of the continuing viability and relevance of American literary naturalism as the fiction of Joyce Carol Oates, the "documentary narrative" as exemplified by Truman Capote's *In Cold Blood* (1965), and the 1978 film *The Deer Hunter* (152). The example of Oates is certainly on target, at least in terms of her early novels and stories, most clearly of all the 1969 novel *them*. Martin Scorsese, who directed *Mean Streets* (1973), *Taxi Driver* (1976), and *Raging Bull* (1980), among others, is an important contemporary director of naturalistic-existential films.

In addition to Howard's and Pizer's, other recent critical studies have brought fresh insights to the continuing discussion and definition of American naturalism. In a 1982 essay Don Graham discusses a number of contemporary naturalists not normally included in treatments of the genre—for example, Algren, Selby, and Willard Motley—and provides a useful way of approaching characterization in naturalistic fiction: "The circumscribed consciousness seems to be the essential element in the naturalistic portrayal of character." He points out that, while "the naturalistic consciousness" may be "capable of some growth," it is "nothing like . . . the supersensitive Jamesian moral seismographs."[13] In fact, the sharp discrepancy between the levels of awareness of author and reader on one hand and fictional characters on the other is perhaps the major source of irony in naturalistic fiction. Walter Benn Michaels's 1987 "new historicist" analysis, *The Gold Standard and the Logic of Naturalism*, treats late-nineteenth-century literary naturalism in the United States as the product of a period of economic unrest and uncertainty. Michaels is especially perceptive in his discussions of Theodore Dreiser.

In *Determined Fictions* Lee Clark Mitchell persuasively refutes the standard charge that late-nineteenth-century American literary naturalism was marred by awkward narrative style by demonstrating the ways in which the literary styles of Crane, Norris, Dreiser, and London contribute to their depictions of deterministic fictional environments. John J. Conder, in *Naturalism in American Fiction: The Classic Phase*, creatively reconciles the doctrine of determinism with the need to posit at least some degree of faith in moral choice. He develops the idea that a kind of "Hobbesian freedom" is central to late-nineteenth-century American literary naturalism. Characters existing in this body of fiction have the freedom to choose in all ways that are not predetermined by heredity and environment, Conder argues. Thus, a severely limited range of choice does exist for them. For example, Crane's Maggie does choose the bartender Pete, but only because he *is* the closest thing to a knight to be found in the degraded environment in which she is trapped.

In sharp contrast to these earlier critics, Michael Davitt Bell, in a new study of American literary realism and naturalism, denies that the late-nineteenth-century writers commonly described as naturalists constitute a separate literary school based on a shared philosophical position. The novels of Frank Norris, Stephen Crane, and Theodore Dreiser represent instead, he argues, contrasting responses to a post–Civil War American ideal based on a clear binary opposition between a "masculine" reality and a "feminine" art. This ideal, according to Bell, was initially expounded by William Dean Howells and then, in an extreme manner, by Norris.[14]

Several of the critical insights discussed here are central to my study of twentieth-century naturalistic ghetto fiction. The novels constituting my focus of study consistently depict determined environments. Michael Gold, Richard Wright, Nelson Algren, Hubert Selby, John Rechy, and Joyce Carol Oates create worlds in which choice is severely limited and often not possible at all. In part for that very reason, it is a matter of enormous significance when it is possible. The inner city is an obvious metaphor for naturalistic determinism; it is a relatively small and vulnerable physical space, often literally surrounded by the rest of the city with all its accumulated wealth and power. Gold's *Jews without Money* (1930) and Algren's *Man with the Golden Arm* (1949) are classic examples of what Blanche H. Gelfant has labeled "the ecological" urban novel that limits its setting to "a small spatial unit within the city."[15] For the characters in these two works the city outside the ghettos in which they live might as well be a continent away. Wright's Bigger Thomas, Selby's Tralala, and Oates's Jules Wendall suffer because they do cross the line separating their ghetto worlds from the affluent areas of the city. Finally, John Rechy's "city of night" is not a single city but the gay subcultures of New York, Chicago, Los Angeles, San Francisco, and New Orleans which merge into one surrealistic universe largely because straight and respectable middle-class U.S. society needs to pretend that they don't exist at all.

Walcutt's and especially Pizer's insights into the protean nature of American literary naturalism offered invaluable assistance to my analysis of the merger of the naturalistic tradition with the existential concept of "the Absurd." Conder's theory of "the Hobbesian choice" in literary naturalism seems relevant, in different ways, to all the works that I have examined.

Before discussing individually the six contemporary novels that constitute the heart of my study, I want to discuss the unique narrative perspectives that control three classic turn-of- the-century American naturalistic works, Stephen Crane's *Maggie: A Girl of the Streets*, Frank Norris's *McTeague*, and Jack London's *People of the Abyss*. The perspectives from which these works are written define them as examples of an "innocent" stage of American inner-city naturalism. It was largely by transcending the narrative perspective at work in these early novels that Gold, Wright, Algren, Selby, Rechy, and Oates gradually made manifest the presence of Stephen Crane's fat man and thus created a "sophisticated" ghetto naturalism.

The central consideration here is one of narrative distance. In the three works of Crane, Norris, and London, the narrator, in different ways and to varying degrees, maintains a narrative distance from his characters and settings. In fact, this distance or detachment has been seen as a defining characteristic of late-nineteenth-century American naturalism.[16] The six twentieth-century novels I have chosen represent key variations on this traditional detachment. In Gold's *Jews without Money* and Wright's *Native Son* (1940) narrative voice virtually merges with character and setting and thereby depicts predominantly sympathetic, and unmistakably human, central characters. Algren's narrator consciously steps back from character, and the fictional figures that dominate *The Man with the Golden Arm* are often absurd and even grotesque; their humanness is overtly and even militantly affirmed.

Among these six works the merging of narrative voice with character and setting is most complete in Hubert Selby's *Last Exit to Brooklyn* (1957). Selby's narrator frequently submerges his voice in the psychopathic collective consciousness of a Brooklyn street gang whose repeated acts of violence result from a complex combination of economic powerlessness, "the sin of pride," and sexual rage. Selby's characters represent the full emergence of Crane's suppressed fat man, the personification of the horror of the inner city, and they are indeed grotesque and frightening. Yet, as with Algren's creations, their essential humanness cannot be denied. In contrast, John Rechy's narrator in *City of Night* (1963), with one significant exception, finds nothing inherently grotesque about the homosexual characters that he encounters in his journey through America's gay subculture. He is always aware, however, that, to mainstream society, these usually tormented individuals are, as practitioners of "sexual deviance," the precise embodiments of the sordid and grotesque. Finally, narration in Joyce Carol Oates's *them* (1969) attains a level of sophistication new to the American naturalistic inner-city novel.[17] Oates, in a metafictional manner, has one of her characters lecture "Joyce Carol Oates" on the impossibility of the middle-class novelist understanding the lives of those individuals trapped in urban slums. Thus, in *them* narrative distance appears, but *only* appears, to return to the detachment of Crane, thereby creating something of a circular effect.

Finally, I want to stress that this book is not intended to be an exhaustive investigation of the American naturalistic ghetto novel. One can easily think of twentieth-century works at least resembling this genre of fiction which I do not discuss in detail: Ann Petry's *The Street* (1946), Willard Motley's *Knock on Any Door* (1947), Thomas McGrath's *This Coffin Has No Handles* (1988), and William Kennedy's *Ironweed* (1983) obviously come to mind. In this book I analyze six novels that exemplify the evolution, after the pioneering works of Frank Norris, Stephen Crane, and Jack London, of this sophisticated variety of the naturalistic inner-city novel. Thus, Gold's *Jews without Money* and Wright's *Native Son* illustrate the merger of the naturalistic urban protest novel with the tradition of the American ethnic novel (at least to some degree, James T. Farrell's *Studs Lonigan* represents the same phenomenon). Similarly, the works by Algren, Selby, Rechy, and Oates that I discuss exemplify the merging of the naturalistic ghetto novel with French existentialism, especially the concept of the Absurd.

Notes

1. Richard Lehan, "American Literary Naturalism: The French Connection," *Nineteenth-Century Fiction* 38 (March 1984): 529.

2. Harvey Swados, "Introduction," *Years of Conscience: The Muckrakers* (Cleveland: World, 1962), 19.

3. Christopher Benfey, *The Double Life of Stephen Crane: A Biography* (New York: Knopf, 1992), 171–81.

4. June Howard, *Form and History in American Literary Naturalism* (Chapel Hill: University of North Carolina Press, 1985), 75–76.

5. Gerd Hurm, *Fragmented Urban Images: The American City in Modern Fiction from Stephen Crane to Thomas Pynchon* (New York: Peter Lang, 1991), 26.

6. Toni Morrison, *Playing in the Dark: Whiteness and the Literary Imagination* (Cambridge: Harvard University Press, 1992), 59.

7. Charles Child Walcutt, *American Literary Naturalism: A Divided Stream* (Minneapolis: University of Minnesota Press, 1956), 3.

8. Frank Norris, "Zola as a Romantic Writer," *The Literary Criticism of Frank Norris*, ed. Donald Pizer (Austin: University of Texas Press, 1964), 71–72.

9. Pizer, *Literary Criticism of Frank Norris*, 69.

10. Donald Pizer, "Frank Norris's Definition of Naturalism," *Realism and Naturalism in Nineteenth-Century American Literature* (Carbondale: Southern Illinois University Press, 1984), 110–11.

11. Donald Pizer, "Late Nineteenth-Century American Naturalism," *Realism and Naturalism*, 10–11.

12. Donald Pizer, *Twentieth-Century American Literary Naturalism: An Interpretation* (Carbondale: Southern Illinois University Press, 1982), 87.

13. Don Graham, "Naturalism in American Fiction: A Status Report," *Studies in American Fiction* 10 (Spring 1982): 10.

14. Michael Davitt Bell, *The Problem of American Realism: Studies in the Cultural History of a Literary Idea* (Chicago: University of Chicago Press, 1993).

15. Blanche H. Gelfant, *The American City Novel* (Norman: University of Oklahoma Press, 1954), 12–13.

16. See, for instance, Howard, *Form and History*.

17. For the concepts and terminology of "innocent" and "sophisticated" narration, I am indebted to James M. Mellard, *The Exploded Form: The Modernist Novel in America* (Urbana: University of Illinois Press, 1980).

Chapter 1

Tour Guides and Explorers

When his 1893 novel *Maggie: A Girl of the Streets* was republished in 1896, Stephen Crane made a number of relatively minor changes in the text. Joseph Katz has described the purpose of Crane's revisions as being "to temper the brutality and to subdue the coarseness of the original."[1] Katz's interpretation of the controlling purpose behind Crane's 1896 minor revisions may also explain the deletion of a crucial paragraph from the original version of the novel. In chapter 17, which describes Maggie's final descent into the horror of prostitution, she encounters, in the 1893 edition, an especially grotesque figure:

> When almost to the river the girl saw a great figure. On going forward she perceived it to be a huge fat man in torn and greasy garments. His grey hair straggled down over his forehead. His small, bleared eyes, sparkling from amidst great rolls of red fat, swept eagerly over the girl's upturned face. He laughed, his brown, disordered teeth gleaming under a grey, grizzled moustache from which beer-drops dripped. His whole body gently quivered and shook like that of a dead jelly fish. Chuckling and leering, he followed the girl of the crimson legions.[2]

Crane's description of this figure is so exaggerated that one must wonder if he intended it to be a surrealistic apparition instead of a real man. This possibility seems especially worth considering in light of the fact that chapter 17, as several critics have pointed out, can only be read as a surrealistic, rather than a realistic, account of Maggie's ultimate destruction and degradation.[3] Whether the fat man is viewed as an actual figure or an apparition, his deletion from the 1896 edition has dramatically affected the way that the novel has traditionally been read. In this later edition Maggie is last seen walking alone through "the blackness of the final block" toward "the deathly black hue of the river."[4] Maggie's aloneness here, the prevailing imagery of blackness, and the fact that the prostitute is not heard from again in the novel until the concluding chapter in which her death is announced have pointed to a long prevailing interpretation that her death is the result of suicide.[5] In an interesting feminist reading of the novel, Elisabeth Panttaja argues that the original 1893 version, in which Maggie is last seen not alone but in the company of the fat man, can be read in quite a different way: "It is possible to infer that the fat man murdered Maggie. . . . It is he who takes actions: he laughs, he stares, he leers, and in the end he follows her right up to the lapping, oily water."[6] Maggie's possible death by murder rather than suicide, Panttaja believes, does much to restore the dignity that, according to Donald B. Gibson, she forfeits through her extreme passivity.[7]

If one views the fat man as a surrealistic apparition, the end of chapter 17 can be read as a symbolic, telescoped account of Maggie's immersion into, and destruction by, the grim horror of prostitution. However one reads this climactic moment in the novel, the fact that Maggie's last companion does not appear in the revised version of his novel has had significant consequences for *Maggie: A Girl of the Streets* and for the development of the American naturalistic inner-city novel as well. In fact, in its twentieth-century evolution, the naturalistic American ghetto novel has not only revived Crane's fat man as metaphor for the uncensored reality of the inner city but sought to give him a voice as well.

It is important to remember that the Stephen Crane of *Maggie*, like the Frank Norris of *McTeague* and other turn-of-the-century literary investigators of the new U.S. city, viewed the startling phenomenon of the ghetto from the perspective of an outsider. June Howard argues, in fact, that the emergence of an inner city populated almost exclusively by immigrants resulted in a psychological crisis for the middle-class, Anglo-Saxon pioneers of American literary naturalism. Howard believes that this internal crisis was intensified by a fundamental shift in the pattern of American immigration: "The shift in the mid-eighties from immigration from northern and western to immigration from southern and eastern Europe exacerbated the tensions of this process of proletarianization" (85). The "foreignness" of this new wave of immigrants, she asserts, made the inner city seem, to the early American naturalists, a strange, but fascinating, place: "The terrain [the urban characters in turn-of-the-century American naturalistic novels] inhabit is imagined as squalid, dangerous, but exciting, even exotic, for it is alien territory to the middle-class perspective . . . from which it is explored" (88). The "exotic" dialects of the immigrants from southern and eastern Europe added significantly to the sense of foreignness which the ghetto communicated to the middle-class writer, according to Howard (106), and the early naturalists came to view the inner city as an exotic "internal colony" existing conveniently next door to recognizably American terrain (173).

Their vision of the ghetto as an internal colony caused the naturalists to adopt a distinctive narrative perspective when writing about it. Moreover, this perspective was inherited, in part, from nonliterary sources; this was especially true for the Stephen Crane of *Maggie*, who, as Alan Trachtenberg has shown, was almost certainly influenced by Jacob Riis's pioneering work of photojournalism, *How the Other Half Lives* (1890).[8] Trachtenberg argues that, in *Maggie* and in his early New York newspaper sketches, Crane was attempting to transcend the tourist-guide narrative perspective that Riis had used in his exposé of New York City tenement life.

How the Other Half Lives

Riis had personally experienced the horror of life as a new immigrant to the United States. He left his native Denmark in 1870 at the age of twenty-one to find work in the new world. Initially, he found only hunger and unemployment and was driven to the brink of suicide; it was not until 1877 that he found work as a police reporter for the New York *Tribune*. While working for the paper, he began investigating in words and photographs the nightmarish world of the city's tenements.[9] Despite this personal experience, or perhaps because of it, Riis, in *How the Other Half Lives*, addresses his readers as a guide taking them on a tour of the tenement district. Having known firsthand the prejudice directed against the immigrant, Riis apparently decided that he could best retain the sympathies of middle-class readers by establishing a fictional bond with them. Thus, his narrator usually speaks as one whose essential experience is no different than theirs except that he possesses unique and privileged insight into the lives of the tenement dwellers.

Moreover, he often shares this insight with a conscious delicacy, as, for instance, when he verbally "shows" his readers the inside of a tenement room:

Be a little careful, please! The hall is dark and you might stumble over the children pitching pennies back there. Not that it would hurt them; kicks and cuffs are their daily diet. They have little else. Here where the hall turns and dives into utter darkness is a step, and another, another. A flight of stairs. You can feel your way, if you cannot see it. Close? Yes! . . . That was a woman filling her pail by the hydrant you just bumped into. The sinks are in the hallway, that all the tenants may have access—and all be poisoned alike by their summer stenches. . . . But the saloon, whose open door you passed in the hall, is always there. The smell of it has followed you up.[10]

Riis directly follows his reference to the saloon with a melodramatic account of a child dying of measles ("that short, hacking cough, that tiny helpless wail—what do they mean?") and the reaction of its parents. The father is particularly bitter: "Hush, Mary! If we cannot keep the baby, need we complain—such as we?" (38). One suspects that Riis did not choose the mother's name accidentally. If fact, a motif that can best be described as Christian melodrama runs throughout his book. His narrator assumes that the middle-class readers share with him a Christian morality and, there-fore, must feel pity and outrage at his graphic descriptions of the sufferings of the inner-city poor.

This calculated tone allows the narrator to identity the villains who are responsible for the existence of the tenements without losing the sympathy of the middle-class reader. The tenement "system," he says, is "the evil offspring of public neglect and private greed" (1). Therefore, he continues, "the remedy that shall be an effective answer to the coming appeal for jus-tice must proceed from the public conscience. . . . The greed of capital that wrought the evil must itself undo it, as far as it can now be undone" (2). Once awakened by *How the Other Half Lives*, the Christian conscience of the public—to which the middle-class reader, of course, belongs—will de-mand that restitution be made for the greedy profits accumulated by capi-talist "speculators," in which the reader has presumably not shared. Such a "Christian" appeal is obviously less threatening than any overtly socialistic message would be.

Further, in order to awaken the conscience of his reader, Riis's narrator is justified in documenting the brutality of tenement life. He is especially graphic when describing the notorious section known as "the Bend":

> Hucksters and peddlers' carts make two rows of booths in the street itself, and along the houses is still another—a perpetual market doing a very lively trade in its own queer staples, found nowhere on Ameri-can ground save in "the Bend." Two old hags, camping on the pave-ment, are dispensing stale bread, baked not in loaves, but in the shape of big wreaths like exaggerated crullers, out of bags of dirty bedtick. There is no use disguising the fact: they look like and they probably are old mattresses mustered into service under the pressure of a rush of trade. (50)

18

Riis's message, of course, is that not only the "queer staples" but also an environment like the Bend is found nowhere else "on American ground." Life there is defined above all by brutal and degrading struggle. Later, when recounting his experience in accompanying the police on a raid of "stalebeer dives," Riis's narrator explains, "I went along as a kind of war correspondent" (61). What he finds there is a horror from which the middle-class reader is sheltered: "Grouped about a beerkeg that was propped on the wreck of a broken chair, a foul and ragged host of men and women, on boxes, benches, and stools. . . . In the centre of the group a sallow, wrinkled hag, evidently the ruler of the feast, dealt out the hideous stuff" (61). A temperance plea runs throughout *How the Other Half Lives*, and Riis's narrator consistently emphasizes the ugly and sordid in his descriptions of drinking in the tenement district.

The temperance message is one key aspect of the Christian melodrama in Riis's book, but this theme is most overt in the narrator's descriptions of the tenement children and young people:

> To [the tenement world] come the young with their restless yearnings, perhaps to pass on the threshold one of the daughters of sin, driven to the tenement by the police when they raided her den, sallying forth in silks and fine attire after her day of idleness. These in their coarse garments—girls with the love of youth for beautiful things, with this hard life before them—who shall save them from the tempter? Down in the street the saloon, always bright and gay, gathering to itself all the cheer of the block, beckons the boys. (124)

The narrator's point, of course, is that, barring social reform inspired by the newly aware and concerned middle-class reader combined with a freshly awakened Christian sensibility within the tenements, the girls, in order to escape the "hard life before them," will inevitably yield to "the tempter" and the boys will seek out the "cheer" of the saloon. It is not at all difficult to see in the prostitute, wrapped "in silks and fine attire," the still innocent girls "with the love of youth for beautiful things" and the boys drawn to the saloon prototypes for Crane's Nell, Maggie, and Jimmie.

In a chapter entitled "The Problem of the Children" Riis's narrator again seems to anticipate Crane's Jimmie in his description of the almost inevitable fate of the tenement boy: "Home, the greatest factor of all in the training of the young, means nothing to him but a pigeonhole in a coop along with so many other human animals. . . . The result is the rough young savage, familiar from the street" (138). Homeless boys in the ghetto not infrequently become the exotic creatures that Riis, in a later chapter, labels "Street Arabs": "The Street Arab has all the faults and all the virtues of the lawless life he leads. Vagabond that he is, acknowledging no authority and owing no allegiance to anybody or anything, with his grimy fist raised against society whenever it tries to coerce him, he is as bright and sharp as the weasel, which, among all the predatory beasts, he most resembles" (153). In Riis's book the Street Arab is associated with the primitive danger of the predatory beast as well as with the exotic appeal of the Arabian "sheik."

Such racist stereotyping runs throughout *How the Other Half Lives* and must have afforded Riis's turn-of-the-century Anglo-Saxon readers a note of comforting familiarity. For instance, Riis's narrator begins his discussion of "The Italian in New York" in this way:

> Certainly a picturesque, if not very tidy, element has been added to the population in the "assisted" Italian immigrant who claims so large a share of public attention, partly because he keeps coming at such a tremendous rate, but chiefly because he elects to stay in New York, or near enough for it to serve as his base of operations, and here promptly reproduces conditions of destitution and disorder which, set in the frame-work of Mediterranean exuberance, are the delight of the art-ist, but in a matter-of-fact American community become its danger and reproach. The reproduction is made easier in New York because he finds the material ready to hand in the worst of the slum tene-ments, but where it is not he soon reduces what he does find to his own level, if allowed to follow his natural bent. (43)

Riis was writing, above all, to those who resided in the "matter-of-fact American communities" of the city, and in this passage his narrator deliber-ately disassociates himself from those "artists" who were stimulated by the exotic appeal of "Mediterranean exuberance." Consciously or not, Riis, in *How the Other Half Lives*, often seems to be trying to have it both ways—emphasizing the exciting foreignness of eastern and southern immigrants while distancing himself from any appeal that might emanate from that same foreignness. Nine years later Frank Norris, in *McTeague*, would em-brace, even if condescendingly, the dangerous exoticism of the most for-eign immigrants.

It is not only the Italian immigrant who suffers from stereotyping at the hands of Riis's narrator. The chapter entitled "Jewtown," contains this comment: "Thrift is the watchword of Jewtown, as of its people the world over. It is at once its strength and its fatal weakness, its cardinal virtue and its foul disgrace. . . . Money is [the Jew's] God" (86). Here again Riis's narrator is expressing a sentiment that would have been endorsed by more than one of the early American naturalists; one remembers, for instance, Norris's sinister and avaricious Polish-Jewish ragpicker, Zerkow. Such anti-Semitism was, of course, also prevalent in most "matter-of-fact American communities." But it is the Chinese immigrant who receives the most harsh treatment from Riis's narrator: "There is nothing strong about him, except his passions when aroused. I am convinced that he adopts Christianity, when he adopts it at all, as he puts on American clothes, with what the politicians would call an ulterior motive, some sort of gain in the near prospect—washing, a Christian wife perhaps, anything he happens to rate for the moment above his cherished pigtail" (77). In fact, Riis's narrator does not overlook any of the negative and even criminal patterns of behavior popularly associated with the Chinese in late-nineteenth-century America—opium addiction, white slavery, "Oriental cruelty," dishonest trading, and so forth. He even succeeds in making a vice out of the alleged Chinese propensity for cleanliness: "[The Chinese man] is by nature as clean as the cat, which he resembles in his traits of cruel cunning and savage fury when aroused" (80). Similarly vitriolic antipathy to the Chinese-American immigrant can be found in much of the popular culture of the period and afterward. It is also present in much of the worst writing of the California naturalists Frank Norris and Jack London; who, for instance, could ever forget the subhuman Chinese pirates of Norris's *Moran of the Lady Letty* (1898)?

Like the temperance message and the emphasis upon the fragile purity of the children, this racial stereotyping is an integral part of Riis's Christian melodrama motif. His clear implication is that the more salvageable immigrant children need to be rescued, before it is too late, from such sinister influences as the Italian, the Jew, and the Chinaman by a program of social reform underscored by a distinctly Christian "morality." In the last part of *How the Other Half Lives* Riis's narrator translates such a program into quite practical and more universally humanistic terms; by that point he has, one hopes, already engaged the sympathies of his implied middle-class Anglo-Saxon readers.

The reader is shown, then, a great deal of the horror of New York City tenement life in Riis's book and from a relatively close-up vantage point. Yet the tour-guide perspective of the narrator still keeps him and the reader at a distance from the immigrant characters who cumulatively constitute the subject of the work. One sees the fat man here, but always in the role of social victim or exotic foreigner. Most certainly, one does not hear him speak.

Maggie: A Girl of the Streets

Though it may not be possible to assert with total assurance that *How the Other Half Lives* influenced Stephen Crane's first novel, it seems reasonable to assume that it did. Crane heard Riis lecture on New York City tenement life at Asbury Park, New Jersey, in the summer of 1892 while he was reworking *Maggie*.[11] In his biography of Crane, Christopher Benfey writes: "It was this urban frontier . . . that needed to be opened, scouted, mapped, and named. Guides appeared on the scene, Kit Carsons of the tenements. None was more famous than the reformist journalist and photographer Jacob Riis . . . whom Crane had heard lecture on the Jersey shore."[12] Moreover, Thomas A. Gullason has pointed out some of the more obvious parallels between Riis's and Crane's works. Gullason cites Riis's account of following a young boy carrying a pitcher through the streets on a cold November night and into a saloon, where he interceded and kept the bartender from serving the boy, and Jimmie's "similar errand" for the neighbor woman in *Maggie*. Most important, he emphasizes the need of both Riis and Crane to believe that pure and innocent young girls could exist in spite of their degrading environments.[13] A Riis photograph entitled "Girl of the Tenements" definitively captures the idealized view, shared by both writers, of the young female. In it a girl, approximately eight or nine years old, is standing in front of a wooden structure of some kind. Her right arm rests on a large board that extends outward toward her, and her left hand and arm are tucked discreetly behind her back. She is wearing a tattered dress of some rough woolen fabric, and her innocent face stares straight ahead (141). The photograph projects the young girl's innocence and strength but also her vulnerability and virtually certain future destruction. The ragged dress is a badge of her poverty, and the phallic shape of the board on which she is leaning, and which dwarfs her in size, symbolizes her inevitable spiritual rape by the harsh tenement world in which she exists.

The "girl of the tenements" might well be the young Maggie Johnson of Crane's novel. From the first she is terrified by the brutality of her battling alcoholic parents and seems, unlike Jimmie, defenseless against them. Most Crane critics have commented on her romanticism, symbolized by her pathetic attempt to hang the lambrequin and her determination to see the crude, chauvinistic Pete as a "knight." He, of course, begins their courtship with what must be one of the most unromantic advances in literature: "Say, Mag, I'm stuck on yer shape. It's outa sight"(19). Crane's central problem in writing the novel was showing Maggie descending into the pit of prostitution without destroying the reader's image of her innocence and romanticism. He attempts to do this by consistently depicting her as a victim and by narratively distancing himself *and the reader* from her in the climactic chapter 17.

She is victimized not only by her mother, Jimmie, and Pete but also by the cumulative environment of the ghetto. Crane utilizes a device that will be echoed by Dreiser in *Sister Carrie* (1900) and later by Nelson Algren in his first novel, *Somebody in Boots* (1935), to convey the desperately limited nature of her choices in life. His narrator juxtaposes descriptions of Maggie's attraction to the fine clothes of the well-dressed women she passes on the street ("She envied elegance and soft palms") and a detailed account of the sordid "collar and cuff establishment" in which she briefly works: "The air in the collar and cuff establishment strangled her. She knew she was gradually and surely shrivelling in the hot, stuffy room. The begrimed windows rattled incessantly from the passing of elevated trains. The place was filled with a whirl of noises and odors" (25). In a note reminiscent of *How the Other Half Lives* Crane also portrays Maggie as a native "American" oppressed by sordid foreigners.[14] She especially loathes the owner of the sweatshop: "She felt she would love to see somebody entangle their fingers in the oily beard of the fat foreigner who owned the establishment. He was a detestable creature. He wore white socks with low shoes" (25). Her drunken mother regularly pawns what few household items the Johnson family possesses "under the shadows of the three gilt balls, where Hebrews chained them with chains of interest" (26).

Apparently knowing that it would be difficult to sustain this image of Maggie as idealized victim while showing her working as a prostitute, Crane limits his account of her working life to the telescoped chapter 17. From the very opening of this surrealistic chapter, the "girl of the painted cohorts of the city" who is seen plying her trade in a path that descends steadily from the glamor and excitement of the theater district ultimately to "the gloomy districts near the river" seems an altogether different creature from the Maggie encountered previously in the novel. She is initially anything but passive in soliciting customers: "She threw changing glances at men who passed her, giving smiling invitations to men of rural or untaught pattern and usually seeming sedately unconscious of the men with a metropolitan seal upon their faces" (52). It is, of course, possible that, by labeling her with a trite and melodramatic phrase instead of calling her Maggie, Crane's narrator is intending to communicate that her experience has already changed and even depersonalized her. At any rate, she does retreat into passivity when the fat man appears at the end of the chapter in the 1893 version of the novel, giving plausibility to Panttaja's reading of her death as murder. It is almost as if Crane's narrator is wanting to say that, through her "smiling invitations" to the men early in the chapter, "the girl of the crimson legions" evokes the specter of the fat man so that he can mete out an instantaneous punishment. That this interpretation can hardly be reconciled with the novel's earlier picture of Maggie as romantic innocent is perhaps one reason that the fat man, the personification of the grotesque horror of prostitution, is removed from the 1896 edition.

Idealizing Maggie is not the only way that Crane creates narrative distance from his characters. Donald B. Gibson, in fact, argues that Crane accepts the naturalistic concept of determinism so totally that he makes his characters "nothing but" animals, apparently not recognizing that, in so doing, "he relinquishes his prerogative as author to judge them."[15] Gibson further argues that, by attempting to use the doctrine of determinism to remove any moral condemnation from Maggie, Crane introduces confusion and contradiction into his novel: "If Maggie is simply a victim of her environment, then so are all of the other characters and so is the rest of society. Nobody is to blame for anything and we cannot help but cringe when Crane attempts with irony to condemn Maggie's fellow victims" (27).

Whatever one thinks of Gibson's argument about determinism and narrative distance, he is undeniably right in his comment about Crane condemning the other characters through irony. Most obviously, there is the name of Maggie's mother, who is anything but a Madonna figure in the novel. (In *Last Exit to Brooklyn* Hubert Selby, who greatly admires Crane, utilizes a trope of ironic "Marys.") In addition, there is the description by Crane's narrator of Jimmie's moment of sensitivity: "He had, on a certain star-lit evening, said wonderingly and quite reverently: 'Deh moon looks like hell, don't it'" (16). Finally, there is Mary Johnson's concluding declaration, inspired by "the woman in black," of forgiveness for her dead daughter (58). This pervasive irony almost makes Crane's narrator seem one with the novel's fictional environment: he too seems to be looking down and mocking the doomed struggles of the characters.

Mary Johnson's given name and her concluding forgiveness of Maggie are only two examples of the ironic Christian symbolism that runs throughout *Maggie*. Crane, in fact, often seems to be giving an ironic twist to Riis's

Christian melodrama, though his interest lies in shocking respectable middle-class readers into an awareness of their own moral hypocrisy rather than in promoting social reform. One remembers the way in which he inscribed several gift copies of his book: "It is inevitable that you will be greatly shocked by the book, but continue, please, with all possible courage, to the end. For it tries to show that environment is a tremendous thing in the world and frequently shapes lives regardless. If one proves that theory one makes room in Heaven for all sorts of souls, notably an occasional steet girl, who are not confidently expected to be there by many excellent people."[16] Much of the time *Maggie* reads like the work of a brilliant young writer who has deliberately set out to upset the Christian morality of those "excellent people" who might happen to read the book. Donald Pizer argues that Crane intends to demonstrate in the novel the fallacy of the idea that slum dwellers should live by a middle-class morality irrelevant to their social and economic reality.[17]

The narrator's propensity for irony can also be seen in his use of the language of medieval romance and courtly love. Like the ironic Christian symbolism, this trope functions as a means of mocking the novel's characters and, thus, distancing the narrator from them. The reader is well aware that Pete is anything but a knight. The opening scene, in which a young Jimmie is shown in a senseless neighborhood brawl on a gravel pit "for the honor of Rum Alley" (one can hardly miss the ironic juxtaposition of *honor* and *Rum Alley*), is dominated by the language of medieval romance—for example, "the little champion of Rum Alley." The narrator's juxtaposition of this academic language and the crude dialect spoken by the characters is intentionally jarring and dramatically distances him *and the reader* from such illiterate people. Obviously, Maggie, Jimmie, and Pete know little, if anything, about the tradition of medieval chivalry. Clearly, they have taken no medieval literature courses. In contrast, the reader who "gets" the allusions presumably has and senses that he or she has discovered a kindred soul in the narrator.[18] Trachtenberg is correct in his thesis that Crane, in *Maggie*, was attempting to transcend Riis's tour-guide narrative perspective in order to convey "the subjective lives of his characters" (144). We do, after all, have some sense of the internal workings of his fictional creations. Yet the final success of his attempt was severely limited by his determined idealization of Maggie and his pervasive irony. Moreover, he avoids confronting the moment of Maggie's decision to become a prostitute, implying instead that, because of the restrictions of her environment, she had no real choice. Even though severely limited, she, of course, did. Crane seems to have been aware of the difficulty in convincingly idealizing Maggie *and* showing her making a moral choice that would have been condemned out of hand by his middle-class readers. Had his interest been in depicting her as a realistic rather than an idealistic character, this particular difficulty might have been significantly lessened.

Maggie's decision to become a prostitute and indeed her entire characterization are classic examples of what John J. Conder has described as the Hobbesian paradox faced by most characters in naturalistic fiction. Conder reconciles the dual existence of determinism and free will in naturalistic fiction in the context of Thomas Hobbes's argument that man is free in only those ways in which his actions are not naturally proscribed.[19] Thus, consistently, Maggie does choose badly largely because her environment offers her a severely limited range of choices. Pete may well be the closest thing to a knight which her world has to offer. Given his deception, the brutality of her mother, the absence of any meaningful loyalty to her on Jimmie's part, the sordid reality of the collar and cuff establishment *and* her envy of "elegance and soft palms," her decision to become a prostitute is a virtually inevitable and, however she dies, certainly a suicidal choice. It remains, nevertheless, a choice.

In order to treat Maggie's climactic decision and ultimate fate in this way, Crane would have had to view her as a sympathetic realistic character, and he was clearly not ready to do so. Thus, he does not directly show the moment of her decision. In addition, in the revised edition of his novel the fat man, who embodies the full horror of prostitution and whose presence Maggie seems unwittingly to have evoked through her "smiling invitations to the men of rural or untaught pattern," is eliminated. The curious narrative distance that distinguishes *Maggie: A Girl of the Streets* originates in Crane's determination to present Maggie as an idealized victim and in his inability to transcend completely Riis's tour-guide narrative model. In contrast, in *McTeague* Frank Norris so drastically eliminates any distance between his narrator and his characters that the novel becomes what William E. Cain has called a kind of prolonged narrative rape.

McTeague

Cain perceptively observes that Norris, in *McTeague*, is concerned, above all, with the dynamics of power and control. He argues that this concern becomes, in fact, a kind of obsession in all of Norris's fiction: "Often exaggerated and heightened, Norris's style reveals his obsessions about power and complicity in its violent enactments. Though anxious to distance himself from McTeague, Norris is enthralled by him, and he even conceives of his novelistic projects in terms of power and victimization, as a grim and demanding theater of cruelty."[20] A crucial element of this theater of cruelty is the denial by Norris's narrator of any rights of privacy for the characters. Cain sees the narrator as a kind of voyeur, unashamedly spying on the most private moments of McTeague, Trina, and the others. This voyeurism originates in Norris's obsession with control: he denies his imaginative creations even the most basic control over their own fictional existence.

Cain is further correct in his observation that Norris's compulsive intrusions into the lives of his characters originated in a unique and complex attitude toward them: "Norris shows a weird mixture of deep empathy for, and snobbery toward, his characters" (201). Even more than Jack London or any of the other early naturalists, Norris consciously wrote as an Anglo-Saxon, often celebrating the historical triumphs of the "race." Strongly influenced by Kipling, he saw the Anglo-Saxon as the historic "force for civilization" in the world. In *The Literary Criticism of Frank Norris* Donald Pizer shows that, in the course of his career, Norris's celebration of the Anglo-Saxon underwent a process of moderation. Initially, he, like Jack London at his worst, luxuriated in writing scenes in which his muscular Anglo-Saxon heroes and heroines brutally subdued representatives of the "lesser races"—for instance, Moran torturing the Chinese pirate by attacking his teeth with a large file. But, as Pizer illustrates, the more mature Norris transformed his veneration of Anglo-Saxon strength into a larger, and at least somewhat more responsible, historical perspective. He came to see the settlement of the American West as the last stage in the "long march," "the latest victory of a restless, fighting people who had begun their journey in the swamps of Friesland."[21] *McTeague*, the first novel that Norris started, shows evidence of both its author's early crude racism and his more mature, if still undeniably racist, glorification of the Anglo-Saxon.

It is hardly surprising, then, that in *McTeague* Norris feels the most empathy for the title character. McTeague is a product of the frontier, the Big Dipper Mine, who has been unnaturally, and it turns out disastrously, grafted onto the city, initially because of the ambition of his mother. (Female characters in *McTeague* uniformly initiate or inspire disaster; the novel is astonishing in its, one suspects, largely unconscious misogyny.) Don Graham succinctly summarizes the shift during the last two decades in the critical response to Norris's central character: "McTeague as sympathetic bottom dog replaces McTeague as animalistic draft horse."[22] Graham views

McTeague as representing the liberating freedom of the frontier and Trina as embodying the restrictive world of the city: "This is an esthetic of space, as opposed to an esthetic of constriction" (53). In fact, much of the bleak tone of *McTeague* is the result of the novel's being, however consciously on the part of its author, an elegy to the corruption and death of the Anglo-Saxon long march when it abruptly confronts the new and increasingly foreign western city.

Certainly, McTeague, the frontiersman and literary descendant of Natty Bumppo, encounters, after an initial honeymoon, an alien world in San Francisco, and he is finally destroyed by his inability to adapt to an environment dominated by greed, sexuality, and exotic "lesser breeds." Critical commentary about the theme of greed in the novel, and especially the crude symbolism with which Norris highlights it, is extensive. McTeague's beloved gold tooth is perhaps the book's most memorable image, and *Greed* is the title of Erich von Stroheim's 1924 film version of *McTeague*. The most curious and fascinating thing about McTeague's and Trina's lust for money is that neither views it primarily as a means of acquiring material goods. For McTeague wealth is essentially a vague, romantic dream, "the old-time miner's idea of wealth easily gained and quickly spent."[23] Warren French places Norris's hero in the context of S. I. Hayakawa's distinction between "thing-handlers" and "symbol-handlers": "McTeague remains a primitive backwoodsman in his thoughts. He has not even the most elementary understanding of how a commercial economy works; thus, as Richard Chase points out, he is 'corrupted and defeated' by the 'evil' city."[24]

Trina's response to money is, to say the least, a much more complicated thing. Walter Benn Michaels sees her miserliness and her sexual masochism as opposing sides of a pervasive psychological disorder: "Trina's passion for McTeague consists . . . in her deep conviction, that '*she was his.*' But her passion for her money involves the equally deep conviction that, whatever might happen, the money is *hers*. . . . The contradiction, then, is that Trina belongs to McTeague but her money doesn't. . . . The simultaneous desires to own and to be owned constitute the emotional paradox Norris sets himself to elaborate in *McTeague*."[25] Michaels is correct in interpreting Trina's psychological abnormalities in the context of the novel's central concern with the dynamics of control and power. Still, Norris specifies another origin of her miserliness which should not be forgotten: "A good deal of peasant blood still ran undiluted in her veins, and she had all the instinct of a hardy and penurious mountain race—the instinct that saves without any thought, without idea of consequence—saving for the sake of saving, hoarding without knowing why" (99). To a degree, then, Trina's miserliness is a manifestation of the "foreignness" of the immigrant, which has transformed San Francisco into an exotic place that can only bewilder and finally outrage a primitive frontiersman like McTeague.

Undeniably, though, Trina's love for money is inextricably linked with her sexuality, making her, in the novel's classic understatement, "a strange woman during these days [the period of her ritualistic sado-masochistic episodes with Mac]" (227). Her habitual fondling of the "chamois-skin bag" containing her beloved gold pieces and the scene in which she strips naked in order to lie in bed with the gold pieces and take "a strange and ecstatic pleasure in the touch of the smooth flat pieces the length of her body are two of the most notorious instances of her unique mode of sublimation. Perhaps her most unforgivable "sin" is introducing McTeague, the innocent frontiersman, to such perverted sexuality or, for that matter, to any form of sexuality at all. One of the remarkable equations in the novel is Norris's association of sex with the exotic city, as if no one on the frontier ever felt such strange and destructive urges.

It is, in fact, too easy to ridicule the treatment of sexuality in all of Frank Norris's work. There is the preposterous Ross Wilbur–Moran love affair, the death of the virginal Dolly Haight by syphilis in *Vandover and the Brute*, published posthumously in 1914, and the fact that any kiss on the mouth between a male and a female in his novels can only be done "grossly." Yet it should be said that, to some extent, the absurdity in Norris's usual treatment of sexuality originates in the fact that he was interested in exploring all ramifications of the subject at a time when censorship barely allowed the American writer to speak of it at all. In *McTeague*, however, it clearly does represent, arbitrarily, the exoticism of the city.

Nowhere is this more evident than in the wildly overwritten Dental Parlors scene in which Mac has Trina unconscious under the influence of ether and, apparently for the first time in his life, becomes sexually aroused. It is, of course, obvious that on one level this scene represents the Sleeping Beauty syndrome, the archetypal male fantasy of assaulting the unnaturally passive, and thus helpless, female. At any rate, it seems safe to say that no — tional character has ever had as spectacular or as traumatic an erection, or one with as anticlimactic a result, as McTeague has in this scene. As he stands over the recumbent Trina, "Suddenly the animal in the man stirred and woke; the evil instinct that in him were so close to the surface, leaped to life shouting and clamoring" (22). What follows is something of a primordial psychic battle between "the brute" (lust?) and "a certain second self, another better McTeague" (civilized restraint?). As if that were not enough, Norris's narrator, on the next page, compares Mac's sexual desire to "the foul stream of hereditary evil": "The vices and sins of his father and of his father's father, to the third and fourth and five hundredth generation, tainted him. The evil of an entire race flowed in his veins. Why should it be? He did not desire it. Was he to blame?" (23–24).

By this point the entire scene has disintegrated into simple incoherence. If "the evil of an entire race" is sexuality, it is certainly a necessary evil if all those generations are to keep on coming. William E. Cain proposes a likely explanation for the contradictions and ultimate absurdity of the writing in this scene. The "exaggerated" and "overblown" style, he argues, is "revealing of Norris's spectacular presence in his own text": "He is as much gripped by sexuality and desire as McTeague, and as obsessed by its violent forms terrifying dynamics, and unnerving hallucinations" (206). Cain's hypothesis of an intrusion by Norris into his fictional world seems convincing. (It should be pointed out that Joseph R. McElrath, Jr., has recently theorized that, in this scene and in other scenes involving sexuality in *McTeague* and *Vandover — the Brute*, Norris is unobtrusively shifting into free and indirect discourse in order to portray his characters as victims of Victorian sexual conventions).[26] Whatever the source and purpose of the almost hysterical rhetoric in this scene, it practically destroys any dignity that the character of McTeague might have. Just as his mother was responsible for his entry into the foreign landscape of the city, Trina, the daughter of urban immigrants, has introduced him to the "evil" of sexuality. The female has set in motion the inevitable destruction of the once pure frontiersman.

The novel's linking of greed, destructive sexuality, and the exotic immigrant is most overt in the characterizations of Zerkow, the "Polish Jew" who roams throughout the city gathering rags and other trash, and Maria Macapa the demented cleaning woman of vaguely Latin-American extraction. Zerkow is clearly a creation of the racism of the young Frank Norris and represents a continuation of the popular tradition, echoed by Riis and Crane, of the rapacious Jew: "It was impossible to look at Zerkow and not know instantly that greed—inordinate, insatiable greed—was the dominant passion of the man. He was the Man with the Rake, groping hourly in the muck-heap of the city for gold, for gold, for gold" (32). Maria Macapa is depicted as a woman of repressed passion who has lost significant contact with reality and, on cue, tells a story of a fabulous service of gold plate which her family once owned. Inevitably, Zerkow marries her in order to discover the location of the probably mythical golden serving pieces. In a twist of pure naturalistic irony she becomes pregnant, has a miscarriage, regains her sanity, and can no longer remember anything about the fabled treasure of gold. Infuriated, Zerkow murders her by slitting her throat. Besides functioning as a double for the darkest reality of the Mac-Trina relationship, the Zerkow–Maria Macapa subplot graphically symbolizes the exotic danger of the city. When Norris's narrator describes the dead child of Zerkow and Maria as "combining in its puny little body the blood of the Hebrew, the Pole, and the Spaniard" (176), one can only feel that, in the world of *McTeague*, it is better off never having lived.

McTeague, an innocent forced to confront the overwhelming forces of sexuality and the city, inevitably evokes empathy from Norris and the reader as well. But he hardly escaped Norris's contempt. His sexual crisis makes him more than a little ridiculous (it is interesting that, when thoroughly bewildered, he regularly exclaims, "You can't make small of me"), and the narrator relentlessly refers to him as "stupid." The dentist is, in fact, the classic example of Don Graham's concept of the character of "circumscribed consciousness" as dominating naturalistic fiction.[27] Norris's condescending attitude toward McTeague and all the novel's characters must be understood in the dual context of his self-definition as a writer and his attitude toward his subject matter. Besides thinking of himself as a spokesman for Anglo-Saxon progress, he unashamedly thought of himself as writing for the bourgeois. In the words of Donald Pizer, Norris viewed himself as a "popular moralist" and "the instructor of the public conscience."[28] He believed that the role obligated him to expose middle-class readers to strange and exotic levels of experience and thus broaden their understanding. In one of his "Salt and Sincerity" essays he wrote: "On the surface and at the very bottom, all people are alike. In the 'middle ground' come the varieties. It is to this 'middle ground' that one looks for strong fiction-characters— unless there should arise a Tolstoy or a Flaubert among us, who dare explore those last and lowest dark places, down at the bottom of things and hearts."[29] In fact, Norris sought to be precisely such an explorer, following in the lead not of Tolstoy and Flaubert but, rather, Kipling and, above all, Zola. Pizer offers the most succinct summary of Norris's highly idiosyncratic concept of literary naturalism: "Norris conceived of naturalism as a fictional mode that illustrated some fundamental truth of life within a detailed presentation of the sensational and low."[30] In his theoretical writings the novelist avoided any discussion of the centrality of determinism or any other philosophical abstraction to naturalism. Instead, he emphasized its affinity to "romanticism" and its superiority to "realism" as a mode of reaching the great and secret truths of life.[31] He praised Zola for taking the reader below the surface of ordinary reality: "We, the bourgeois, the commonplace, the ordinary, have no place nor lot in the *Rougon-Macquart*, in *Lourdes*, or in Rome; it is not our world, not because our social position is different, but because we are *ordinary*. . . . The naturalist takes no note of common people, common in so far as their interests, their lives, and the things that occur in them are common, are ordinary. Terrible things must happen to the characters of the naturalistic tale."[32]

In *McTeague* Norris was concerned about "social position"; he intuitively saw the ghetto as a place in which he could show his ordinary reader "terrible things" happening to exotic characters. Moreover, as June Howard points out, the foreignness of the ghetto inspired a crucial subtext in his novel; he created in McTeague, Trina, Zerkow, and Maria Macapa a cumulative image of "the brute," a symbolic embodiment of the Other. The extremity of Norris's mode of characterization is necessitated by his compulsion, however conscious, to personify the repressed and even denied depths of the ordinary reader's psyche. The world of Polk Street functions as both social and psychological Other, the exotic and dangerous world of the ghetto *and* the dark regions of the respectable, middle-class subconscious. Polk Street is not precisely the ghetto; rather, it is a working-class "accommodation street" that forms a fragile border between a world of small shops and the menacing slums lying just behind it. At the first of the novel McTeague, with his "huge porcelain pipe" and "steam beer," is passive and content, but, after he is abruptly introduced to sexuality and an especially perverted form of greed, he is transformed into the very prototype of the naturalistic brute. Polk Street is, then, a complex metaphor for the thin lines separating the urban middle class from the threatening slum and respectable, civilized beliefs and behaviors from repressed savagery.

As Howard has shown, *McTeague*'s subtext of the exploration of the social and psychological Other makes the novel a prototype for subsequent naturalistic fiction: "[In naturalism] we encounter the brute in its far-flung manifestations as a creature perpetually outcast, yet perpetually to be cast out as it inevitably reappears within self and within society" (95). The degree of conscious intent in Norris's exploration of the psychological Other must remain an open question; as William B. Dillingham has shown, he was always an artist who worked by instinct more than by deliberate design.[33] Still, it is undeniable that, in *McTeague* and in much of his other fiction, he did deliberately set out to investigate the boundaries of sexual perversion, especially sadomasochism. His fascination with the dark regions of the mind is, of course, a factor in what Cain describes as his constant violation of his characters' privacy and in the frequent and awkward intrusions of his self into the fictional text. An observation by June Howard about *Vandover and the Brute* is also relevant to *McTeague:* "Norris is profoundly revolted by and yet obsessed with dirt, as he is with sex. And in both cases he attempts to exclude the horror from the familiar precincts of middle-class life, attributing it to the brutal Other" (68).

It should be said that many readers find *McTeague* to be an extremely depressing work because it is the most thoroughly deterministic of all Norris's novels. There is little Hobbesian paradox in it; with the exception of the old couple, its characters are pawns of external and internal forces. This thorough determinism is especially surprising in Norris, who, as Donald Pizer points out, does not emphasize it, or any other abstract doctrine, in his theoretical writings about naturalism. It is, in fact, the philosophical openness customarily underlying Norris's brand of naturalism which Pizer sees as its most important legacy for subsequent American fiction.

Certainly, in its creation of the narrator-as-explorer simultaneously probing the depths of the ghetto and of the human psyche, *McTeague* pointed the way for such twentieth-century naturalistic explorers as Richard Wright, Nelson Algren, Hubert Selby, Jr., John Rechy, and Joyce Carol Oates. Norris had, in fact, left work for them to do. He did show the fat man, the personification of the full horror of the slum *and* of the repressed areas of the human psyche, directly. Approaching his subject matter as an explorer of the most secret depths of the social and psychological abyss, he did, more successfully than Crane, transcend the limitations of Riis's tour-guide narrative perspective. But he did not give the fat man a voice. Instead, he exhibited him to the middle-class, ordinary reader as an exotic specimen discovered in his exploration of dangerous and forbid

den terrain. As the twentieth century progressed, Wright, Gold, Algren, Selby, Rechy, Oates, and other contemporary naturalists would redefine the fat man, humanize him, and give him a voice.

Another, and now little known, work by one of the turn-of-the-century naturalists also anticipated these twentieth-century explorations of the depths of the inner city. In *The People of the Abyss*, an account of his brief, voluntary submersion in the ocean of suffering that was the East End of London,

England, Jack London combined the tour-guide and explorer perspectives to create his own vision of the social and psychological Other.

The People of the Abyss

As discussed, Stephen Crane, in *Maggie: A Girl of the Streets*, was attempting to escape the tourist-guide narrative perspective that dominated early American writing about the slums and which according to Trachtenberg, had been definitively established by Jacob Riis in his classic work on photojournalism, *How the Other Half Lives*. Again, Trachtenberg posits the idea that, in the tourist-guide perspective, it is essential to create a fictional bond between narrator and reader: both are assumed to be enlightened individuals of goodwill who would alleviate the brutal and sordid reality of the American slum if they had the power to do so.

In contrast, Frank Norris, in *McTeague*, utilized the informed outsider perspective for quite a different purpose than had Riis. *McTeague*'s narrator functions as an explorer, sharing insights about the exotic world of the slum and its inhabitants with the middle-class reader. The novel's characters emerge both as exotics living in a foreign colony and as projections of the Other, the repressed areas of the respectable middle-class reader's psyche.[34] Norris's purpose seems not to promote social reform but, rather, to shock with images of sordid and savage characters existing within the new American city and to tantalize with glimpses of denied and forbidden impulses and behavior.

Jack London's *People of the Abyss*, his 1903 account of living for a short time in the East End, exhibits variations of both Riis's tour-guide and Norris's explorer perspectives to create his own unique narrative perspective. (It should be specified that I am not attempting an influence argument here.) London begins his preface to *The People of the Abyss* by establishing his identity as an explorer of a foreign and dangerous world: "The experiences related in this volume fell to me in the summer of 1902. I went down into the under-world of London with an attitude of mind which I may best liken to that of the explorer. . . . I took with me certain simple criteria with which to measure the life of the under-world. That which made for moral life, for physical and spiritual health, was good; that which made for less life, which hurt, and dwarfed, and distorted life, was bad."[35] An imagery of submersion dominates London's account of his descent into the "under-world" of the East End: the narrator becomes a kind of deep-sea diver, gradually, but inexorably, moving downward into an uncharted and dangerous ocean filled with grotesque subhuman creatures.

In fact, this controlling metaphor is made overt in several ways. In addition to the preface, the book's first chapter is entitled "The Descent." Finally, there is this key passage: "The streets were filled with a new and different race of people, short of stature, and of wretched or beer-sodden appearance. . . . And as far as I could see were the solid walls of brick, the slimy pavements, and the screaming streets; and for the first time in my life the fear of the crowd smote me. It was like the fear of the sea; and the miserable multitudes, street upon street, seemed so many waves of a vast and malodorous sea, lapping about me and threatening to well up over me" (20).

London's narrator will continue to emphasize the motif of the East End dwellers as a "new and different race" throughout the book—ultimately depicting them, in fact, as a subhuman species. For this reason, among others, *The People of the Abyss* is central to understanding London's fictional application of the evolutionary concept of atavism; consistently in his work, reversal to animalistic states and/or behavior is destructive in an urban setting while usually beneficial, if not redemptive, in a frontier setting.[36] The male denizen of the East End has been dehumanized, in part by a cynical and emotionless sexuality: "[The East End male], has already solved the mysteries of girl's love and wife's love, and childs love, and found them delusions and shams, vain and fleeting as dewdrops, quick-vanishing before the ferocious facts of life" (138).

The facts of life, as depicted by London, in the East End are "ferocious" indeed. Every aspect of existence from sexuality to sheer survival occurs on a primarily, if not solely, bestial level, and the book's setting seems increasingly a territory inhabited by faintly recognizable, but ultimately terrifying, nonhuman creatures: "[East End males] become indecent and bestial. When they kill, they kill with their hands, and then stupidly surrender themselves to the executioners. . . . They wear remarkable boots of brass and iron, and when they have polished off the mother of their children with a black eye or so, they knock her down and proceed to trample her very much as a Western stallion tramples a rattlesnake" (134). Near the end of his book London expresses the dehumanization of the East End male in a powerful jungle metaphor:

[Males in the East End] reminded me of gorillas. Their bodies were small, ill-shaped, and squat. There were no swelling muscles, no abundant thews and wide-spreading shoulders. They exhibited, rather, an

elementary economy of nature, such as the cave-men must have exhibited. But there was strength in those meagre bodies, the ferocious
primordial strength to clutch and grip and tear and rend. . . . As valley
and mountain are to the natural savage, street and building are valley
and mountain to them. The slum is their jungle, and they live and
prey in the jungle. (166–67)

London's narrator has submerged himself in water as well as in mythical space and time. The ocean, the jungle, and the "primordial" have merged
into an image of a strange and dangerous world, which modern civilized
man enters only at his peril. Yet within *literal* space and time this alien world
exists next door to one of the most thoroughly civilized places in the world.
Similarly, of course, the Other, those repressed and denied parts of the civilized psyche, exist intermingled with acknowledged and "appropriate" impulses and behavior. The implied vision of the Other in *The People of the
Abyss* is truly primordial, an "abyss" of prehuman and nonhuman behaviors.
In *McTeague* Frank Norris had portrayed the new immigrant to the United
States through the prism of a comparable vision. There is, of course, considerable irony inherent in London's depicting inhabitants of the capital of
the British Empire as personifications of such a primordial, bestial Other.
At the turn of the century the middle-class reader must have found it much
easier to equate subconsciously the foreign-appearing and often foreign-
sounding immigrant with a subhuman Other than to do so with even the
most obviously depraved resident of London.

At any rate, the abyss of the human psyche which emerges to the surface through London's exploration contains nothing redemptive; it is entirely grotesque and frightening. Such an approach is consistent with
London's fiction, in which such irrational impulses as sexuality and violence
can only be transformed from the grotesquely subhuman to the transcen-
dently superhuman when experienced by an Anglo-Saxon in a frontier, rather
than an urban, setting. In fact, London's many tales of heroic Anglo-Saxon
explorers physically beating non-Anglo-Saxons can be read, on one level, as
allegories of the purification of inherently bestial desires and impulses, and,
throughout *The People of the Abyss*, he contrasts adventure on the "primitive" and redemptive frontier with existence in the primordial and degrading East End.

June Howard points out that London's narrator has a privileged status
quite uncommon for naturalistic explorers of the primordial abyss: "In *The
People of the Abyss* . . . the naturalist transgresses the boundary between classes

with impunity" (152). Howard also notes that London adopts a costume of old clothing which allows him to move easily into and out of the abyss (153). Metaphorically, the narrator's "costume" also represents an externalization of the primitive Other, which he can discard at will. The primary element in the narrator's costume is an old "stoker's singlet," which becomes the most important symbol of his ability to move back and forth between social classes and between his respectable civilized self and the primordial abyss of the psychic Other. London describes in detail the first time the narrator envelopes himself in the stoker's singlet: "Inside my stoker's singlet, in the armpit, I sewed a gold sovereign (an emergency sum certainly of modest proportions); and inside my stoker's singlet I put myself. And then I sat down and moralized upon the fair years and fat, which had made my skin soft and brought the nerves close to the surface; for the singlet was rough and raspy as a hair shirt, and I am confident that the most rigorous of ascetics suffer no more than I did in the ensuing twenty-four hours" (22). The gold sovereign, the coin of social respectability and the emblem of a civilized psyche, serves as a constant reminder of the narrator's ability to surface, when necessary, from his exploratory immersion in the abyss of social and psychic degradation. That London's explorer persona is a superficial one is made manifest through the juxtaposition of his "soft" skin and "close to the surface" nerves and the "rough and raspy" texture of the singlet.

The temporary nature of the narrator's immersion is further exemplified by the arrangements that he makes to facilitate his exploration: "While living, eating, and sleeping with the people of the East End, it was my intention to have a port of refuge, not too far distant, into which I could run now and again to assure myself that good clothes and cleanliness still existed." He needs the assurance that he can, at will, return to the reassuring "port" of civilization, which exists "not too far distant" from the foreign world he is exploring. In order to find such a haven of refuge and return, he seeks the assistance of "a detective of thirty-odd years' continuous service in the East End," known appropriately as Johnny Upright (26). When the narrator calls on Upright, the detective has not yet returned from church, but his two daughters are present to greet visitors. Upright is, of course, a personification of civilization and respectability: the narrator immediately associates him with the trappings of church and family. Like the gold sovereign sewn inside the stoker's singlet, Johnny Upright serves as a reminder that the safety and comforts of civilization exist, in terms of space and time, not far from the narrator's realm of exploration. A distinct and important subtext of *The People of the Abyss* parallels, then, the central focus of Norris's *McTeague*—exploration of the primordial and frightening Other, the submerged and denied urges of the civilized psyche. On the most conscious level, however, "London's purpose in this book is," as June Howard points out, "to expose social injustice" (153). These two motifs are potentially quite contradictory, and they create an underlying sense of narrative schizophrenia, which becomes more overt in, and almost destroys the effectiveness of, the last half of *People of the Abyss*. To expedite his exploration London adopts a narrative strategy similar to those of Riis and Crane. The book's reformist strand necessitates that his narrator, like theirs, establish an alliance with an implied reasonable middle-class reader. The underlying narrative assumption in all three works is that these middle-class readers are men and women of decency and goodwill who have been sheltered from shock and outrage at the horrors of the ghetto by their ignorance.

It then becomes the challenge of the three writers to strip away this ignorance without alienating the sensitivities of their readership. To accomplish this goal Riis's narrator assumes the persona of a tour guide revealing the brutal reality of New York City tenement life to his privileged readers in a gradual and systematic fashion, while regularly reminding them that the teachings of Christianity necessitate the alleviation of such horror and that those same teachings provide assurance that such reform is possible. The New Testament, after all, emphasizes that no man or woman, however depraved, is beneath the possibility of redemption, and assimilation of the economically downtrodden into safe and respectable society would constitute the mode of redemption with which Riis is concerned.

In contrast, the frequently discussed Christian symbolism in *Maggie: A Girl of the Streets* is generally ironic in tone and, therefore, allows Crane to establish a working contrast between the hypocritical and judgmental Christianity that middle-class society practices and the humanistic teachings of Christ. One goal of Crane's narrator is, then, to evoke a sense of shame in middle-class readers without so alienating them as to lose their sympathy. His narrator establishes a distance between the title character and himself *and the reader* which is highly unusual in the fiction of the period. Crane's reader never sees, but only receives an impressionistic sense of, Maggie's final spiritual destruction and physical death.

To establish his bond with the middle-class reader London devises a narrative strategy that recalls both *How the Other Half Lives* and *Maggie*. Like Riis's, his narrator assumes the obligation to inform, in quite dramatic ways, the reader about the extreme suffering in the slums. In order to succeed at this, he has to inform the objects of his investigation of his purpose. Early in the book London's narrator decides to treat two particularly desperate denizens of the East End to toast and tea; this act of generosity necessitates the removal of the gold sovereign from the stoker's singlet, an act that naturally arouses the suspicion of the two recipients of his generosity. The coin is extricated with a knife, and the language describing this act is surprisingly violent. The narrator's surgical determination even frightens one of the two men: "Possibly he took me for a latter-day Jack-the-Ripper with a penchant for elderly male paupers." It is essential, then, that he quickly reassure them: "Of course I had to explain to them that I was an investigator, a social student, seeking to find out how the other half lived" (59).

This revelation, not surprisingly, creates an immediate distance between London's narrator and the two men, but it signals the assumed bond between the narrator and the middle-class reader. Jack London, of course, knew more than a little bit about "how the other half lived" in the United States, if not in England, long before he voluntarily submerged himself in the ocean of suffering that was London's East End. Throughout *The People of the Abyss* there are echoes of London's exploits on the frontier but only indirect clues of the poverty of his early years. His narrator emerges, then, as an adventurer exploring a new kind of frontier as initially strange and remote as the Yukon had once been. By having his narrator adopt this particular persona, he can address the comfortable, respectable reader from the perspective of a man with a background somewhat more exotic, but fundamentally no different in kind. Narrator and assumed reader become partners investigating the East End with the implied scientific detachment of social scientists. This detachment is ultimately a mask assumed by a narrator who will be soon discard it.

The narrative affinities between London's book and *Maggie* are, in comparison with the echoes of Riis, more subtle. Again, there is no argument here for a direct influence by Crane on *The People of the Abyss*. In contrast to Crane, London holds back few details of the horror of slum life: the last half of *People of the Abyss* is, in fact, saturated in such detail. In addition, Christian symbolism is not so pervasive in London's work as in Crane's novel. Still, London's narrator, like Crane's, assumes a shared humanism, which recalls the New Testament, with the reader. After describing the death of a seventy-five-year-old woman, whose vermin-covered body was discovered abandoned in a desolate room, the narrator comments: "If it is not good for your mother and my mother so to die, then, it is not good for this woman, whosoever's mother she might be, so to die" (131). Such a passage indicates that London's purpose in recounting his investigation of the East End was, in part, not unlike Crane's famous statement of his motive for telling the story of Maggie Johnson: "For it [*Maggie*] tries to show that environment is a tremendous thing in the world and frequently shapes lives regardless. If one proves that theory one makes room in Heaven for all sorts of souls, notably an occasional street girl, who are not confidently expected to be there by many exalted people."[37] Similarly, London wants to convince his socially exalted readers that there is room in heaven for abandoned, "vermin-covered" mothers just as there is for the mothers of the well-to-do. This strand of London's work, existing side by side with its exposé approach, creates the narrative schizophrenia previously mentioned. Again, its narrator has already emphasized that the poor of England's capital are so degraded by suffering and poverty as to be "a new and different race of people," who not infrequently become "indecent and bestial" and who are physically reminiscent of "gorillas." It is as if the subtext of the narrator's exploration of the abyss of the psyche, the repressed Other, collides with his scientific investigation of the life of the poor and oppressed. Moreover, in the concluding section of the novel London's exploration of the abyss as the home of the middle-class Other is virtually abandoned as the narrator identifies a villain or class of villains who are responsible for transforming London's urban poor into a new and often bestial race of people.

Again, having established a bond of shared humanism with his readers, London's narrator, in contrast to Crane's, pulls very few punches and gradually creates a cumulative shock effect through the accumulation of sordid details of the suffering of the denizens of the East End. He describes, for instance, his experience in a "spike," a charity ward in which the poor receive food, a place to sleep, and a bath in exchange for performing menial labor. The individuals in charge of the spike make certain that the recipients of the charity are made even more aware than they already were of their lack of any social status and of their resulting vulnerability. While waiting in line to enter the spike, the narrator carefully observes his fellow sufferers: "Some were poor, wretched beasts, inarticulate and callous, but for all that, in many ways very human" (65). He is particularly struck by an old "'Hopper' and his female mate." In an unguarded moment the "Hopper" instinctively reaches over to touch a strand of gray hair "back properly behind her ear." This instinctive act prompts an observation from the narrator: "It was a sturdy affection [the old Hopper] bore [toward the woman]; for man is not prone to bother his head over neatness and tidiness in a woman for whom he does not care, nor is he likely to be proud of such a woman" (66).

Once inside, however, the old man's affection, like all his humanizing qualities, needs to be very sturdy indeed to withstand the filth and systematic degradation of the spike. The "skilly," which passes for food is "gross," "bitter," and "repulsive" (69), and the water for bathing is filthy. Attempting to sleep on a brutally uncomfortable bed, the narrator is rudely awakened by "a rat or some similar animal" on his chest (72). To pay for the charity he has received the narrator is, the next morning, assigned to do scavenger work at Whitechapel Infirmary. Reflecting on the ease of picking up a contagious disease from the sordid refuse he is forced to handle, the narrator speculates that "perhaps there is a wise mercy in all this": "These men of the spike, the peg, and the street, are encumbrances. They are of no good or use to anyone, nor to themselves. They clutter the earth with their presence, and are better out of the way. Broken by hardship, ill fed, and worse nourished, they are always the first to be struck down by disease, as they are likewise the quickest to die" (73). Despite all this, the spike is considered so desirable by the denizens of the East End that they line up outside for hours hoping for admission.

London's motif, in the spike episode, of having his narrator first realize the still lingering humanity of the oppressed and, shortly thereafter, be shocked into a new awareness of the surrounding environment's threat to that humanity is repeated in his account of a night in a doss-house, "a poor man's hotel." Observing the sleeping young men, the narrator once again indulges in a moment of introspection: "They were not bad-looking fellows. Their faces were made for women's kisses, their necks for women's arms. They were lovable, as men are lovable. They were capable of love. . . . And I wondered where [the] women were, and heard a 'harlot's ginny laugh.' Leman Street, Waterloo Road, Piccadilly, The Strand, answered me, and I knew where they were" (146).

Like Riis and Crane, London intends to make the point that this dehumanizing environment can be reformed and changed, and, like Riis, he understands that it exists in its present state not by accident but, rather, by social design. In the last half of the book he becomes quite specific in identifying the East End as the calculated creation of the lords of British capitalism. His narrator, for instance, after observing homeless men sleeping in Green Park, lectures the reader: "And so, dear soft people, should you ever visit London Town, and see these men asleep on the benches and in the grass, please do not think they are lazy creatures, preferring sleep to work. Know that the powers that be have kept them walking all the night long, and that in the day they have nowhere else to sleep" (78).

Having established his bond of shared humanistic values with the reader in the first half of the book, the narrator risks shattering that bond through an increasingly ironic and angry tone. He begins to demand that his "dear soft" readers abandon their present allegiance to "the powers that be," who have created and subsequently profited from the horrors he has depicted, and acknowledge the full and obvious implications of the humanistic values to which they pretend to ascribe. As long as they choose to remain "dear soft people," they help to preserve the morally intolerable status quo. It has been, after all, several pages since the narrator's confession that, inside the stoker's singlet, he is himself "soft."

Not surprisingly, London's political radicalism leads him to a sweeping condemnation of British capitalism and imperialism. Watching the public celebration of the coronation of King Edward, his narrator is both impressed and disgusted by the mass display of England's military might, and he does not miss the implications of the empire's army being immediately followed in the procession by a representative body of London's constabulatory: "And as it was thus at Trafalgar Square, so was it along the whole line of march—force, overpowering force; myriads of men, splendid men, the pick of the people, whose sole function in life is blindly to obey, and blindly to kill and destroy and stamp out life. And that they should be well fed, well clothed, and well armed, and have ships to hurl them to the ends of the earth, the East End of London, and the 'East End' of all England, toils and rots and dies" (89). The narrator perceives the ghettos of England as internal colonies, brutally exploited in a cruel and misguided design to further the power of the empire. In his opinion the British constabulatory does not function to insure justice but, instead, as an internal army to repress those who are viewed as having nothing to contribute to the preservation of the empire.

Such a system of enforced and pervasive injustice, the narrator argues, will not result in the preservation of the empire but, rather, in its deterioration and ultimate destruction. In fact, he believes, a kind of reversed Darwinism has been operative in England for some time, with the best of the "race" abandoning the island for the new world, leaving behind only a stunted and inferior breed of people. Further, an impending collapse of British society can be averted only by a new vision of the essential interrelationship of all elements of society: "We cannot understand the starved and runty toiler of the East End . . . till we look at the strapping Life Guardsmen of the West End, and come to know that the one must feed and clothe and groom the other" (89–90). The narrator is also quite clear about the principal impediment to the implementation of such a saving vision: it is not ignorance so much as greed. London's Marxism becomes increasingly overt as his narrator begins to ascribe a profoundly unpatriotic avarice to the British powers that be: "And in these latter days, five hundred hereditary peers own one-fifth of England; and they, and the officers and servants under the King, and those who go to compose the powers that be, yearly spend in wasteful luxury $1,850,000,000 or £370,000,000, which is thirty-per cent. of the total wealth produced by all the toilers of the country" (91).

This kind of profligate self-indulgence by the British aristocracy prohibits any realization of a saving vision of social equality and has already set in process the inevitable disintegration of the empire. In a passage that echoes Crane's *Maggie*, London's narrator expresses his outrage that the social class devoted to perpetuating such pervasive greed wraps itself in the external trappings of Christianity:

> In London the slaughter of the innocents goes on on a scale more stupendous than any before in the history of the world. And equally stupendous is the callousness of the people who believe in Christ, acknowledge God, and go to church regularly on Sunday. For the rest of the week they riot about on the rents and profits which come to them from the East End stained with the blood of the children. Also, at times, so peculiarly are they made, they will take half a million of these rents and profits and send it away to educate the black boys of the Soudan. (165–66)

Having located his villain in the British upper classes and made his prophecy of their destructive legacy for the future of the empire, London devotes much of the last part of his book to statistical and anecdotal evidence in support of his charge of the pervasive injustice of English society. June Howard calls this London's "documentary strategy" in *The People of the Abyss* and says that it results in a work that fits no conventional literary genre. Also useful is her insight that the first half of the book, which depicts the stages of the narrator's submersion into the abyss, functions like the literature "of plot," which we are accustomed to designating as "fiction" (152–53). In fact, in its stress upon the concept of determinism—the inhabitants of London's East End have been transformed into a new and bestial race by socioeconomic oppression—*The People of the Abyss* is clearly a work that falls into the tradition of the naturalistic novel and anticipates the Marxist naturalism of Michael Gold and Richard Wright. Moreover, it is especially interesting in its echoes of Riis and Crane as well as of Norris. It provides the respectable middle-class reader with a tour of the lower depths of society and an exploration of the forbidden and repressed areas of the civilized human psyche. Even though this dual approach ultimately weakens the artistic integrity of the work, it is valuable for what it portends about the twentieth-century naturalistic inner-city novel in the United States.

Notes

1. Joseph Katz, "[Art and Compromise: The 1893 and the 1896 *Maggie*]," in Stephen Crane, *Maggie: A Girl of the Streets*, ed. Thomas A. Gullason (New York: W. W. Norton, 1979), 194.

2. Gullason, *Maggie*, 53.

3. See, for instance, Edwin Cady, *Stephen Crane* (Boston: Twayne, 1962); and Joseph X. Brennan, "Ironic and Symbolic Structure in Crane's *Maggie*," in Gullason, *Maggie*, 173–84.

4. Stephen Crane, *Maggie: A Girl of the Streets and George's Mother* (New York: Fawcett, 1960), 81.

5. For an interesting discussion of the history of the deletion of the "fat man" and resulting interpretation of Maggie's suicide, see Hershel Parker and Brian Higgins, "Maggie's 'Last Night': Authorial Design and Editorial Patching," in Gullason, *Maggie*, 234–45.

6. Elisabeth Panttaja, "Interpreting *Maggie*" (paper presented at the 1989 MLA national convention, Washington, D.C., December 1989).

7. Donald B. Gibson, *The Fiction of Stephen Crane* (Carbondale: Southern Illinois University Press, 1968).

8. Alan Trachtenberg, "Experiments in Another Country: Stephen Crane's City Sketches," in *American Realism: New Essays*, ed. Eric J. Sundquist (Baltimore: Johns Hopkins University Press, 1982). For an informative discussion of other possible nonliterary influences on *Maggie*, such as Charles Loring Brace's *The Dangerous Classes of New York; and Twenty Years Work among Them* (1872); the Reverend Thomas De Witt Talmage's *The Evil Beast: A Sermon* (1871); and the theological writings of Crane's father, see Marcus Cunliffe, "Stephen Crane and the American Background of Maggie," Crane, *Maggie: A Girl of the Streets*, ed. Thomas A. Gullason (New York: W. W. Norton, 1979), 94–103; and Thomas A. Gullason, "The Sources of Stephen Crane's *Maggie*," *Philological Quarterly* (October 1959): 497–502.

9. Charles A. Madison, "Preface," *How the Other Half Lives*, by Jacob A. Riis (New York: Dover, 1971).

10. Riis, preface, *How the Other Half Lives*, 38.

11. R. W. Stallman, *Stephen Crane: A Biography* (New York: George Braziller, 1968), 49.

12. Christopher Benfey, *The Double Life of Stephen Crane* (New York: Knopf, 1992), 59.

13. Gullason, "Sources of Crane's *Maggie.*"

14. In a recent article Josef Grmela discusses the narrative coldness toward slum dwellers which is revealed in *Maggie* and the shorter pieces "The Men in the Storm" and "A Christmas Dinner Won in Battle." This coldness, he believes, reflects some authorial prejudice against immigrants (Grmela, "Some Problems of the Critical Reception of Stephen Crane's *Maggie: A Girl of the Streets,*" *Brno Studies in English* 19 [1991]: 149–55).

15. Gibson, *Fiction of Stephen Crane*, 27.

16. In Joseph X. Brennan, "Ironic and Symbolic Structure in Crane's *Maggie,*" in Gullason, *Maggie*, 183–84.

17. Donald Pizer, "Stephen Crane's *Maggie* and American Naturalism," *Criticism* 7 (Spring 1965): 168–75.

18. Michael Davitt Bell brings an interesting fresh perspective to the source of Crane's narrative distance:

> The distance achieved by Crane's irony, the distance between the reader and the characters, stems from our recognition of the parodic emptiness of the characters' conceptions of reality. . . . It is not enough to say that these characters are trapped by the styles they imitate; for the most part they are eager to indulge in the ferocious exuberance of empty stylistic display, and such indulgence is all that really "happens" in *Maggie.* There is no social interaction here, only a collision of self-referential performances, as if each of the characters were doing exercises in front of a mirror. (Bell, "Irony, Parody, and 'Transcendental Realism': Stephen Crane," *The Problem of American Realism: Studies in the Cultural History of a Literary Idea* [Chicago: University of Chicago Press, 1993], 140)

19. John J. Conder, *Naturalism in American Fiction: The Classic Phase* (Lexington: University Press of Kentucky, 1984), 10–12.

20. William E. Cain, "Presence and Power in *McTeague,*" in Sundquist, *American Realism*, 205.

21. Donald Pizer, ed., *The Literary Criticism of Frank Norris* (Austin: University of Texas Press, 1964), 100. Norris outlined his theory of the settlement of the American West as representing the last stage of the Anglo-Saxon "long march" in an essay entitled "'The Literature of the West': A Reply to W. R. Lighton," *Boston Evening Transcript*, 8 January 1902; reprinted in Pizer, *Literary Criticism of Frank Norris*, 103–7.

22. Don Graham, *The Fiction of Frank Norris: The Aesthetic Context* (Columbia: University of Missouri Press, 1978), 43.

23. Frank Norris, *McTeague* (New York: Holt, Rinehart, and Winston, 1950), 97.

24. Warren French, *Frank Norris* (New Haven: College and University Press, 1962), 72.

25. Walter Benn Michaels, *The Gold Standard and the Logic of Naturalism* (Ber-

keley: University of California Press, 1987), 122–23.

26. Joseph R. McElrath, Jr., *Frank Norris Revisited* (New York: Twayne, 1992).

27. Don Graham, "Naturalism in American Fiction: A Status Report," *Studies in American Fiction* 10 (Spring 1982): 10.

28. Pizer, *Literary Criticism of Frank Norris*, xxi.

29. Reprinted in Pizer, *Literary Criticism of Frank Norris*, 207–8.

30. Pizer, *Literary Criticism of Frank Norris*, 69.

31. Michael Davitt Bell, who is almost completely unsympathetic to Norris, emphasizes the considerable confusion in the novelist's use of the terms *realism* and *romance*. Not infrequently, Bell points out, Norris uses them almost interchangeably as inherently "masculine" concepts that are preferable to a distinctly "feminine" art. Bell sees Norris as struggling, throughout his formulation of a "naturalist" agenda, to reconcile his devotion to the "art" of writing with his constant need for reassurance of the intactness of his masculinity. Bell locates the origin of this central conflict in Norris's psyche in the tensions emanating from his complex responses to his businessman father and his artistic mother (Bell, "The Revolt against Style: Frank Norris," *The Problem of American Realism*, 115–30.

32. Frank Norris, "Zola as a Romantic Writer"; reprinted in Pizer, *Literary Criticism of Frank Norris*, 71–72.

33. William B. Dillingham, *Frank Norris: Instinct and Art* (Boston: Houghton Mifflin, 1969).

34. June Howard, *Form and History in American Literary Naturalism* (Chapel Hill: University of North Carolina Press, 1985).

35. Jack London, *The People of the Abyss* (London: Arco Publications–Fitzroy Edition, 1963), 11.

36. See my essay "Jack London 'Down and Out in England': The Relevance of the Sociological Study *People of the Abyss* to London's Fiction," *Jack London Newsletter* 2 (September–December 1969): 79–83.

37. In Joseph X. Brennan, "Ironic and Symbolic Structure in Crane's *Maggie*"; reprinted in Gullason, *Maggie*, 183–84.

Chapter 2

The Fat Man Finds His Voice, Part 1
Michael Gold's *Jews without Money*

A central element in the creative strategies of Riis, Crane, Norris, and London is a narrative voice that can assume a bond of shared values and experience with an implied middle-class reader. This must have seemed an obvious device to Crane and Norris. Crane was, after all, the son of a small town minister, while Norris grew up in a comfortable, even affluent, environment. Riis and London probably came to use this kind of narrator much more consciously and deliberately. To do so, Riis had to suppress that part of his past when he was a new and desperately poor first-generation immigrant from Denmark. *The People of the Abyss* contains allusions to London's trip to the Yukon, but none to his earlier experiences of poverty in San Francisco and Oakland. It is as if London had to confront his bitter early years obliquely through an immersion in London's East End in order to obtain the psychological distance necessary to produce his masterpiece, *The Call of the Wild* (1903). *Call of the Wild* was, at any rate, the next book London wrote after *The People of the Abyss*.[1]

Because of the comparable narrative strategies found in *How the Other Half Lives*, *Maggie*, *McTeague*, and *The People of the Abyss*, a clear separation between narrative voice and subject matter exists in each work. In large part because of the novel's pervasive irony, Crane's narrator seems to be looking down on the Johnson family and on Pete and Nellie from a position safely above them. Norris's narrator, in contrast, so regularly and thoroughly invades the privacy of his characters that they often come to seem mere devices in an exploration of the exotic and the erotic within the lower depths. Riis adopts the persona of a guide taking the reader on a tour of the ghetto. He is much more overtly sympathetic to the oppressed inhabitants of the tenement than Crane and Norris are to their characters, though his racial stereotyping often dilutes this sympathy. London gives his narrator the unique privilege of moving freely back and forth between the desperate ugliness of London's East End and the "Upright" world on its border. Riis and London both employ narrators who see themselves as social scientists investigating an alien world.

As an almost inevitable result of such narrative detachment, these four works are marked by varying degrees of dehumanization in the characterizations of their central subjects. In making them prototypes of the exotic, Norris especially dehumanizes such important secondary characters as Zerkow and Maria Macapa. Riis, in the weakest parts of his work, presents not individual human beings but, rather, "the assisted Italian," the avaricious Jew, and the cruel Chinaman. London presents to us denizens of the East End who have been transformed by capitalistic oppression into a "new and different race." Crane reveals the most obvious ambivalence in his authorial approach to his characters. He desires to create a distinctly Christian sympathy for Maggie and thus generally idealizes her. Consequently, he depicts her descent into prostitution in a surrealistic and detached manner. In the first edition of his novel he briefly confronted the full grotesque horror of prostitution in his depiction of the fat man who accosts her just before her death. In the next edition, for whatever reason or reasons, this emblematic figure is deleted.

Crane's creation of and the subsequent suppression of the fat man as a personification of the ugly brutality of prostitution can be seen as an extreme example of the ways in which all four of these early biographers of the inner city view and approach their central subject matter. They were drawn to the ghetto as a rich field for the dramatic and obvious human suffering that they wanted to record in their writing. Yet, because of their own distance from this subject matter, their awareness of such a distance for implied middle-class readers, or both, they ultimately pulled back from real identification with the characters who people their works. To some degree at least, they had to be aware that, for the safe middle class, the ghetto seemed hardly less grotesque and ugly than prostitution. Moreover, Norris and London, however consciously, saw the inhabitants of the inner city in part as personifications of the psychic Other, socially forbidden and thus commonly repressed and denied inner needs and urges.

The most important development in the twentieth-century inner-city novel has been the disappearance of such narrative distance. This happened naturally and quickly when the fictional portrayers of the inner city became those products of it who wished to emphasize rather than suppress their origins. In their work Riis's money-hoarding Jew, Norris's insane and sadistic Zerkow, and Crane's "Hebrew" pawnbrokers are transformed into complex and generally sympathetic human beings. A desire to be seen as products of the oppressed inner city was especially strong in the group of writers who pioneered the emergence of "proletarian fiction" in the United States.

The Promise of the Golden Bear

No one is more closely associated with the emergence and the history of American proletarian fiction than Michael Gold. He produced in 1930 one of the first examples in this country of the politically committed inner-city novel, *Jews without Money*. Moreover, nine years earlier he had elaborated, in the *Liberator* magazine, a formula for the leftist writer, entitled "Towards Proletarian Art," which came to be seen as a manifesto for this kind of fiction in the United States. Gold remained so loyal and committed to the Communist Party and to revolutionary fiction that, by the time of his death in 1967, he was known as the "chief literary assassin for the Communist party of America."[2] His abiding importance, though, is as the author of "Towards Proletarian Art" and *Jews without Money* and as an editor of such historically important leftist journals as the *Masses*, the *Liberator*, and the *New Masses*.[3] In 1930 he issued, under the title "Proletarian Realism," another proclamation of what proletarian fiction should be. Still, it is the 1921 manifesto, "Towards Proletarian Art," which most reads like a preface for *Jews without Money*, his only novel, which would not appear for almost a decade.

Michael Brewster Folsom describes this manifesto as "essentially an explanation of [Gold's] own experience and practice blown up in bombast." He then quotes a central passage from it:

> The tenement is in my blood. When I think it is the tenement thinking. When I hope it is the tenement hoping. I am not an individual; I am all that the tenement group poured into me during those early years of my spiritual travail. Why should we artists born in tenements go beyond them for our expression? Can we go beyond them? "Life burns in both camps," in the tenements and in the palaces, but can we understand that which is not our very own?
>
> The masses are still primitive and clean, and artists must turn to them for strength again. The primitive sweetness, the primitive calm, the primitive ability to create simply and without fever or ambition, for primitive satisfaction and self-sufficiency—they must be found again.[4]

From its beginning *Jews without Money* establishes a crucial bond of identity between its first-person narrator and the New York City East Side tenement in which he grows up:

I can never forget the East Side street where I lived as a boy.

It was a block from the notorious Bowery, a tenement canyon hung with fire-escapes, bed-clothing, and faces.

Always these faces at the tenement windows. The street never failed them. It was an immense excitement. It never slept. It roared like a sea. It exploded like fireworks.[5]

Gold consistently maintains and emphasizes this bond between narrator and setting throughout the novel. As a result, one critic credits him with a kind of summing up of one established literary form and the resulting creation of a new one: "Fictionalized memoirs of the ghetto had been published before, but the success of *Jews without Money* in effect established a contemporary genre."[6] Gold's novel does generally succeed in a kind of dual effect: it conveys the feeling of a personal memoir while nevertheless imposing on its material the requisite unity of successful art. Still, critics have debated whether the work reads most successfully as an autobiography or as a novel. Walter Rideout, for instance, writes that *Jews without Money* "is perhaps more accurately characterized as a book of personal reminiscence rather than a novel."[7] Similarly, Allen Guttmann says that it "has no plot in the conventional sense" and "is more like an unstructured memoir than a novel."[8] Other commentators on the work have seen that its autobiographical elements are, in fact, ultimately less important than they initially appear to be. After comparing *Jews without Money* in its final form to previously published selections from it and to what we do know for certain about Gold's life, Richard Tuerk concludes that, to the extent that the book is autobiographical, "it is the autobiography of an invented character that vaguely resembles one of Gold's favorite books during his formative years, [Mark Twain's] *Adventures of Huckleberry Finn*."[9]

Tuerk's insight is especially perceptive in two ways. To a considerable degree the "autobiographical" elements in the novel represent an artistic strategy on Gold's part, a calculated attempt to make the work seem more "realistic." The comparison of Gold's novel to *Huckleberry Finn* is instructive for more reasons that what it tells us about this Jewish writer's taste in literature. *Jews without Money* is, like Twain's novel, an episodic work that often *appears* to be heading toward no clear, definitive ending. Its episodic structure has encouraged the perception that it is a work of loosely connected memoirs rather than an aesthetically controlled and unified work of fiction. Tuerk is also onto something in his comment that the book is a kind of "autobiography of an invented character." The novelist Michael Gold constructs the character "Michael Gold" out of his personal experience and his imagination in order to convey an artistic and a political vision.

Diane Levenberg, in an earlier essay, to some degree anticipates Tuerk. She also argues that the book's autobiographical feel is a calculated literary effect, though she ascribes to Gold a somewhat different motivation for this approach:

> Gold was trying to revive the original purpose of the novel. In the 18th century, novels were invented to convey, in a time-bound realistic manner, the story of one person's life. Mostly, they were written by the middle-class for the middle-class reader. Those who did the most to popularize this new literary amusement, however, were its real readers—an oppressed class of servants and apprentices who found the time, borrowed the books and stole the necessary candles.
>
> What Gold was calling for, in 1930, was a working-class writer who would write for the working class. Having finished *Jews without Money*, he could feel secure that he had answered his own call.[10]

Whatever one thinks about her concept of the history of the rise of the novel, Levenberg's idea that Gold was, in effect, attempting to adapt the most familiar convention of the early British novel, a plot that disguised itself as a realistic account of the life of a "real person," to a twentieth-century proletarian readership seems valid. For an implied modern working-class reader, "Michael Gold" would function in much the same way that Tom Jones had for eighteenth-century middle-class readers. The two characters embody sufficient familiarity to make each seem believable to his targeted audience. Certainly, the most truly revolutionary aspect of Gold's art was his desire to create and inspire fiction that would appeal to a new kind of readership—the largely uneducated working class for whom, in England and the United States at least, literature and art had traditionally been considered irrelevant.

It must be said that the experiences of "Michael Gold" do parallel, in several crucial ways, those of his creator. Gold the novelist was born Itshok Isaac Granich on 12 April 1893 and grew up in poverty, living with his family in a tenement on New York City's East Side. The most sympathetic, and in many ways most perceptive, Gold critic, Michael Brewster Folsom, describes the evolution of Itshok Granich into Michael Gold, revolutionary editor, playwright, and novelist: "As a schoolboy, Gold adopted Irwin for a Christian name; he wrote as Irwin Granich until 1921; during the Palmer Raids he took Michael Gold for a protective pseudonym, and it stuck" (223). Like his fictional counterpart, Gold was an intelligent and sensitive boy and young man who deeply felt the pain of his severely prescribed educational opportunities.

He was able to attend Harvard for less than a semester before he had to drop out because of insufficient funds; he experienced just enough of an academic life to tell him that it was what he desperately needed and wanted. Along with the novel's episodic structure, the close similarities between the careers of author and character are the principal reasons that *Jews without Money* is sometimes mistakenly dismissed as essentially artless autobiography.

Gold's underlying and subtly controlling artistic approach is perhaps best illustrated by the novel's abrupt and usually condemned ending. Events leading up to the book's conclusion have forced the main character into what seems a dead end. His father has been reduced by a series of misfortunes into peddling apples on the street, a fate that destroys the little pride the older man has somehow managed to retain, and his son has decided, after much pain and with considerable bitterness, that he cannot move on to high school. Michael finds first a job running errands "in a silk house" but quickly loses it as the result of anti-Semitism: "How often was I made to remember I belonged to the accursed race, the race whose chief misfortune it was to have produced a Christ" (306). He then goes to work in the suffocating hell of "a factory where incandescent gas mantles are made" (306). Despite the physical and psychological torments of a grotesque supervisor called "Monkey Face," Michael, still a boy, lasts for six months in the factory: "Monkey Face tortured me. I lost fifteen pounds in weight. I raced in nightmares in my sleep. I forgot my college dreams: I forgot everything, but the gas mantles" (308).

Rescued from this hell, significantly by his mother, he undergoes a long and desperate time before finding any peace, any sanctuary from the desperate poverty that seems his only future: "Jobs, jobs. I drifted from one to the other, without plan, without hope. I was one of the many. I was caught like my father in poverty's trap. I was nothing, bound for nowhere" (308). As several critics have pointed out, a symbolic pattern of entrapment, primarily economic in origin, runs throughout *Jews without Money*. Adolescence is a desperate time for the character, Michael Gold. The pain resulting from his feeling that he can never escape the poverty of the East Side is intensified by extreme psychological pressures, which result in recurrent thoughts of suicide. Moreover, the pressures of his awakening sexuality are transformed into a religious fanaticism: "Sex began to torture me. I developed a crazy religious streak. I prayed on the tenement roof in moonlight to the Jewish Messiah who would redeem the world" (309). In anger and despair he begins to attach himself to Nigger, a violent boy from the neighborhood who is clearly headed toward a future as a criminal.

Clearly standing on the brink of self-destruction, Michael is suddenly rescued in an unexpected manner. He hears one night "a man on an East Side soap-box" proclaim the coming Marxist revolution that will reform and redeem the world. Instantly, he is converted, and the novel ends:

O workers' Revolution, you brought hope to me, a lonely, suicidal boy. You are the true Messiah. You will destroy the East Side when you come, and build there a garden for the human spirit.

O Revolution, that forced me to think, to struggle and to live.

O great Beginning! (309)

Michael's conversion to Marxism takes all of five such brief paragraphs and initially seems unconnected to anything that has preceded it in the novel. Not surprisingly, it has generally been criticized as being forced and arbitrary. Marcus Klein, for instance, writes that "the scene has a duration of exactly six sentences and is remarkable chiefly for being so abrupt as it is, and so actually discordant with what has gone before" (186). Similarly, Diane Levenberg asserts that "this final epiphany is only twelve lines long and it occurs very abruptly. In no way have we been prepared for young Mike's sudden espousal of Communism" (237).

For most critics the fact that his character's Marxist conversion is obviously based on an experience of Gold's only makes this ending seem even more forced and arbitrary as well as adding to the perception that *Jews without Money* is closer to being an autobiography than a novel. One April afternoon in 1914, as he was returning home after unsuccessfully looking for a job, Gold wandered into Union Square and heard the female radical Elizabeth Gurley Flynn preaching that communism was the only answer to "the unemployment problem." Soon a riot broke out in which Gold, a mere bystander, was assaulted by a policeman. Michael Brewster Folsom points out that the real Michael Gold's initiation into political radicalism was, in fact, almost as sudden as his fictional character's:

Before he blundered into Union Square that afternoon . . . heard Gurley Flynn, and had his head cracked when the cops busted up the rally, Gold did not know there was [except on a strictly personal level] an "unemployment problem," much less a movement to abolish it. His "conversion" was more like an awakening, for he had been converted from nothing but ignorance, and it was that quick, if not that easy. After the melee he was taken in by the proprietor of an anarchist bookshop off the square. He was soon out on a soapbox himself. (238–39)

Folsom believes that, in the ending of Gold's novel, the separation between author and character virtually disappears as the novelist locates in his personal experience a way to conclude his book.

In fact, when one realizes that *Jews without Money* is held together by a kind of subtle poetic unity rather than the more controlled and obvious structure traditionally associated with fictional realism, its ending no longer seems quite so forced and arbitrary. To understand fully how this unconventional structure works, it is necessary to remember that Gold's book belongs to a second literary tradition in addition to that of the urban proletarian novel. It also has an important place in the evolution of the American Jewish novel. Levenberg views it in company with Anzia Yezierska's *Bread Givers* (1925) and Henry Roth's *Call It Sleep* (1934) as virtually defining the Jewish-American urban protest novel. (*Jews without Money* is not infrequently compared to *Call It Sleep*.) In *The Invention of the Jew* Bernard Sherman discusses Gold's book in the context of the Jewish-American "education novel": "As the first author of an education novel to be born in the United States, [Gold] marks the second stage of the education novel."[11] Especially perceptive is Helge Norman Nilsen's argument that Gold's Jewish-American sensitivity and experience enabled him to produce a novel of more depth and complexity than can always be expected in a naturalistic protest novel: "In *Jews without Money* the narrator's vision of slum life and struggling humanity is both sensitive and compassionate. The Jewish milieu is rendered with an authority and understanding which is not diminished by the author's radical naturalism. These qualities are the ones that characterize all the important works of Jewish-American writers, irrespective of period and subject matter."[12]

Jews without Money is most clearly naturalistic in its emphasis upon environmental determinism. Gold extensively, and sometimes with quite purple prose, documents the sordid and violent nature of his ghetto setting. For most of his novel it seems that such a brutal environment must inevitably crush any gentleness or compassion that might miraculously flower within it, and, in fact, the young narrator, Michael, develops considerable guilt over the ways in which he allows the brutality of the ghetto to compromise his inherent decency. Yet there is in the book, virtually from the beginning, a counter-stress upon the abiding strength and decency of several of its characters—most important of all, Michael's mother. These strong characters, even though they know little or nothing about international communism, foreshadow Michael's concluding conversion and salvation in that they embody a communal strength among the Jewish tenement dwellers which can momentarily be eclipsed but not permanently erased. As Folsom points out, there is, in Gold's vision of the ghetto, a kind of affirmation bordering on nostalgia decidedly absent in Jack London's treatments of comparable environments: "London was always terrified by the degradation of the 'abyss'; Gold found honor, if not love, on a garbage dump" (228). "Love on a Garbage Dump" is, in fact, the title of one of Gold's short stories.

Gold achieves the poetic unity of *Jews without Money* by juxtaposing grim details of the destructive effects of the tenement environment with examples of the indestructible kindness and humanity of the novel's affirmative characters. This subtle unity rests upon three underlying assumptions, which are developed gradually in the novel. From the beginning of his book Gold emphasizes the brutality of the tenement setting as the direct legacy of U..S. capitalism, thus clearly identifying a negative force that must be somehow overcome. Less overtly and more gradually, he develops the idea that such an abstract and yet pervasive barrier to a humane existence can be meaningfully opposed only by the communal strength and decency of the Jewish inhabitants of the tenement. This communal strength is personified by the novel's affirmative characters and represented initially by the Jewish religion. The longing for the coming of a Messiah who will liberate an oppressed people is a recurrent emphasis in the novel. Michael, the young narrator, has become sufficiently assimilated to U.S. culture to feel the need to secularize the Messiah concept, and he wants a savior who closely resembles Buffalo Bill. He has "learned" that the mythical frontiersman vanquished the Native American through brute force, and he wants his Messiah to do the same thing to American Gentiles. Not surprisingly, when he describes such a longing to his rabbi, the holy man is horrified and lectures the boy that the Messiah, when he appears, will conquer through love rather than brute force.

Still, Gold's implicit point is that the old-world faith is not adequate to oppose the exigencies of life in the capitalistic United States. Two secondary characters in the novel reflect Gold's complex response to the old-world Jewish faith. The Hasidic rabbi, Reb Samuel, personifies the historical power and integrity of European Judaism as well as the inflexibility that renders it inadequate to the new world. He is described as communicating an almost biblical spirituality: "He had that air of grandeur that surrounds so many old pious Jews. The world can move them no longer; they have seen and suffered all" (191). Consequently, he functions as the moral conscience of the tenement world that Michael and his family inhabit. He is so rigid and unyielding concerning observation of Hasidic rituals, however, that he has begun to drive away some members of his congregation.

In sharp contrast there is no ambiguity in the characterization of Michael's Chaider instructor, Reb Moisha: "This man was a walking, belching symbol of the decay of orthodox Judaism. What could such as he teach any one? He was ignorant as a rat. He was a foul smelling, emaciated beggar who had never read anything, or seen anything, who knew absolutely nothing but this sterile memory course in dead Hebrew which he whipped into the heads and backsides of little boys" (65). There is a comparable character in Roth's *Call It Sleep*, and in both books these mindless sadists signal the imminent death of a religion that has degenerated into empty and sterile practice. Ironically, despite his obvious sanctity, Reb Samuel's uncompromising advocacy of Hasidic ritual prevents him from being, in a new and increasingly secularized society, an effective countering voice for the preservation of old-world faith. In fact, his intense devotion merely allows him to be easily victimized in the United States.

At one point Reb Samuel attempts to revive the devotion of his congregation by recruiting Rabbi Schmarya, a supposedly devout rabbi from Europe, to come to New York. During the celebration of the new rabbi's arrival in the United States, young Michael senses that this eagerly anticipated holy man is, in reality, a selfish hypocrite and tries to communicate his misgivings to Reb Samuel, who refuses to listen. The boy proves to have been perceptive, indeed, when Schmarya immediately becomes thoroughly Americanized and uses his new position solely for his own power and comfort. It is significant that it is the young narrator who intuits Schmarya's corruption and Reb Samuel who refuses to hear such unpleasant truth. Michael will discover a new religion suited to the secular power and turmoil of U.S. society, while Samuel, "the saint of the umbrella store," will be unable to surrender his devotion to the old European faith.

Gold's response to traditional Judaism is not, then, simple, unqualified repudiation. He sees it as a reflection of the communal strength and goodness emanating from the pure souls of such people as his mother. But he also believed that it was an inadequate weapon against the pervasive corruption of U.S. capitalism. A more worldly and more militant faith was needed to resist capitalistic oppression. At the end of his novel he allows his narrator to discover and be instantly converted by just such a religion—international communism. *Jews without Money* often seems to lack a controlling narrative structure because Gold does not make apparent his dual thesis that Marxism is a necessary substitute for old-world Judaism and that both religions emanate from the integrity and conviction of the oppressed urban masses until the novel's abrupt ending. He seems to have felt it unnecessary to elaborate on the significance of young Michael's encounter with the "man on an East Side soap-box" because it is never necessary or even possible to explain an overwhelmingly emotional religious conversion. It is not an accident that just two paragraphs before his unexpected moment of salvation the narrator confesses having "developed a crazy religious streak" and praying for a "Jewish Messiah who would redeem the world." It is also not surprising that Gold uses some of the same characters who personify the integrity of Judaism to foreshadow, especially in the last half of the book, the narrator's concluding discovery of the true faith of international communism.

For much of *Jews without Money* the hope embodied in these affirmative characters is almost engulfed in Gold's often emotional, if not lurid, documentation of the deterministic power of the ghetto setting. A causal relationship between the suffering of the immigrants and the exploitative nature of U.S. capitalism is established early in the novel:

> America is so rich and fat, because it has eaten the tragedy of millions of immigrants.
>
> To understand this, you should have seen at twilight, after the day's work, one of our pick and shovel wops watering his can of beloved flowers. Brown peasant, son of thirty generations of peasants, in a sweaty undershirt by a tenement window, feeling the lost poetry. Uprooted! Lost! Betrayed! (41–42)

"Betrayed" specifically by America, the new nation that promised a life of unlimited possibilities but which, in actuality, proved to be a land of degrading oppression. Bernard Sherman argues that Gold's novel depicts a central shift in the perception of America by its immigrant characters. They cease, he points out, viewing their adopted country as *"die goldene medineh"* (the golden country) and come to resent it as *"Amerika ganif "* (America, the thief) (79). They have been robbed of any dream of a decent life and, in many cases, of the capacity for faith in any future.

Having diagnosed the illness ineluctably destroying the inhabitants of the tenements as capitalistic oppression, Gold need only document its symptoms and, finally, prescribe a cure. Certainly one of the most memorable of his details concerning the poverty of life in the tenements is his description of the bedbugs that torment Michael and his family every night:

> Did God make bedbugs? One steaming hot night I couldn't sleep for the bedbugs. They have a peculiar nauseating smell of their own; it is the smell of poverty. They crawl slowly and pompously, bloated with blood, and the touch and smell of these parasites wakens every nerve to disgust.
>
> (Bedbugs are what people mean when they say: Poverty. There are enough pleasant superficial liars writing in America. I will write a truthful book of Poverty; I will mention bedbugs.) (71)

Gold is, of course, doing much more than simply "mentioning" bedbugs; he is, in fact, making them a kind of emblem of poverty and oppression. In his reference to the "pleasant superficial liars writing in America," one assumes a satiric dig at those who wrote about poverty without having experienced it and who consequently romanticized it. His novel, in contrast, bears the unmistakable stamp of the insider. "Bedbugs" are obviously not what most people "mean when they say: Poverty," but they are a memorable example of the kind of grotesque or sordid detail not uncommonly used by naturalistic writers to validate the factual integrity of their work. Nelson Algren, for example, makes comparable use of a cockroach to testify to the accuracy of his description of a jail cell in *The Man with the Golden Arm*.

There is, however, a key difference in strategy between Algren's account of the cockroach and Gold's description of the bedbugs. Algren is consciously writing for a safe, middle-class reader who most probably had never been inside a jail cell. His cockroach functions, then, as a bit of esoteric knowledge, as evidence of his narrator's privileged status in describing jail cells. Lacking the relevant experience to confirm or deny the novelist's testimony concerning the presence of roaches in jails, the sheltered reader will, he hoped, react by thinking that the detail sounds right and, by extension, that Algren is a reliable expert concerning such sordid settings. In contrast, Gold's implied working-class reader should respond to his account of the assault of the bedbugs with a personal and immediate sense of outrage. In *Jews without Money* the bedbugs function as a call for working-class resistance to an oppressive capitalism.

The novel offers related examples of the unsanitary condition of life in the tenements. For instance, it describes the way in which many of the inhabitants of these suffocating structures dispose of their garbage during the summer months:

> Summer. Everywhere the garbage. Plop, bung, and another fat, spreading bundle dropped from a tenement window. Many of the East Side women had this horrible custom. To save walking downstairs, they wrapped their garbage in newspapers and flung it in the street. In summer the East Side heavens rained with potato peelings, coffee grounds, herring heads and dangerous soup bones. Bang, went a bundle, and the people in the street ducked as if a machine gun sounded. (56–57)

This description of the torrential downpour of the garbage is a central detail in Gold's narrative strategy. First, it functions as a metaphor for the corrupting power of capitalistic America. The garbage literally rains down upon the tenement streets from above, just as capitalistic power controls from a privileged external position life in the East Side ghetto. In addition, the fact that the tenement dwellers themselves are, in this case, responsible for desecrating their streets is evidence that they have already been corrupted to some degree by life in the United States. As the novel progresses, Gold's young narrator will become increasingly aware of, and guilty about, his own actions that mirror those of his oppressors.

He comes to regret, for instance, the ways in which he, like most of those around him, mistreats the hordes of cats that roam the ghetto streets. The tortured cats, in fact, function as a metaphor for the brutalization of Michael, the narrator, and his young male ghetto companions:

> It was a world of violence and stone, there were too many cats, there were too many children.
> The stink of cats filled the tenement halls. Cats fought around each garbage can in the East Side struggle for life. These cats were not the smug purring pets of the rich, but outcasts, criminals and fiends.

... They were so desperate they would sometimes fight a man. ... We tortured them, they tortured us. It was poverty. (63–64)

Gold's underlying thesis, of course, is that the cruelty of life in the ghetto often inspires a comparable cruelty in the behavior of those who live there. This idea leads directly to discussions of the ways in which sex becomes a bestial activity in the tenements and of the appeal of gangs and criminal activities to young boys trapped there.

One of the first images in the novel is of prostitutes crowding the ghetto streets and openly selling themselves there. The narrator emphasizes that this scene constituted his introduction to sex and that he was consequently unable, for some time, to believe that it could be "good as well as evil" (26). More than one critic has pointed out the novel's seemingly disproportionate emphasis upon sex. This motif, however, is more aesthetically relevant and valid than it may initially appear. Gold characterizes Michael as a boy and young man who is frightened, more or less consciously, by his intense sexuality. He thus seeks, often without realizing that he is doing so, less threatening outlets for his "evil" needs and desires. He displays an intense religiosity and is suddenly converted to Marxism when his initial faith fails.

Gold never makes very explicit a thesis that one expects to be a major thrust in the novel; he does not overtly argue that prostitution in the tenement is deliberately perpetuated by U.S. capitalism. His response to this subject is too emotional to sustain any prolonged rational analysis. The treatment of prostitution in *Jews without Money* recalls the work of earlier naturalistic writers, especially Frank Norris. Gold and Norris both seem, at times, to view sexuality as a particularly upsetting manifestation of the human propensity to atavistic reversal. At their worst both depict sexuality as irredeemably animalistic, as a dangerous force that must be caged and repressed. As with much of Norris, there is an unmistakable puritan subtext in *Jews without Money*. It can be seen in Gold's idealization of Michael's mother as well as in his treatment of the young narrator's response to the tenement prostitutes. In this context a key early scene in the novel describes the mother's corporal punishment of Michael after he joins his street companions in cruelly taunting Rosie, an especially grotesque prostitute. From his mature perspective the narrator comments upon the futility of such discipline: "Vain beating; the East Side street could not be banished with a leather strap. It was my world; it was my mother's world, too. We *had* to live in it, and learn what it chose to teach us" (19). The narrative thrust of *Jews without Money* is that such knowledge can only be transcended through the true faith of Marxism.

The mother is similarly helpless in preventing her son from responding to the appeal of the street gang. Through two secondary characters Gold makes clear the close link between young gangs and adult criminality. Nigger is a perennially angry youth who personifies the temptation of gangs and gang warfare to young Michael. Gold makes even his physical appearance seem ominous: "He was built for power like a tugboat, squat and solid. His eyes, even then, had the contemptuous glare of the criminal and genius. His nose had been squashed at birth, and with his black hair and murky face, made inevitable the East Side nickname: 'Nigger'" (42). The boy's facial disfigurement is a metonymic representation of the moral and spiritual damage that he has sustained through life in the tenements. Yet Gold succeeds in making him something of a romantic character, a prototype of the young urban outlaw. His rebellion against the ghetto adds a heroic dimension to his characterization that is totally lacking in such a comparable figure as Crane's Jimmie Johnson, even though most of the battles he fights are as futile and even destructive as Jimmie's fights for the honor of Rum Alley.

Nigger is, for instance, the dominant figure in the brutal and senseless battles that young Michael's gang wages against any and all intruders. From his mature perspective the narrator emphasizes the absurd and twisted "patriotism" that inspired this potentially deadly warfare: "The East Side, for children, was a world plunged in eternal war. It was suicide to walk into the next block. Each block was a separate nation, and when a strange boy appeared, the patriots swarmed" (42). This senseless gang warfare functions in *Jews without Money* as a metaphor for the ways in which U.S. capitalism controls the masses by dividing them. The street battles are a grim and bloody kind of competition and foreshadow the class warfare that necessarily supports laissez-faire capitalism. Thus, Michael's sometimes eager participation in them contributes to the unfocused, yet intense, guilt that haunts him until his conversion to Marxism. Nevertheless, there is, despite his mature repudiation of it, an unmistakably heroic dimension in Gold's account of this adolescent warfare, and Nigger is the most heroic of all the youthful warriors: "We often boasted about our remarkable bravery to each other. But Nigger was bravest of the brave, the chieftain of our brave savage tribe" (43).

The inevitable adult fate of Nigger is personified in the character of Louis One Eye, an adult gangster who keeps pigeons on his tenement roof. Gold's treatment of Louis anticipates the ambivalent narrative response to the Jewish gangster that one finds in Daniel Fuchs's trilogy of novels about the New York Jewish ghetto—*Summer in Williamsburg* (1934), *Homage to*

Blenholt (1936), and *Low Company* (1937)—and in E. L. Doctorow's brilliant novel *Billy Bathgate* (1989). While Louis is depicted as being cruel and even savage, he is also shown to be a victim of societal injustice and brutality. A "legend" concerning Louis's conversion to criminality is repeated throughout the tenement world in which he lives. When he is fourteen he nearly kills his father while attempting to prevent the man from physically assaulting Louis's mother. As a result of this act, he is sent to a reform school, where, as punishment for breaking a "rule," he is lashed with a leather belt for an hour by a "keeper." During the beating the belt buckle strikes and destroys one of his eyes. Gold wants to take no chance that a reader might miss the implications of this brutal story and rhetorically asks, "Is there any gangster who is as cruel and heartless as the present legal State?" (128). Moreover, he validates the legend by depicting Louis's mother as being still devoted to her son.

The pigeons function as a metaphor for the residue of sensitivity that survives within Louis's soul. They are thus an example of the literary naturalist's fondness for the one incongruous detail that calls attention to, and thus reinforces, the contrasting dominant elements contained in a characterization or a setting, for example, McTeague's beloved canary. In addition, however, the birds constitute an image of the ghetto's seemingly unshakable control over Louis and the members of Michael's gang. Twice each day the gangster releases his pets and thus allows them a brief moment of freedom before he calls them back to their cages: "He whistled the long mysterious signal known to pigeon fanciers. From the glimmering sky the pigeons descended like a heavenly chain gang, and returned meekly to their prison. They were not free. We children always marveled at this, but now the secret is known to me; pigeons, like men, are easily tamed with food" (129). Until his salvation through Marxism Michael is also unable to fly free of the ghetto.

Despite his devotion to his mother and his love of his pigeons, Louis is predominantly a cruel and selfish character, and it is these traits that ultimately destroy him. He makes the mistake of angering Nigger, who has his own kind of family loyalty. What dooms the gangster is his decision to corrupt Lily, Nigger's older sister, in order to turn her into a prostitute. Subsequently, the gang leader organizes his followers for a retaliatory raid on Louis's pigeon house:

We entered and cut the throats of forty pigeons.
    They fluttered their wings as we murdered them, then lay silent and gory.

We whispered to each other, and stared about us, expecting Louis. Our hands reeked with blood. (267–68)

The slaughter of Louis's pigeons is merely the curtain raiser for Nigger's real revenge. Seven years after Lily dies "of what the East Side called 'the black syphilis,'" Nigger has grown up and become a gangster himself. Of course, "one of his first deeds as a gangster was to kill Louis One Eye" (272). It is as if Louis had been tracked down and destroyed by a personification of his own brutalized childhood. The naturalistic determinism that underscores virtually all of *Jews without Money* is nowhere stronger than in Gold's accounts of the doomed and savage lives of Nigger and Louis One Eye.

It is crucial to the theme and narrative strategy of the novel that Michael participates in the killing of the pigeons. At this point the direction of his life is very much up for grabs. In fact, he is on the brink of becoming another Nigger, who will in turn grow up to emulate Louis One Eye. What saves him is his own evolving sense of family. Throughout much of *Jews without Money* the street gang and Michael's actual family are joined in battle for the ultimate possession of his soul. His mother, especially, stands in opposition to the destructive influence of Nigger. Gold's thorough idealization of this maternal figure inspired Leslie Fiedler to write that "it is not for nothing that Mike Gold has been called the Al Jolson of the Communist Movement."[13] In a preface to a 1935 republication of his novel he left little doubt that his own mother was the model for his fictional character and elevated both the real and the fictional women to the realm of secular sainthood:

My mother, who is the heroine of "Jews without Money," died just a year ago this month. She lived, to the last, in the same East Side tenement street, and prayed in the same synagogue. This was her world; though her sons born in America were forced into a different world.

We could not worship her gods. But we loved our mother; and she loved us; and the life of this brave and beautiful proletarian woman is the best answer to the fascist liars I know.[14]

In fact, Gold may or may not have been so close and devoted to his mother, but the actual biography matters much less here than the novelist's intention to confuse the boundary between his own life and that of his character. By 1935 Gold's was a prominent name in U.S. leftist circles, and in this preface he is casting himself as someone to be emulated, as a heroic individual who is not unlike one of his heroes, Lincoln. He had, after all, like Lincoln, transcended an obscure background in which he had suffered from poverty and ignorance. Still, it was crucial to his political purpose that he not treat his hard-won prominence as a strictly individual accomplishment. It had to be seen, rather, as an example of the kind of personal triumph which was only possible to those who found, in their roots, an abiding strength and determination. It was necessary, in other words, to identify a source of faith which had sustained him before his conversion to Marxism and which had, in fact, anticipated that conversion. For the purposes of fiction that early faith had to be embodied in certain characters in the novel; it could not remain a strictly abstract fictional motif. His mother, and the mother of "Michael" in the novel, become emblematic figures, personifications of the indestructible strength and integrity of the Jewish tenement community.

At one point Gold virtually explains the role of Michael's mother as a symbolic figure in the novel: "Mother! Momma! I am still bound to you by the cords of birth. I cannot forget you. *I must remain faithful to the poor because I cannot be faithless to you! I believe in the poor because I have known you.* The world must be made gracious for the poor! Momma, you taught me that!" (158; my italics). In selflessly caring for other people, whether they are family or not, the mother becomes a kind of Jewish saint. As a mother to the entire tenement community, she anticipates later maternal-political figures in American literature, most clearly Steinbeck's Ma Joad. Significantly, her capacity for generous sacrifice is representative of the tenement wives: "How often have I seen my mother help families who were evicted because they could not pay rent. She wrapped herself in her old shawl, and went begging through the tenements for pennies. . . . But this is an old custom on the East Side; whenever a family is to be evicted, the neighboring mothers put on their shawls and beg from door to door" (161–62). Her inherent kindness and compassion are so strong that, even though she hates Gentiles in the abstract, she unfailingly helps them as well. Gold's novel, and its ending especially, imply a political application of this kindness which crosses religious boundaries—the lesson that, after Marxist conversion, one should hate capitalists as an abstract class but still be willing to reach out to them on a personal, individual level. It is, after all, difficult to convert others through pure hatred.

In addition to Michael's mother, four other characters in the novel personify the positive and sustaining qualities of the tenement community. The first, Michael's sensitive young friend Joey Cohen, is introduced into the novel primarily in order to be destroyed. Joey dies horribly when he is run over by a horse cart and, through his death, attains the status of one who has been martyred by capitalistic oppression: "Joey Cohen! you who were sacrificed under the wheels of a horse car, I see you again, Joey! I see your pale face, so sensitive despite its childish grime and bruises" (50). Marcus Klein points out that, on a strictly logical level, the Joey Cohen episode makes no clear sense: "There has been nothing in the novel to motivate such grief, and the observation that Joey has been 'sacrificed' is patently absurd—there is an important lesson here for little boys, but not so grandiose a one" (187–88). In fact, there is nothing inevitable about Joey's dying because he hitches a ride on a horse cart: Michael and his other friends do it all the time, and none of them dies because of it.

Yet it may make sense in the context of literary naturalism. It is one of those completely arbitrary events so common in naturalistic fiction that seem, in retrospect, to have been part of some indecipherable design; one thinks, for instance, of Trina's winning the lottery prize in Norris's *McTeague*. Klein is also correct in saying that Joey's tragedy is hardly prepared for in the novel. It is, however, immediately preceded by this poetic description of the boy: "Joey was the dreamy kid in spectacles who was so sorry when he killed the butterfly. He was always reading books, and had many queer ideas. It was he who put the notion in my head of becoming a doctor. I had always imagined I wanted to be a fireman" (49). Joey's fictional role is so intensely symbolic that it verges on allegory. He represents, in part, the sensitive, idealistic side of Michael, which the brutality of life in the ghetto threatens to destroy. This symbolic mode of characterization necessitates that he be a one-dimensional figure barely glimpsed in the novel. It is worth noting that his only memorable contribution to the novel, other than dying horribly, is to be approached on the street by a grotesque pederast. Before crushing him, the ghetto attempts unsuccessfully to corrupt him. Michael would undoubtedly have been corrupted or crushed had it not been for his mother's care and the lesson of her generosity, Joey's martyrdom, and the examples of three other characters.

His Aunt Lena begins the necessary process of translating the communal strength of the ghetto into political action. She nearly sees her beauty and kindness destroyed by the hard drudgery of a sweatshop. In describing this common mode of exploiting women in U.S. urban centers, Gold's novel follows the naturalistic tradition of Crane's *Maggie* and Dreiser's *Sister Carrie*. Like Carrie Meeber, but for different reasons, Lena is too strong to be ground up by working in a sweatshop. Whereas Dreiser's heroine discovers and is rescued by Drouet and Hurstwood, Lena is saved by her involvement in a labor union. After disappearing for most of the novel, she reappears near the end, when she shocks Michael's father by describing her participation in a strike: "She was thinner, she had wrinkles. The sweatshops aged people prematurely. But her mind had grown in the struggle. She amazed us all by her eloquence, by her proud courage and dignity. And her eyes were still beautiful" (236). She has also grown tougher in ways that the generation of Michael's parents cannot reconcile with their old-world concepts of femininity. She is, for instance, unapologetically involved in a physical struggle with some men who have been hired to break up the strike: "'But how we scratched their faces,' she chuckled grimly. 'They will remember us girls.' My mother was horrified. She begged my aunt not to go into the fire again. But my aunt smiled. 'It's war,' she said, and went every morning as usual" (237).

Young Michael will also remember this first lesson in the necessity of class warfare and, unlike his saintly mother, will not be horrified by it. He is not, however, the only character in the novel to fall in love with Aunt Lena. For thematic reasons Gold develops a contrast between two doctors: they are the thoroughly Americanized Dr. Axelrod, whom the tenement community respects precisely because of the condescension and arrogance with which he approaches his patients, and young Dr. Solow, whose unconventional and selfless approach to medicine causes him to be distrusted by that same community. Nevertheless, Michael's family, like most of their neighbors, usually seek treatment from Dr. Solow simply because he does not demand payment in advance. Gold is utilizing this generous young man as an emblematic figure in the novel: he is a prototype of the revolutionary social commitment represented by Marxism, which is unselfish and scientific in nature. Gold is implying that, because of its strangeness, communism, like the good doctor, initially inspires distrust in the very people it seeks to help. It is hardly surprising, then, that Solow is motivated in part by an essentially leftist political stance or that he quickly falls in love with Lena.

He, for instance, baffles the tenement world with this advice to one chronically ill worker in a sweatshop: "Brother, no medicine can cure you. You must join a labor union" (233). It would seem that, when Solow asks Aunt Lena to marry him, she would be predestined to accept him. In the tradition of sexual stereotyping Gold would have thus set up a marriage between the scientific and, of course, *male* mind and the nurturing and, inevitably, *female* soul of the political Left. It comes as no little surprise that Lena refuses the doctor's proposal because she is already engaged. Thematically, it is not so surprising that her fiancé is a strike leader *or* that the manner in which Solow accepts her refusal constitutes one of the more dramatic *and obvious* gestures of political correctness in American literature: "'Hurrah for the unions! Down with the sweatshops!' the Doctor suddenly shouted" (239).

Aunt Lena and Doctor Solow thus begin to give young Michael a political context for the example of communal and religious integrity and solidarity he has received from his mother and Joey Cohen. All that is still needed to prepare him for his climactic conversion is some sense of the role of intellectual history as a catalyst for individual self-renewal, and the potential for such awareness is given him by a character who is hardly more than a plot device in the novel. When he is forced to forgo high school because of his family's poverty, he feels intense bitterness. Sensing the boy's pain, Miss Barry, his teacher, volunteers to provide Michael a list of the readings required for a high school certificate if he will promise her that he will study at night. Initially, he rejects her overture: "I was trying to be hard. For years my ego had been fed by every one's praise of my precocity. I had always loved books; I was mad about books; I wanted passionately to go to high school and college. Since I couldn't, I meant to despise all that nonsense" (304).

Still, Miss Barry persists in her attempt to encourage the promising youth and challenges him with the examples of two American icons. First, she agrees that studying every night will be difficult but points out that "Abraham Lincoln did it, and other great Americans" (304). Those familiar with Gold and his work knew that Lincoln was a particular hero of his. As with the idealized portrait of the narrator's mother, Gold is intentionally blurring the boundary between autobiography and fiction and for essentially the same didactic purpose. Michael, the fictional creation, is told that the example of Lincoln will help him escape the pain and suffering of the tenement world; Michael Gold, the novelist and admirer of Lincoln, had, in actuality, so escaped it. Thus, young tenement readers of *Jews without Money* should be encouraged and inspired to examine the story of the frontier president who transcended his lack of formal education as well as the life of the well-known political activist whose book they held in their hands.

In the novel the example of Lincoln is not immediately sufficient to relieve young Michael's bitterness. An undaunted Miss Barry next presents him with "a volume of Emerson's Essays, with her name and my name and the date written on the flyleaf" (305). But the angry boy refuses to examine the hope this gift symbolizes just as he had rejected the example of Lincoln. Yet, when the student of Gold learns that he was intent on incorporating the political and intellectual legacy of America into Marxist ideology, the importance of the gift of Emerson becomes clear. Though the persistent Miss Barry appears only in this one brief scene, she plays an important symbolic role in the novel. By providing Michael with the examples of Lincoln and Emerson, she introduces him to a national and an intellectual tradition from which he can view the political protest advocated by Aunt Lena and Doctor Solow. At the novel's end he does not yet realize the significance of the Lincoln and Emerson examples, but the reader can assume that, after his dramatic conversion, he soon will. Once again the deliberate blurring of the boundary between fiction and autobiography points the reader to precisely this insight. Gold's implied working-class reader would presumably know something about his personal vision of Lincoln and Emerson as examples of a natural link between American traditions and Marxism.

The affirmative theme underlying *Jews without Money* is developed, then, in three stages. Michael, the young narrator, realizes the roles of his mother and Joey Cohen as personifications of Jewish strength and integrity; Aunt Lena and Doctor Solow illustrate to him the necessity of directing this communal strength into an ongoing protest against exploitative capitalism; and Miss Barry provides him with a national heritage that will provide *historical* legitimacy for this essential social resistance. It only remains for the young narrator to discover in international communism an immediate language into which the historical examples of Lincoln and Emerson can be (even if rather violently) translated. Of course, he makes this discovery in the novel's last scene. Gold, then, resolves the potential conflict between naturalistic determinism and a thematically necessary freedom in essentially the same way that, according to Charles C. Walcutt, Zola and other politically conscious naturalists do: while depicting most of the novel's characters as being overwhelmed by external social forces, he assumes the freedom of his readers to initiate saving social change and reform.[15] In addition, like other literary naturalists writing from a Marxist perspective, he allows his central character to escape, through the discovery of international communism, the environmental determinism that otherwise controls the society in which he lives. This dramatically liberated character is then able to guide the implied working-class reader in choosing a specific political direction for his freshly awakened political consciousness.

Having attained a saving political maturity before telling his story, Michael, the narrator of Gold's novel, has been able to subdue the guilt that originated in his childhood when he disobeyed his mother and joined a gang, taunted the prostitutes, and tortured the cats. His three-stage discovery of escape and affirmation has further inspired him to tell his personal story as a potential source of inspiration for other young men trapped in the tenements. Gold subtly foreshadows young Michael's eventual miraculous salvation in a story told by the narrator's father. The father tells about a Rumanian hunter who has had, since childhood, a dream of journeying to Turkey, where "it is warm" and "the roses bloom in December and the birds sing." The hunter, as an adult, is hopelessly trapped by his marriage, his family, and his poverty, and, as a result, Turkey seems only a distant dream. One "bitter cold morning" he journeys forth to find food for his family and discovers three bear cubs in a cave. He is about to shoot them, when their mother, "the largest and most beautiful bear he had ever seen," appears and begs him for the lives of her cubs. She offers him "magic secrets known only to Golden Bears," if he will spare the cubs. When the hunter asks if she can take him and his family to Turkey and discover land for them in this warm southern sanctuary, the mother bear promises that she can and further adds that the hunter "will never need money all [his] life" (84–86).

Michael's father never discovers a magical "Golden Bear" to rescue him from the trap of the tenement, but, on the novel's final page, his son does, even if he does not equate Marxism quite yet with his father's mythical animal. In the context of Gold's faith in the indestructible vitality of the Jewish-American tenement community as the soil from which Marxist salvation will ultimately grow, it is proper that the story of the Golden Bear is a Jewish folk tale imported to the United States from Europe. The real role of the novel's autobiographical elements is best summarized by Michael Brewster Folsom:

> To the extent that *Jews without Money* is autobiographical, it is perhaps the most self-effacing autobiography ever written. The individual is there in the narrative and in the informing sensibility, but he serves mainly as the perceiver of and relater of that community life which is the subject of the book. *Jews without Money* is the autobiography of the tenement in Gold's blood, a record of the tenement thinking. (246)

Notes

1. I am indebted to Earl Wilcox for most of this insight into the relationship between *The People of the Abyss* and *The Call of the Wild*. He developed it in response to a paper that I presented at the first Jack London Society Summer Session in

Sonoma, California, in August 1992. For especially good discussions of London's childhood, including his years as a young "work beast" in San Francisco and Oakland, see Earle Labor, *Jack London* (Boston: Twayne, 1974); and Russ Kingman, *A Pictorial Life of Jack London* (New York: Crown, 1979).

2. Marcus Klein, *Foreigners: The Making of American Literature 1900–1940* (Chicago: University of Chicago Press, 1981), 231.

3. For informative discussions of Gold's background, relationship to the American Communist Party, and editorship of the *Masses*, the *Liberator*, and the *New Masses*, see Klein, *Foreigners*; as well as Daniel Aaron, *Writers on the Left* (New York: Harcourt, Brace, and World, 1961); Walter B. Rideout, *The Radical Novel in the United States, 1900–1954* (Cambridge: Harvard University Press, 1956); and Michael Brewster Folsom, "The Education of Michael Gold," *Proletarian Writers of the Thirties*, ed. David Madden (Carbondale: Southern Illinois University Press, 1968).

4. Folsom, "Education of Michael Gold," 245.

5. Michael Gold, *Jews without Money* (New York: Carroll and Graf, 1984), 13.

6. Klein, *Foreigners*, 184.

7. Rideout, *Radical Novel in the United States*, 151.

8. Allen Guttmann, *The Jewish Writer in America: Assimilation and the Crisis of Identity* (New York: Oxford University Press, 1971), 141.

9. Richard Tuerk, "*Jews without Money* as a Work of Art," *Studies in American Jewish Literature* 7 (Spring 1988): 68.

10. Diane Levenberg, "Three Jewish Writers and the Spirit of the Thirties: Michael Gold, Anzia Yezierska, and Henry Roth," *Book Forum* 6 (1982): 236.

11. Bernard Sherman, *The Invention of the Jew: Jewish-American Education Novels (1916–1964)* (New York: Thomas Yoseloff, 1969), 74–75.

12. Helge Norman Nilsen, "The Evils of Poverty: Mike Gold's *Jews without Money*," *Anglo-American Studies* 4 (April 1984): 50.

13. Leslie A. Fiedler, *To the Gentiles* (New York: Stein and Day, 1972), 89–90.

14. Reprinted in the Carroll and Graf 1984 edition of *Jews without Money* (n.p.).

15. Charles C. Walcutt, *American Literary Naturalism: A Divided Stream* (Minneapolis: University of Minnesota Press, 1956).

Chapter 3

The Fat Man Finds His Voice, Part 2
Richard Wright's *Native Son*

Richard Wright's *Native Son* appeared in 1940, exactly one decade after *Jews without Money*, and a comparison of the two novels will illustrate some of the tensions and complexities behind the evolution of Marxist protest fiction during the turbulent decade of the 1930s. Wright, like Gold, was a convert to the Party but, unlike the militant editor and novelist, did not remain a true believer until the end. In fact, though conceived in part as a work designed to advance the U.S. Communist movement, *Native Son*, especially in its long third section entitled "Fate," reveals a considerable degree of ambivalence on the part of its author toward the American Communist Party and, consequently, made Party officials more than a little uneasy. At times, in fact, Wright seems almost to be deliberately taunting his more politically correct colleagues, and, in 1942, he quietly left the Party. In a 1955 letter to Edward Aswell, his editor at *Harper's*, Wright reviewed the factors behind this break and inadvertently revealed much about the unique tensions underlying *Native Son*, tensions that unfortunately damage the aesthetic integrity of the novel:

> When I was a member of the Communist Party, I took that party seriously, and when I discovered that I was holding a tainted instrument in my hands, I dropped that instrument.

> As anyone with common sense could easily guess, I was a Communist because I was Negro. Indeed the Communist Party had been the only road out of the Black Belt for me. . . . To me the racial situation was a far harder matter than the Communist one and it was one that I could not solve alone.[1]

Wright had, in fact, already started to feel that the Party was a "tainted instrument" while writing *Native Son*. He had misgivings about a number of things, but the center of his growing unhappiness was his, in fact accurate, perception that racial justice was not the high priority of the Party he had initially believed it to be. His conversion to the Party had been inextricably bound up with his African-American identity, and that identity transcended his political commitment. Still, a part of him struggled while writing *Native Son* to produce a novel that his Party associates would find acceptable. Max's long defense of Bigger Thomas at the young man's trial, in part, represents Wright's capitulation to Marxist orthodoxy. Wright, of course, retracts much of the logic of Max's speech in the concluding jail cell scene between the lawyer and his client. Moreover, he had already significantly undermined it in his characterizations of Max and Mary Dalton. It seems that, in spite of his conscious intentions, Wright was incapable of producing a novel that his Party colleagues would find completely acceptable. His inability to do so was a direct result of the precedence that his racial identity held over his political allegiance.

Jews without Money and *Native Son* can both be described as proletarian protest novels that exhibit a strong ethnic consciousness. A distinguishing difference between them is the degree of emphasis each gives to its proletarian and ethnic themes. While directly introducing his theme of Marxist conversion only in the last scene of his novel, Gold carefully and deliberately focuses upon Jewish-American ethnic pride as the soil from which Marxist commitment can grow. His ethnic theme is then subordinated to a concept of proletarian awareness. Wright is torn throughout *Native Son* by conflicting desires to stress proletarian *and* racial consciousness. However intentionally, the theme of racial identity ultimately attains the greatest significance in his novel. This tension in his work is echoed in more than one African-American novel set in the late 1930s or early 1940s—Ralph Ellison's *Invisible Man* (1952) and William Attaway's *Blood on the Forge* (1941) come quickly to mind. In part, the political ambivalence in these novels is the result of a crucial shift in strategy on the part of the American Communist Party as World War II began. Racial justice in America was more or less put on the back burner by the Party until Hitler was defeated. Yet what Wright began to feel in the late 1930s was an inherent conflict between proletarian unity and Black Nationalist consciousness. In fact, African Americans had never been accepted by much of the American working class and had often been scapegoated by it. *Native Son*, at times, anticipates the Black Nationalist literature of the 1960s in what it implies about the necessary African-American response to such rejection and oppression.

Focusing in part on *Jews without Money* and *Native Son*, John M. Reilly has published an important essay concerning the essential characteristics of an ethnic novel. Reilly first stresses the importance of using the term *ethnic literature* carefully: "It would be best if we were to discard easy definitions altogether and attempt to describe the object of our criticism—ethnic literature—from the assumption that it is an autonomous, but not separate, way by which authors imaginatively render the significance of ethnic experience in the United States."[2] He then argues that ethnicity in fiction is a matter of "strategy" and not simply "identity": "Identity can be assumed without reflection, but a *statement* of identity involves consciousness and serves as the premise for an effort to see oneself in history and to become the subject of historical processes" (3). Reilly further clarifies this essential point:

> Ethnic literature is not so designated because of the authors' race, color, creed, national origin or associations. If it were, then Auchincloss or Marquand would be appropriate for inclusion in a multi-ethnic literature anthology since the class for which they generally write is Anglo-American in origin. What we designate "ethnic literature" are the products of authors who choose to feature the significance of ethnicity in their writing. (4)

Jews without Money and *Native Son* represent interesting variations upon this distinction. Gold *apparently* chooses to feature ethnicity in his novel, but, at the end, treats it as a means to the higher end of proletarian unity. Wright goes back and forth between featuring ethnic identity and political consciousness throughout *Native Son*, but still ethnicity ultimately overwhelms politics in the novel.

Reilly's next point is also especially relevant to Gold and Wright. He describes a recurrent plot in ethnic literature, along with its major variations:

> (A) A character is established in the context of an American ethnic group. (B) That character conflicts with the facts of social organization as they are embodied in established patterns of power and discriminatory relationships. There is, then, a movement either to (C) destruction of the character, or (D) character growth that transcends in some manner the historical-material facts of social organization. The basic variations suggested by (C) and (D) are that the narrative will be constructed either to represent victimization of the ethnic character by American social realities, or to dramatize the character's achievement of a degree of self-determination through growth of consciousness. (5)

For much of *Jews without Money* Michael seems as much the victim of the dominant social power as Nigger, Louis One Eye, and Joey Cohen, but his encounter with the "man on the East Side soap box" allows him to transcend the oppressive social order in the United States. On the novel's last page Michael escapes victimization and achieves self-determination.

Given this familiar emphasis upon character as victim of social forces, it is hardly surprising that one finds a special bond between the ethnic novel and the naturalistic novel. Reilly argues that literary naturalism is especially common in ethnic fiction that utilizes the plot of victimization, while other models "ranging from the *Bildungsroman* to the exempla of the 'self-made man' are central to the stories of ethnic self-determination" (5). *Native Son*, he adds, exemplifies the most common kind of variation upon the recurrent ethnic novel plot. Wright's novel, he points out, combines the tropes of "character destruction" and "growth of consciousness." Bigger Thomas travels a path of destruction, but still achieves, in the last half of the novel, a new level of awareness. This dual effect, Reilly believes, is made possible by the "insider's" point of view from which his story is told; this mode of narration makes it possible to chart a path of destruction for Bigger while still allowing him "to experience life as do most human beings, with some sense of choice" (5).

Certainly, this insider's point of view makes possible much of the rich complexity of *Native Son*, but it is also the source of much of the artistic confusion in the novel. In "Fear," the novel's first section, Wright does a generally good job of keeping the narrative voice separate from Bigger Thomas. One has little difficulty, then, in comprehending Bigger as the violent, frightened leader of a street gang. After the murder of Mary Dalton narrative distance in the novel becomes increasingly fragile and in places breaks down completely. This problem was probably inevitable in Wright's novel because of the number of not always harmonious, and at times flatly conflicting, motifs which he brought to it. He wanted to write a proletarian novel *and* a naturalistic novel of ethnic victimization. In addition, he intended the last half of the book to reflect an existentialist perspective. Finally, as recent publication of the first "final" version of the novel makes clear, Wright meant to depict Bigger as being partially destroyed by a twisted and uncontrollable sexuality.

Bigger Thomas and the Masturbatory Life

In his often reprinted 1940 essay "How 'Bigger' Was Born," Wright directly addresses the proletarian and ethnic elements in his novel and in so doing provides some clues about the difficulties he faced in attempting to reconcile them. Not surprisingly, *Native Son* has been frequently analyzed from these two perspectives. Much of "How 'Bigger' Was Born" reads as if written deliberately to pacify an imaginary Party censor sitting at Wright's side and reading over his shoulder:

> I made the discovery that Bigger Thomas was not black all the time; he was white, too, and there were literally millions of him, everywhere. The extension of my sense of the personality of Bigger was the pivot of my life; it altered the complexion of my existence. I became conscious, at first dimly, and then later on with increasing clarity and conviction, of a vast, muddied pool of human life in America. . . . I sensed, too, that the Southern scheme of oppression was but an appendage of a far vaster and in many respects more ruthless and impersonal commodity-profit machine.
> Trade-union struggles and issues began to grow meaningful to me. The flow of goods across the seas, buoying and depressing the wages of men, held a fascination.[3]

Wright almost certainly believed, at least in one part of his mind, in such abstract Marxist ideas, and his novel does contain some passages of indirect discourse in which Bigger, in prison and awaiting execution, begins to realize, and somewhat fearfully hope for, a saving epiphany of universal proletarian brotherhood. Still, such a limited perspective is finally inadequate as a means of "defining" as complex a character as Bigger Thomas. There may, indeed, be "millions" of Biggers but not in the sense meant here. James Baldwin has famously insisted that all African Americans contain within them a Bigger Thomas, and the dominant logic of Wright's novel makes clear that it is Bigger's specifically black rage that most defines, and most twists, him. It seems evident that Wright was clearly aware of this and was attempting in much of "How 'Bigger' Was Born" to deny and disguise a major emphasis of his novel in order to retain his standing within the American Communist Party.[4]

Even within the essay the disguise is hardly complete. Wright acknowledges in it that, while Bigger "was an American, because he was a native son," "he was also a Negro nationalist in a vague sense because he was not allowed to live as an American" (xxiv). In delineating Bigger's stunted black nationalism, Wright utilizes W. E. B. Du Bois's concept of the inescapable dual identity that threatens to push African Americans toward a bitter and self-destroying paranoia: "What made Bigger's social consciousness most complex was the fact that he was hovering unwanted between two worlds—between powerful America and his own stunted place in life—and I took upon myself the task of trying to make the reader feel this No Man's Land" (xxiv). Taking the reader on an exploration of the frightening "No Man's Land" of the African-American psyche necessitates an acknowledgment by Wright that its most distinguishing feature is a profound and pervasive hatred for white people. He readily grants this crucial fact but quickly stresses his regret about it and implies that such crippling hatred is not, in fact, inevitable: "Of this dual aspect of Bigger's social consciousness, I placed the nationalistic side first, *not because I agreed with Bigger's wild and intense hatred of white people*, but because his hate had placed him, like a wild animal at bay, in a position where he was most symbolic and explainable" (xxiv; my italics). In his defense speech in the novel Max will also stress the significance of Bigger as a symbolic being.

His certain awareness of the destructive potential of such blind racial hatred for the realization of any viable proletarian unity must have been one motivation for Wright's overtly repudiating it in his essay. Yet he did place "the nationalistic side [of Bigger's 'social consciousness'] first" and not only, one suspects, for symbolic purposes: it is blackness that lies at the heart of the young man's identity. On the most immediately obvious level *Native Son* is, as Reilly points out, a classic example of the naturalistic ethnic novel. From its famous opening scene Bigger Thomas is depicted as a victim of overpowering social forces. He is intensely aware of being physically in but legally and economically outside U.S. society and feels deeply the pain resulting from such alienation. Ultimately, the bitterness of his ostracism is a central factor in his destroying two other human beings and thus assuring his own imminent destruction. Before he dies, illustrating Reilly's pattern, he is allowed a transcendent vision.

In the first two sections of the novel, "Fear" and "Flight," the proletarian and naturalistic ethnic strands of the novel exist in a kind of uneasy harmony; at times, in fact, they come together brilliantly. One political implication of Wright's book is that Bigger is a victim of a brutally unjust society that needs sweeping political reform. In part, then, he is dealing with the issue of determinism and free will in the way that Gold does in *Jews without Money:* he is depicting his characters largely as pawns, while granting his readers the free will to reform society. Sometimes the novel points the reader toward a Marxism that will negate the legacy of class *and* racial injustice in the United States. In order to present this concept Wright must work from a clear and definite narrative strategy.

In a second essay John M. Reilly outlines the way in which Wright develops this essential strategy. He first points out that "in civilization, history, family patterns, language, art, psychology, the white is always the norm; the black is forever the 'other.'"[5] Reilly then argues that Wright, like other African-American writers, had to establish his authority to depict the world of his text. To do so, he says, Wright sought validation in a narrative method deliberately modeled on that found in the discipline of social science: "To take up the challenge presented to him by the political configurations of American discourse on race, Richard Wright had to do more than create a narrative that would be recognizably accurate in its localized detail. Since the problem was political, its solution lay in adoption of narrative techniques that would recreate the literary form of the social novel as a black text" (41). It would be accurate to be even more specific than this. In part, Wright is attempting, in *Native Son*, to recreate the proletarian novel as a naturalistic black text.[6]

The novel's famous opening scene brilliantly realizes this merger of narrative approaches. An alarm clock brutally jars Bigger into consciousness of the claustrophobic existence that constitutes his everyday reality: he is forced to sleep in the same tenement room with his mother, sister, and younger brother. A central tension throughout the novel results from Bigger's desperate struggle to escape from a pervasive physical and psychological claustrophobia that threatens to suffocate him. At times he literally finds it difficult to breathe in the harshly constricted world of the black ghetto. Almost immediately upon waking he must chase down and kill a rat that has invaded the narrow room in which he and his family are trying to dress. It is now a critical commonplace that Bigger's pursuit and killing of the rat functions in the novel as a metaphor for the hatred and rejection that confront him, and all black men, in virtually every avenue of American society. Wright deliberately portrays Bigger as a terrifying personification of an especially frightening American middle-class nightmare, the black male Other who, by his mere existence, evokes white images of rape and murder. Bigger's encounter with the rat is also commonly seen as foreshadowing his own flight from, and inevitable capture by, the police, whom he tries to escape by hiding out in abandoned tenement rooms on Chicago's South Side. Rodents, reptiles, and insects appear not uncommonly in naturalistic fiction as metaphors for human vulnerability and degradation. Less commonly noticed is the importance of the scene as a symbolic depiction of the psychological damage that the young man has suffered. His reaction after killing the grotesque rodent should be noted:

He kicked the splintered box out of the way and the flat black body of the rat lay exposed, its two long yellow tusks showing distinctly. Bigger took a shoe and pounded the rat's head, crushing it, crying hysterically:
"You sonofa*bitch!*"[7]

His rage and hysteria at this moment result from more than disgust and fear at the intrusion of the rat into his family's cramped living quarters, though such feelings are, of course, involved. On a deeper and thus more potentially damaging level Bigger feels an identification with the rat—a sensation he attempts to destroy by crushing the head of the invading beast. He knows that he is viewed by white American society as being every bit as grotesque as the yellow-tusked monster he has just destroyed, and, despite himself, he has been unable to deny his own monstrosity. His sordid and claustrophobic existence has forced him to acquiesce in his own dehumanization, and he is attempting to crush the part of his psyche which made such a debilitating surrender. In addition, Wright subtly points to Bigger's ultimately fatal sexual rage by italicizing the last five letters of the epithet that the young man shouts at the corpse of the rat.

The reader understands implicitly through Wright's social science narrative model that Bigger's claustrophobic existence and his damaged psyche are the products of an oppressive white-controlled capitalism *before* this point is made overtly and repeatedly in the last half of the novel. Bigger's destruction of the rat functions effectively, then, as a trope for the book's ethnic, proletarian, and psychological motifs.

The ethnic and proletarian motifs also come together brilliantly in the early scene in which Bigger and Gus "play white." Reilly points out that the scene is based on the African-American linguistic practice of "signifying," which works primarily through contradiction, extreme exaggeration, and deliberate "inversion of standards." He adds that "the circumstance of being always viewed first of all as black guarantees that one's language must be broadly political": "Signifying is, thus, an example of creative politics that draws upon a store of knowledge about the ways of white folks to achieve ends that custom and prevalent racial assumptions deem improper."[8]

Utilizing the signifying practice also underscores Wright's authority to depict the black world of his text. The particular linguistic game played by Bigger and Gus is based upon an understanding of their social positions as victims of a racist capitalism as well as their resistance to such victimization.

Initially, they see a plane flying overhead and feel intensely, if inarticulately, the overwhelming distance between the freedom of the pilot and their own entrapment in the ghetto. Bigger voices, "as though talking to himself," the frustration, which pervades his very being, over his inhumanly restricted existence: "I could fly one of them things if I had a chance." Gus immediately reminds his companion, as if he needed to, of the overwhelming impediments to the realization of such an ambition: "If you wasn't black and if you had some money and if they'd let you go to that aviation school, you *could* fly a plane." His companions' harsh summary of the specifics of his restricted life inspires in Bigger a bitter and angry response: "Maybe they right in not wanting us to fly. . . . Cause if I took a plane up I'd take a couple of bombs along and drop 'em as sure as hell" (460). This outburst reflects the vague and stunted black nationalism that lies, barely controlled, within the soul of the young man. Wright makes overt later in the novel the ironic and explosive potential of Bigger's nationalistic rage when he shows his young character responding positively to media images of Hitler and Mussolini. His point is that such intense irrationality might one day be directed toward allegiance to fascism. Only a new and just society, achieved through Marxist rebellion, can be certain of negating the attraction of fascist power to significant numbers of the African-American population. This implication of Wright's novel, in 1940, shocked and offended readers at all levels of the political spectrum; they did not always get his point that allegiance to fascism was a potential, not a desirable, result of racist oppression in the United States.

For the remainder of this conversation Bigger and Gus return to the signifying mode, which allows them the opportunity for satiric commentary about the symbiotic relationship of big business and government in the United States. Further, they mock the degree to which national economic and political structures are dependent upon racism in U.S. society. Here Wright seems to anticipate Du Bois's 1953 revision of his 1903 assertion, in *The Souls of Black Folk*, that "the problem of the twentieth century is the problem of the color line." Fifty years after the publication of his seminal work, Du Bois significantly broadened his analysis: "Today I see more clearly than yesterday that back of the problem of race and color, lies a greater problem which both obscures and implements it: and that is the fact that so many civilized persons are willing to live in comfort even if the price of this is poverty, ignorance and disease of the majority of their fellow men; that to maintain this privilege men have waged war until today war tends to become universal and continuous, and the excuse for this war continues largely to be color and race."[9] Over a decade earlier Wright emphasized, through the signifying of Bigger and Gus, that racism was inextricably tied to "privilege" and class inequalities. Again, the implied remedy is pervasive Marxist reform.

The artistic unity of the novel's proletarian and ethnic emphases begins to be strained, however, virtually from the moment that Bigger leaves the ghetto. It is relevant to point out here that, unlike most of the works discussed thus far, *Native Son* is not a pure example of Blanche H. Gelfant's category of the "ecological novel," the fictional work that restricts itself to a single oppressed urban area.[10] Wright, like Joyce Carol Oates in *them*, requires a more inclusive urban canvas to paint his vision of class conflict in the United States. Bigger is forced by family economic necessity to leave Chicago's South Side and accept a chauffeur's job in the heart of white privilege and power. Almost immediately he feels isolated and threatened in this new and alien world.[11]

Initially, it is the wealthy Dalton family for whom he goes to work who unnerve him. Wright has no difficulty in keeping the proletarian and ethnic thrusts of the novel unified in his treatment of Mr. and Mrs. Dalton, who are known for their generous contributions to black charities and who own and charge exorbitant rents for the South Side tenement in which the Thomas family lives. Critics have frequently emphasized that Mrs. Dalton's physical blindness is a metaphor for the absence of insight into black suffering that characterizes the dangerously limited vision of herself and her husband.[12] Mr. and Mrs. Dalton primarily represent a devastating satire of misguided white liberalism. They attempt to atone through meaningless philanthropic gestures for their guilt as exploitative capitalistic landlords. By doing so, they succeed only in temporarily confusing black rage and, thus, delaying essential social reform.

It is in the characterizations of Mary Dalton and her Communist boyfriend, Jan Erlone, that the aesthetic unity of the novel begins to unravel. Mary is portrayed as a shallow and insensitive young woman, who because of an attraction to Marxist ideology (an attraction that seems primarily a kind of flirtation with politics) seeks to befriend a badly frightened Bigger. Her characterization and her murder are central to the novel in several ways, and it is difficult not to feel at times that Wright comes close to trivializing all four of the novel's central motifs (the proletarian, the Black Nationalist, the existential, and the sexual) by making her such a superficial character. Michel Fabre argues that Wright's ambivalence toward the Party made him incapable of realizing Mary as a complex and coherent character.

Fabre points out that Wright insisted upon naming his creation Mary "because [the name] had been the 'nom de guerre' of a New York Communist sent to Chicago as a Party official in 1934. Without knowing her very well, Wright had heartily disliked this girl, and it gave him pleasure to think that people like Harry Haywood and John Davis [Communist Party officials] would get the subtle allusion if he used her name in this context" (170).

The depiction of Jan Erlone also results in some narrative incoherence. Wright wants to make him an ultimately sympathetic character yet intentionally complicates this goal through his account of Jan's own insensitive and dangerously careless behavior on the night when Bigger first meets him. In contrast to Mary Dalton, Jan is firmly and clearly committed to a realization of the Marxist agenda in the United States. His determination to convert Bigger to the Party before really knowing him makes the young black man extremely uneasy; the apolitical Bigger knows little about Communists except that they are, if possible, more hated than black people in the United States. It is, then, the genuine sincerity of Jan's political commitment that results in some incoherence in his characterization.

With Bigger on that first and tragic night, Jan is guilty of his own kind of blindness. His determination to see the chauffeur as a potential convert prohibits him from realizing the black youth's essential humanness. He co-operates with Mary in pressuring Bigger into taking them to eat at Ernie's Kitchen Shack, where he, of course, orders fried chicken.[13] He further frightens Bigger by forcing Party pamphlets and whiskey upon him. But it is after the three characters leave Ernie's that Jan most graphically demonstrates his inability to see the black youth as a human being by asking the chauffeur to drive aimlessly through a park while he and Mary engage in some heavily sexual activity in the backseat. The inevitable and disastrous effects of this exhibitionism upon Bigger are especially clear in the new Library of America edition of the novel, but, even in the previously accepted text, it is clear that Jan and Mary, in order to give release to their pent-up sexual desire, have reduced their "new friend" to a subhuman status. They have made him, in fact, the very personification of Ralph Ellison's concept of black invisibility.

Jan then cements the inevitability of tragedy by leaving Bigger alone to get a drunken and sexually aroused Mary to her bedroom. He, as a rebel against repressive and brutal racism in the United States, should certainly understand the danger in which he places both of his companions. It is as if Wright is presenting Jan, in this first section of the novel, as something of a personification of the limitations of the American Communist Party's commitment to racial understanding and justice. This in itself would not be a cause for criticism except that, beginning almost immediately after Mary's murder, he attempts to redeem the character and make him less politically threatening.

Jan is remarkably, if not unbelievably, forgiving of Bigger not only for the murder of Mary but also for attempting to frame him for the crime. As the novel's last scene shows, it is Jan, and not the defense lawyer Max, who breaks through Bigger's elaborate psychological defenses and makes human contact with the young black man. In the last half of the novel Jan seems to embody not ambivalence by the Party toward the pursuit of racial justice in the United States but, rather, unquestioning commitment. Wright might have dramatized his character experiencing a process of growth which would have made this metamorphosis possible, but he, in fact, only superficially tries to do so.[14] Jan is never really the narrative focus in the last section of the novel; thus, Bigger's final request that Max "Tell. . . . Tell Mister. . . . Tell Jan hello . . ." (850) seems to leap off the page at the reader.

As with Mary, Fabre believes that much of the inconsistency in Wright's treatment of Jan results from his conscious anticipation of the reaction of future Party readers:

[Wright] was not at all satisfied with the portrait of [Jan] that had emerged by the end of the second book [of the novel]. . . . Jan was in fact the only person who eventually managed to elicit a friendly reaction from Bigger. (His first name seems to have been taken from Jan Wittenber, Wright's old friend from the John Reed Club.) . . . He could feel the critical eyes of certain members of the Party— people whom he considered his friends and whose judgment he respected and even depended on—fixed upon him. He admitted, though, that he did not expect them to praise him for the novel, even if he finally succeeded in presenting Jan Erlone in a more favorable light. (173–74)

Fabre goes on to argue that the cumulative depictions in the novel of Jan and of the Party itself avoid an aesthetically damaging inconsistency through adroit manipulation of point of view. The reader, he believes, comprehends Jan gradually, precisely as Bigger does, and comes to understand only at the novel's conclusion the young radical's capacity for a transcendent human compassion.

Again, the problem with this thesis is that the reader has not seen Jan enough in the "Fate" section to be able to credit him with any significant growth. There is simply insufficient artistic reason to understand that he is fundamentally different from the careless young man of the novel's early scene who leaves his wealthy girlfriend in a situation that will claim her life as well as that of her killer. What the character of Jan most personifies is the way in which the unifying bond between the novel's proletarian and ethnic thrusts begins to deconstruct as soon as Bigger leaves the ghetto.

Native Son's existential emphasis, which becomes dominant only after Bigger's murder of Mary, has been frequently discussed by Wright critics and scholars. In an influential early essay Nathan A. Scott, Jr., expressed a preference for the later and overtly existential novel, *The Outsider* (1953), which he called Wright's "finest achievement" after *Black Boy* (1945) and "the one emphatically existentialist novel in contemporary American literature."[15] In contrast, Scott argues, the existentialism of *Native Son* is aesthetically undercut and compromised by the inarticulate black rage that defines the characterization of Bigger Thomas. Its origins were felt rather than discovered in other literature, and the existential content of *Native Son* reveals much, Scott believes, about the artistic and intellectual limitations of Richard Wright in 1939: "[Wright] simply did not *know* enough about the labyrinthine interiorities of the human soul" (154). Scott's Richard Wright is, in fact, a special kind of victim of American racism, an artist whose sensibility was severely restricted by rage at being forced into the status of victim until he escaped the United States and found refuge in the France of Sartre and Camus.

In another important essay on Wright, Irving Howe did not find the nonliterary nature of the novelist's early existentialism to be problematic: "Wright was an existentialist long before he heard the name, for he was committed to the literature of extreme situations both through the pressures of his rage and the gasping hope of an ultimate catharsis."[16] It seems clear, in fact, that Wright intuitively understood racism in the U.S. to be a strikingly clear and dramatic example of the Absurd in human conduct and society. In this intuition Wright anticipated Jean-Paul Sartre's pronouncement in *What Is Literature?* that social protest fiction constituted an especially viable literary form for the African-American writer because of the pervasiveness of racism in the United States as well as Sartre's 1946 play *The Respectful Prostitute*.

Certainly, a central theme of *Native Son* is that the black American lives a life of "extreme situations," which not uncommonly finds its only outlet in violent reaction. Violence lies at the core of much of Wright's work, and some of the best recent criticism of the novelist focuses upon the existential overtones of his obsession with violent behavior. Steven J. Rubin, for instance, compares *Native Son* to Camus's *Stranger* (1942), both works representing, he believes, examples of the modern novel of existential revolt:

> The literature of revolt is born from the recognition on the part of many modern writers that meaning and purpose are not an integral part of the universe in which man finds himself. *Native Son*, written at a time when Wright was preoccupied with social issues, also represents an examination of the nature of personal rebellion, a theme which dominated much of the thinking of such modern European writers as André Malraux, Jean-Paul Sartre, and especially Albert Camus.[17]

Rubin believes that Bigger Thomas, like Camus's Meursault, finds freedom and identity in murder, though not with the same metaphysical awareness: "Bigger is forced into an alien existence because of the irrational and unjust nature of the society in which he lives. For Bigger, the opposite poles of aspiration and satisfaction can only be briefly united through violence" (16).

Jerry H. Bryant also utilizes a comparison between *Native Son* and *The Stranger* as a context for analyzing Bigger's inarticulate striving for self-definition. He sees Wright's novel as emerging out of three strands of twentieth-century philosophical thought: José Ortega y Gasset's concept of modern "mass-man," Sartre and Camus's existentialism, and Marxist humanism. Bryant's thesis is that Wright initially presents Bigger Thomas as an embodiment of Ortega y Gasset's mass-man, a character so fundamentally alienated and isolated by the purposeless anonymity of twentieth-century life that he is irresistibly attracted to violent personal conduct and totalitarian political thought. The character is allowed, however, a degree of redemption through the novel's existential and Marxist humanist strands.[18]

It seems clear that Wright intended an existential dimension for Bigger and his acts of "creative" murder, however literary or nonliterary his inspiration was. Two real aesthetic problems for the novel do result, however, from this thematic emphasis, the first being a matter of balance. The novel's existential strand emerges almost exclusively in the last half of the novel, gaining a clear focus only after Bigger's murder of Bessie. Though Wright will repeatedly stress that the earlier killing of Mary Dalton constitutes the basis for an emerging sense of self for the young man, the wealthy white girl's death is too inextricably tied to accident and warped sexuality for him to be truly convincing.

Michel Fabre believes that Wright consciously used Bessie's murder to give the novel an existential slant. The novelist, he says, was responding from the start to two diverse literary influences, Dreiser's *American Tragedy* (1925) and Dostoevsky's *Crime and Punishment* (1866) and

> saw no obstacle to combining in one character two types of people— the murderer who kills as an act of creation and the one who kills in response to a social determinism. If Bigger resembled Clyde Griffiths at the beginning of the novel, he was by now gradually turning into another Raskolnikov. Bigger's murder of Bessie marked a new stage in Wright's literary evolution; everything that he had learned from his naturalist models up to this point had prevented him from allowing his characters to give in to these demonic temptations, but now Bigger claimed his right to "create," in the existential meaning of the word, by rejecting the accidental nature of his first murder with this further proof of his power to destroy. (171)

Bigger, in this view, is naturalistic victim in the first book of the novel, "Fear," and increasingly existentialist rebel in the last two, "Flight" and "Fate." There is nothing inherently wrong with such a dual approach to character—Wright's problem here is that the transformation of Bigger from a black Clyde Griffiths into an African-American Raskolnikov doesn't seem so much gradual and inevitable as abrupt and forced.[19]

The reader's sense of a sudden shift in the definition of Bigger is directly related to the second problematic result of the existential emphasis that Wright begins to develop after the murder of Mary Dalton. He chooses to delineate this aspect of the novel largely through passages of indirect discourse intended to reflect Bigger's thought process rather than narrative action, and, as more than one critic has noticed, the rhetorical level of these passages often seems foreign to the Bigger Thomas whom we have seen in the first part of the novel. At one point Wright describes Bigger as thinking at this level of sophistication:

> He had murdered and had created a new life for himself. . . . His crime was an anchor weighing him safely in time; it added to him a certain confidence which his gun and knife did not. . . . The hidden meaning of his life—a meaning which others did not see and which he had always tried to hide—had spilled out. . . . It was as though he had an obscure but deep debt to fulfill to himself in accepting the deed. (542)

It is not that one is unable to conceive of Bigger thinking in such an abstractly probing manner: Wright goes to some trouble to show him as possessing an impressive, if untutored, level of intelligence. The difficulty in accepting such a passage lies, instead, in its distinctly "literary" language, a language obviously more natural to Richard Wright than to Bigger Thomas; Scott and Howe to the contrary, the existential strand of *Native Son* was not wholly without literary influences. As Wright developed it, the distance between author and character sometimes collapsed. It should not be forgotten that, in 1949, a forty-one-year-old Richard Wright played the role of Bigger Thomas (after Canada Lee was forced to drop out of the project) in the first film version of *Native Son*.

The concept of Bigger's creation of an existential identity through killing Mary Dalton is undercut in other ways as well. Responding to his Marxist humanism, Wright, in an impressionistic description of a nightmare that torments Bigger, demonstrates that his character does feel guilt over the young woman's gruesome death. In the nightmare Bigger carries his own bloody head wrapped in a package through a public street: despite himself, the murderer feels a human bond with his victim. Most crucially, the violent deaths of both Mary and Bessie are the results of Bigger's twisted sexuality, which had become inextricably linked with his capacity for violence.

In his defense summary at Bigger's trial his Communist Party lawyer Max (read Marx) shocks the courtroom with the information that the defendant and "boys like him" frequented a movie theater and "committed acts of masturbation in the darkened seats." He then asks two rhetorical questions: "Was not Bigger Thomas' relationship to his girl a masturbatory one? Was not his relationship to the whole world on the same plane?" (823). Especially given Bigger's seeming repudiation of Max's defense summary in the novel's last scene, the degree to which the reader is meant to take this approximately twenty-page "explanation" of the black youth seriously is open to question.[20] Still, his questions concerning Bigger and masturbation do provide a clue to the hidden and dangerous complexity of the young protagonist. Bigger Thomas is indeed trapped in a masturbatory existence, though the degree to which this is true was not clear until the Library of America publication of the original version of Wright's novel.

At the request of the Book-of-the-Month Club Wright revised his original version of the novel, cutting some overtly sexual language throughout and rewriting the early scene in which Bigger and Jack attend a movie. (He made one other significant revision, which strengthened the novel: he cut some of the repetitiousness out of Max's defense summary.) The original and subsequently deleted movie theater scene paints a graphic picture of the potentially explosive sexual anger that Bigger must struggle to repress. He and Jack are drawn inside the theater by a poster advertising *Trader Horn*, an older film released in 1931 which they have apparently seen before. Once inside the darkened auditorium and waiting for the film to start, each begins to masturbate. When Jack realizes that his companion is doing the same thing he is, he issues a challenge: "I'll beat you." Onanism becomes in part, then, a form of competition and not simply a way to attain sexual gratification and release.

More important, the two young men describe their penises in language containing overtones of aggression and repressed violence. Bigger describes what he is doing as "polishing my nightstick," referring to the kind of club ordinarily used by police officers to subdue suspects who resist arrest or threaten violence. Without his being aware of the full implications of his metaphor, he has compared his erect penis to an instrument of brutal repression. He is then acknowledging, without meaning to, the societal repression of his sexuality and of his very self. Jack, "with intense pride," responds by asserting that "mine's like a rod." In popular culture *rod* was a term commonly used during the 1930s to refer to a handgun.[21] In "tough-guy" detective novels and films the lone wolf antihero as well as the criminals he seeks to subdue always "pack rods." Jack then also describes, without necessarily meaning to, his sexual organ as a weapon and as one commonly utilized by both the agents of and the rebels against law enforcement. Like Bigger's, his sexual identity has become inextricably linked to the social repression that he can never fully escape as well as to his desire to rebel violently against that repression.

A male's association of his phallus with weapons of violence obviously negates for him any possibility of a healthy sexuality. In addition, it can only have frightening implications for any female who might be or who might become his sexual partner. While masturbating, Jack expresses regret that his girlfriend is not present: "I could make old Clara moan now." He and Bigger then discuss the possibility that a woman who has just walked down the aisle past them has seen what they are doing:

> "If she comes back I'll throw it in her."
> "You a killer."
> "If she saw it she'd faint."
> "Or grab it, maybe."
> "Yeah." (472–73)

Wright does not clearly signal which of the young men is speaking in this exchange; it really doesn't matter because both have experienced the same perversion of their sexuality. Both view sexual intercourse as an act of violence in which the female is assaulted and made to feel pain, even "killed" symbolically.

It must be said, however, that some recent Wright criticism approaches the novel's obvious misogyny as being relevant to more than its mode of characterization. Alan W. France, for instance, emphasizes what he calls "the misogynistic underside of the text" in *Native Son*, arguing that, in addition to the novel's "reigning dialectic" of "racial oppression," it contains "a repressed dialectic" concerned with "the violent and phallocentric appropriation of women": "From underneath, *Native Son* is the story of a black man's rebellion against white male authority. The rebellion takes the form of the ultimate appropriation of human beings, the rape-slaying, which is also the ultimate expropriation of patriarchal property, the total consumption of the commodified woman."[22] France's thesis has validity, especially in the context of the indirect discourse in the passage where Bigger, still in the Dalton home, luxuriates in a newfound sense of power after having killed Mary: "He was conscious of . . . the wealthy white people moving in luxury to all sides of him, whites living in a smugness, a security, a certainly that he had never known. The knowledge that he had killed a white girl they loved and regarded as their symbol of beauty made him feel the equal of them, like a man who had been somehow cheated, but had now evened the score" (598). Here Bigger feels avenged and magnified as a result of appropriating and consuming, in the literal furnace and in the metaphorical furnace of his sexual rage, Mary, the young woman who personified the white privilege that oppresses him.

Moreover, France correctly points out that "signification by which sexual penetration becomes confused with murder" spills over at one especially frightening moment in Wright's text. Two white men, members of the party searching for Bigger through the abandoned tenements of Chicago's South Side, see a nearly nude "brown gal" in one of the buildings. One of them then expresses a degree of mystification: "I wonder what on earth a nigger wants to kill a white woman for when he has such good-looking women in his race" (689). In this passage the equation of sex with murder is not restricted to the consciousness of Bigger or of one of his friends; it seems, instead, to be embedded in the psychology of the dominant white capitalist male society. Wright may consciously be making the political point that the U.S. system of economic and racial oppression reduces everyone except the privileged white man to the level of a commodity intended to be consumed and thus destroyed. If so, Bigger's psychosis makes him a truly "native son," a young man who has instinctively adopted the brutal sexual mores of the society in which he is trapped.

A controlling irony of his life, then, is the fact that his victimized social and economic position allows him virtually no outlet for his barely repressed sexual aggression. Even with Bessie he lives a truly masturbatory existence, finding release for his rage only in random acts of meaningless violence. France, for example, describes his slashing Doc's pool table with his knife as a "sexually symbolic" act of violence against Gus (4–5). In fact, Bigger's rage over society's negation of his very existence has penetrated his sexual identity and transformed it into something monstrous and frightening. Life is, for him, a state of constant frustration and impotence: he can dream of someday flying a plane, but he cannot escape for long the awareness that society will never let him do so. Instinctively, he locates a necessary and sustaining pride in his sexuality, the tangible proof of his "masculinity," but even that can only be released through unfeeling sex with Bessie or in aggressive masturbatory fantasies in darkened theaters. There are thus two extreme poles of sexuality and of existence itself open to Bigger: acts of masturbatory rage, which are generally safe because they do not threaten to impinge upon the dominant white society (he can slash a pool table at Doc's but does not dare rob a white-owned store), and outbursts of hostility, which are always a form of rape.

However accidental it is, the murder of Mary Dalton is a liberating experience for Bigger. As the language of the text makes clear, his sexual response to the drunken young woman is a central factor in her death:

He lifted her and laid her on the bed. Something urged him to leave at once, but he leaned over her, excited, looking at her face in the dim light, not wanting to take his hands from her breasts. She tossed and mumbled sleepily. He tightened his fingers on her breasts, kissing her again, feeling her move toward him. He was aware only of her body now; his lips trembled. Then he stiffened. The door behind him had cracked.

Mary's fingernails tore at his hands and he caught the pillow and covered her entire face with it, firmly. Mary's body surged upward and he pushed downward upon the pillow with all of his weight, determined that she must not move or make any sound that would betray him. His eyes were filled with the white blur moving toward him in the shadows of the room. Again Mary's body heaved and he held the pillow in a grip that took all of his strength. (524–25)

Sexual excitement inspired by her present and vulnerable body prevents his leaving "at once" and thus escaping the tragedy that will engulf him and the rich young white woman as well. Wright's description of Mary's body "surging upward" as he "pushed downward upon the pillow" indicates that her suffocation is, in part, a grotesque and deadly form of intercourse. With virtually no warning Bigger is shocked to discover that he has Mary, the embodiment of the capitalistic society that simultaneously tempts and denies him, in a position of passivity and vulnerability, an extreme form of the defenseless state in which he prefers to find Bessie.

He experiences the momentary illusion of an escape from his masturbatory existence. In her drunken state Mary, by responding to his sexuality, however unconscious that response is, has affirmed his sexual identity, his "masculinity." She has unknowingly inspired the sudden release through sexual arousal of that essential self, which he has learned to hide and even appears to deny. But Mrs. Dalton's presence in the room dooms such a self-affirming release. The ghostly figure of Mary's mother induces an overwhelming fear in Bigger, and, as always happens when his fear becomes too much for him to bear, he finds release through violence. As the rat in the novel's opening scene metaphorically foreshadows, Bigger lives a cornered life, forced by U.S. racism and economic oppression into such a restricted area of existence that he can hardly breathe. The poles of his life are consequently extreme and destructive, the customary "masturbatory" state in which he survives through repression of his rage and those moments in which the rage breaks free in acts of literal or symbolic rape, such as slashing the cloth of the pool table at Doc's in a grotesque parody of sexual penetration. Mary's drunken response to him gives him a tantalizing, and thus infuriating, glimpse of a life lived outside the masturbation-rape polarity. By shocking him into a renewed awareness of the suffocating taboos of U.S. racism, Mrs. Dalton's entry into the room abruptly forces him back into his masturbation-rape mode of existence. Her entry into Mary's bedroom thus dooms her daughter and Bigger.

It is impossible to determine the degree, if any, to which Bigger's assertion that so frightens Max in the novel's last scene, is intended to indicate a belated understanding on the part of the young man of the full range of the abrupt emotional changes that so disoriented him on that fatal evening in

Mary's bedroom and of the ways in which they inevitably contributed to his eventual destruction. But his words to Max, pointing as they do toward a perception of himself as both murderous agent and passive victim, may well indicate at least the beginning of such awareness: "I didn't want to kill! . . . But what I killed for, I *am!* It must've been pretty deep in me to make me kill! I must have felt it awful hard to murder . . ." (849). Most obviously, Wright is using this speech, and this entire concluding scene, to back away from Max's defense summary, with its overly simplified explanation of Bigger as a naturalistic victim of society and to move toward an overtly existential vision of Bigger. The never fully resolved narrative tension that results from the combination of a naturalistic and an existentialist view of Bigger is the principal reason that *Native Son* deconstructs in part 3, "Fate." Moreover, Wright's somewhat desperate attempt to unify these at least somewhat contradictory approaches to his character results in his minimizing the motif of Bigger's sexual identity in the novel's concluding scenes. Still, Bigger's speech, which so frightens Max, may represent a narrative trace of the sexual identity theme.

Of course, because of the insistence of the Book-of-the-Month Club, Wright tried, fortunately without success, to remove or at least disguise the motif of Bigger's masturbatory sexual identity. After the movie theater scene and some aesthetically beneficial cuts in the courtroom summaries, the most significant revision that Wright made in his original manuscript is in the paragraph describing Bigger's rape of Bessie just before he murders her. The original version emphasizes even more strongly than the revision that what occurs is, in fact, a rape and that it is another instance of Bigger's attempts to escape the prison of masturbation in which he is relentlessly trapped. Both versions describe Bigger "ignoring the cold" and flinging the covers away from Bessie's body and then, despite her silent protest, preparing to have sex with her. In one brief sentence both emphasize that Bigger feels that he cannot control what he is about to do: "He had to now."

Then the two versions become very different. The original emphasizes Bigger's attempt to escape the masturbatory trap and to force from Bessie a recognition of his essential self:

Yes. Bessie. His desire was naked and hot in his hand and his fingers were touching her. Yes. Bessie. Now. He had to now. . . . He was sorry, but he had to. He. He could not help it. Help it. Sorry. Help it. Sorry. Help it. Sorry. Help it now. She should. Look! She should should should look. Look at how he was. He. He was. He was feeling bad

91

about how she would feel but he could not help it now. Feeling. *Bessie.*
Now. All. He heard her breathing heavily and heard his own breath
going and coming heavily. *Bigger.* Now. All. All. Now. All. *Bigger.* . . .
(664)

The fragmented prose in this section corresponds to Bigger's accelerating desperation as he fails to evoke the recognition he so badly needs
from Bessie. He even fails to fully awaken her. (Wright makes it impossible
to know whether the italicized exclamations of his name come from Bessie
or from the furnace of Bigger's mind.) At any rate, she does not indicate any
awareness that he is, in fact, "All." Perhaps rather than any fear that she
might betray him to the police, this is the real reason that he must kill her.
As with Mary, he has found himself in an intensely sexual moment with a
drunken, half-sleeping woman, and, once again, he has been unable to force
from that moment a recognition of his essential self. On the first occasion
the sudden appearance of Mrs. Dalton thrusts him back into the masturbation-rape polarity that is the norm of his existence. With Bessie, while he
does succeed in sexual penetration, he fails, because of his inability to awaken
her into consciousness, to force a sign from her that "He. He was."[23]

Significantly, just before describing Bigger's brutal and fatal assault on
Bessie with the brick, Wright repeats the phrase used to describe the black
youth's terror when Mrs. Dalton enters Mary's bedroom: "He stiffened"
(666). The two words with their connotation of male sexual arousal effectively telescope Wright's motif of utilizing Bigger's constrained and twisted
sexuality as a metaphor for his anger and rage at being a perennial victim of
socioeconomic oppression. It is this motif that the novelist sought to mini-
mize in his revision of *Native Son:* in the first *published* version of the novel
the passage communicating Bigger's desperate need and struggle to force
an acknowledgment of his identity during sexual intercourse with Bessie is
changed into a poetic, and more safely abstract, description of his riding
"roughshod" over the passive female body beneath him like "a frenzied horse
down a steep hill in the face of a resisting wind."[24]

Especially in the original version of *Native Son,* Wright presents, from
an insider's perspective, an unforgettably complex and frightening vision of
the fat man residing in the inner cities of America. The creation of Bigger
Thomas, the black youth helplessly torn between the extreme poles of metaphoric masturbation and deadly outbursts of violence, was intended to shock
the middle-class reader into recognition of a tortured and twisted, but still
undeniable, humanity. Now, in the newly published original version of the

novel, the use of Bigger's warped and deadly sexuality as metaphor for his doomed struggle to attain a saving self, while still not fully and clearly developed, aesthetically transcends the inconsistency and confusion that results from Wright's failure in the last half of the novel to reconcile the naturalistic and existentialist motifs.

The original *Native Son* is a clearly superior work to the novel as revised and first published. Despite some confusion, it is also superior in its complexity and daring to Gold's *Jews without Money*. Wright's very ambivalence toward Marxism led him to write a less politically correct but more humanly meaningful novel than Gold's. Writing almost a decade after the publication of *Native Son*, Nelson Algren, influenced by such European masters as Kuprin, Gorky, Sartre, and Céline more than by Karl Marx, would paint, in *The Man with the Golden Arm*, an even more deliberately grotesque portrait of the urban fat man.

Notes

1. Quoted in Michel Fabre, *The Unfinished Quest of Richard Wright* (New York: Morrow, 1973), 230–31.

2. John M. Reilly, "Criticism of Ethnic Literature: Seeing the Whole Story," *MELUS* 5 (1978): 3.

3. Reprinted in Richard Wright, *Native Son* (New York: Harper and Row Perennial Library, 1987), xiv–xv.

4. In discussing an essay called "Blueprint for Negro Writing," which Wright published in 1937, Barbara Johnson emphasizes the degree to which the novelist's Marxism rested from the first upon his identity as an African American:

> He urged Negro writers to abandon the posture of humility and the bourgeois path of "individual achievement," and to develop a collective voice of social consciousness, both nationalist and Marxist. "The Negro writer must realize within the area of his own personal experience those impulses which, when prefigured in terms of broad social movements, constitute the stuff of nationalism. . . . It is through a Marxist conception of reality and society that the maximum degree of freedom in thought and feeling can be gained for the Negro writer." Negro writing, in other words, could fulfill itself only by becoming at once black and red. (Johnson, "The Re[a]d and the Black," *Richard Wright's Native Son: Modern Critical Interpretations*, ed. Harold Bloom [New York: Chelsea House, 1988], 115)

5. John M. Reilly, "Giving Bigger a Voice: The Politics of Narrative in *Native Son*," in *New Essays on Richard Wright*, ed. Keneth Kinnamon (Cambridge: Cambridge University Press, 1990), 36.

6. *Native Son* has often been discussed as a naturalistic novel, and in *Black Boy* Wright discusses the shock of recognition he felt upon first discovering the tradition of literary naturalism. For an especially good analysis of Wright's debt to Emile Zola, see Robert James Butler, "Wright's *Native Son* and Two Novels by Zola: A Comparative Study," *Black American Literature Forum* 18 (1984): 100–105.

7. Richard Wright, *Native Son*, in *Richard Wright: Early Works*, ed. Arnold Rampersad (New York: Library of America, 1991), 450. (This volume represents, of course, a new and definitive text of *Native Son*.)

8. Reilly, "Giving Bigger a Voice," 41–42.

9. W. E. B. Du Bois, "Fifty Years After," *The Souls of Black Folk* (Greenwich, Conn.: Fawcett, 1961), n.p.

10. Blanche H. Gelfant, *The American City Novel* (Norman: University of Oklahoma Press, 1954).

11. Joyce Ann Joyce, in refuting the standard critical charge that Wright is a careless and clumsy stylist, points to the novel's consistent use of references to black and white to symbolize Bigger's psychological and emotional turmoil: "Ubiquitous in the novel, *black* presages fear and humiliation while *white* warns of danger and insensitivity" ("Style and Meaning in Richard Wright's *Native Son*," *Black American Literature Forum* 16 [Fall 1982]: 114).

12. James Nagel places Mrs. Dalton's blindness in the context of a pervasive imagery of vision in the novel (Nagel, "Images of 'Vision' in *Native Son*," in *Critical Essays on Richard Wright*, ed. Yoshinobu Hakutani [Boston: G. K. Hall, 1982], 151–58). Keneth Kinnamon discusses it in the context of Wright's familiarity with the condition of color blindness known as Daltonism (Kinnamon, "*Native Son:* The Personal, Social, and Political Background," in Hakutani, *Critical Essays on Richard Wright*, 120–27).

13. Keneth Kinnamon writes that the fictional Ernie's "is a slight disguise for an actual restaurant called 'The Chicken Shack,' 4647 Indiana Avenue [in Chicago], of which one Ernie Henderson was owner" ("*Native Son:* The Personal, Social, and Political Background," 121).

14. For an interesting defense of the coherence of Jan's character as well as the novel's Marxist theme, see James G. Kennedy, "The Content and Form of *Native Son*," *College English* 34 (1972): 269–83.

15. Nathan A. Scott, Jr., "The Dark and Haunted Tower of Richard Wright," in *Richard Wright: A Collection of Critical Essays*, ed. Richard Macksey and Frank E. Moorer (Englewood Cliffs, N.J.: Prentice-Hall, 1984), 158. (The essay first appeared in *Graduate Comment* [Wayne State University] in 1964 and was then included in *Five Black Writers*, ed. Donald B. Gibson [New York: New York University Press, 1970], 12–25.)

16. Irving Howe, "Black Boys and Native Sons," *A World More Attractive* (New York: Horizon, 1963), 103.

17. Steven J. Rubin, "Richard Wright and Albert Camus: The Literature of Revolt," *International Fiction Review* 8 (Winter 1981): 12.

18. Jerry H. Bryant, "The Violence of *Native Son*," *Southern Review* 17 (Spring 1981): 303–19.

19. For an interesting comparison of the story of Bigger Thomas to Dostoevsky's antihero, see Tony Magistrale, "From St. Petersburg to Chicago: Wright's *Crime and Punishment*," *Comparative Literature Studies* 23 (Spring 1986): 59–70.

20. Two interesting recent essays take conflicting positions concerning the relevance of Max's defense speech to the characterization of Bigger and the thematic focus of the novel. In "The Dissociated Sensibility of Bigger Thomas in Wright's *Native Son*" Louis Tremaine sees Max as a fantasy "mouthpiece" for Bigger:

> Max has been characterized by various readers as a mouthpiece for the Communist Party. In fact, he is much more importantly a mouthpiece for Bigger, a fantasy come true: he possesses a vast audience, commands the language (words, imagery, frame of reference) of that audience, and stands in a privileged forum from which to address it. In every sense of the word, he *represents Bigger* to the world in a way that Bigger could never represent himself. (*Studies in American Fiction* 14 [Spring 1986]: 62–76)

In contrast, Laura E. Tanner sees Max playing a largely ironic role in the novel. She argues that Max's speech signals, through linguistic similarities, the unreliability of the narrative voice in the rest of the novel: "Max functions in the plot exactly as the narrator's presence functions in the novel; the limitations of Max's speech expose to the reader the unreliability of the narrative voice through which Bigger's consciousness has been articulated throughout the work" ("Uncovering the Magical Discourse of Language: The Narrative Presence in Richard Wright's *Native Son*," *Texas Studies in Language and Literature* 29 [Winter 1987]: 412–31). Tanner's reading obviously has interesting implications for the overtly existentialist indirect discourse passages discussed earlier in this chapter.

21. Kathleen Gallagher offers an incisive study of the ways in which Bigger's mind is controlled by images and stereotypes originating in the mass media of the 1930s, in "Bigger's Great Leap to the Figurative," *CLA Journal* 27 (March 1984): 293–314.

22. Alan W. France, "Misogyny and Appropriation in Wright's *Native Son*," *Modern Fiction Studies* 34 (Autumn 1988): 2.

23. Robert James Butler sees Mary and Bessie as personifications of the duality of Bigger's existence: "Whereas Mary represents a side of Bigger which may be called 'romantic' because it is centered in an idealized set of longings for a radically new life based upon expanded possibilities, Bessie epitomizes an aspect of his personality which may be called 'naturalistic' since it is severely conditioned by the economic, political, and social pressures of his actual environment" (Butler, "The Function of Violence in Richard Wright's *Native Son*," *Black American Literature Forum* 20 [1986]: 11).

24. Wright, *Native Son* (Harper and Row Perennial Library), 219–20.

Chapter 4

Encountering the Urban Grotesque
Nelson Algren's *Man with the Golden Arm*

Twelve years after his death Nelson Algren remains something of a cultural icon in Chicago, his lasting literary importance militantly defended by Studs Terkel, Mike Royko, and other Chicago literary figures. Despite this local popularity and even though he was the first winner of the National Book Award (in 1950, for *The Man with the Golden Arm* [1949]), Algren has yet to be welcomed without reservation into the canon of twentieth-century American literature. Throughout his career his work, on occasion, provoked undisguised and quite irrational hostility in certain influential academic and establishment reviewers. In 1956 Leslie Fiedler contemptuously dismissed Algren as "the bard of the stumblebum,"[1] and Norman Podhoretz expressed dismay and disgust at the novelist's obsession with drug addicts, prostitutes, and other members of the urban lumpenproletariat.[2] Today few critics pay any attention at all to Algren's work.[3]

An important factor in the current critical neglect of Algren's work and his marginal status in relation to the literary canon can be traced back to his arrival on the national literary scene. Algren's first novel, *Somebody in Boots*, which appeared in 1935, is essentially a conventional naturalistic protest novel, narrated from the usual proletarian perspective of such Great Depression fiction. Appearing at the beginning of Algren's career, it inspired a perception of the novelist as a writer of naturalistic protest in the tradition of Stephen Crane and Theodore Dreiser, artists whom Algren did, in fact, respect. In a literary age of modernism and postmodernism Algren has often, and not surprisingly, been dismissed as an exponent of an outdated and irrelevant literary tradition. Further, even those critics who have asserted the continuing importance of naturalistic social protest, and who might thus have been his most determined defenders, have sometimes been made uncomfortable by his work.

Maxwell Geismar, for instance, was an enthusiastic Algren champion until the appearance in 1956 of one of the novelist's best *and most unconventional* works, *A Walk on the Wild Side*. Geismar saw *Walk* as being something of a betrayal of the naturalistic tradition. In contrast, he admired *The Man with the Golden Arm*, Algren's richest novel, which preceded *A Walk on the*

Wild Side. Geismar's 1958 essay "Nelson Algren: The Iron Sanctuary" remains one of the most incisive discussions of *Man with the Golden Arm* and contains an important clue concerning the complexity of Algren's aesthetic. Without developing or clearly explaining the basis of his comparison, Geismar mentions Sherwood Anderson's 1919 classic examination of the alienation of small-town America, *Winesburg, Ohio,* as being a work that anticipated *The Man with the Golden Arm.* Specifically, he writes that *Man with the Golden Arm* "is a *Winesburg, Ohio* of the slum dwellers; and one remembers that Sherwood Anderson wrote his nostalgic country tales while living in these miserable Chicago buildings, at the ragged end of life, where the streets run on and on, 'out of nowhere into nothing.'"[4] Geismar's implication that one can sense, in *Winesburg,* traces of the urban setting in which the book was written is an interesting concept but one that cannot be developed here.

What is of immediate interest is the Anderson-Algren comparison itself. The probable basis of Geismar's linking of these two writers is that, in their books, both explore idiosyncratic visions of grotesque characters. Anderson's collection of stories is introduced by a preface entitled "The Book of the Grotesque," which explores, in a highly symbolic manner, the transformation of human beings into "grotesques." Essentially, Anderson says that finite human beings attempt to define, to validate, themselves by adopting as their own one or two "truths" from the wide complex range of abstract truths that are potentially relevant to human life and which exist in an interrelated manner in the universe. By adopting such limited, and limiting, self-definitions, human beings thus distort and isolate themselves. Loneliness and alienation in a culturally barren small-town Midwest are the felt causes of suffering for Anderson's people, and their most grotesque actions result primarily from an inevitable, even if self-imposed, distortion of identity, which makes truly meaningful communication with others impossible.

It should be emphasized that *Winesburg, Ohio* is a book written at a time when the end of the American frontier was, especially for the Midwest, still a recent and personally felt loss, a historic moment after which an infinitely expanding American life and character no longer seemed possible. It also appeared at the end of World War I, an event that would seem to the Lost Generation, a group of romantic writers directly influenced by *Winesburg, Ohio,* to have been a traumatic national betrayal of youthful ideals and creeds. Geismar is right, then, to describe Anderson's stories as "nostalgic country tales"—the volume is distinguished from beginning to end by a tone of nostalgia for a lost American innocence. Moreover, Anderson's nostalgia, which at times lapses into sheer sentimentality, leads him to depict even his most clearly grotesque characters (e.g., Wash Williams and Doctor Parcival) as ultimately sympathetic victims of external forces.

Nelson Algren did not use the word *grotesque* to describe his characters. But he certainly might have. His best novels, *Man with the Golden Arm* and *Walk on the Wild Side*, examine the ugly and sordid lives of his ghetto characters in unflinching detail. The characters who people these novels are drug addicts, dealers, prostitutes, petty thieves, and world-weary, and not infrequently corrupt, police officers. Moreover, Algren is normally not interested in positing a hidden and potentially redeeming decency within them. Kurt Vonnegut has asserted that Algren "broke new ground (in American literature) by depicting persons said to be dehumanized by poverty and ignorance and injustice as being *genuinely* dehumanized, and dehumanized quite *permanently*."[5] Vonnegut's assessment is not quite accurate, but it is accurate enough to provide an important insight into the reason that *A Walk on the Wild Side* seemed a betrayal to a Marxist critic like Geismar. In that novel Algren's aesthetic denies the essential consolation of the naturalistic protest novel—the faith that social reform can, by ameliorating the sordid and exploitative conditions in which socioeconomic victims live, transform them into productive and useful citizens of society. The characters of *A Walk on the Wild Side* are, in fact, far beyond the reach of even the most thorough social reform. An interesting question is why Geismar did not see that this was equally true of the individuals depicted in *The Man with the Golden Arm*, a novel that is, in fact, fundamentally more pessimistic and despairing than Algren's *A Walk on the Wild Side*.

Charles C. Walcutt, in *American Literary Naturalism: A Divided Stream* (1956), did perceive the bleakness of Algren's vision in his 1949 novel and was as offended by the book as Geismar would be by *A Walk on the Wild Side*. For Walcutt it was *The Man with the Golden Arm* that represented a perverse distortion of the tradition of American literary naturalism:

Algren seems to have given up even the pretense that society could be improved or purified. For him it has become a jungle of viciousness and injustice beyond reclamation; only the waifs and strays merit attention because only they are capable of tender and beautiful feelings. One may be deeply moved by *The Man with the Golden Arm* but must, I believe, finally regard it as irresponsible and inaccurate— a sentimental contrivance that has little to do with reality but rather explores a cul-de-sac in the author's imagination. Algren's subject matter, considered alone, would seem to be firmly in the naturalistic tradition; but his total attitude toward it is not so at all.[6]

Especially given the brilliance of Walcutt's extensive study of the origins and nature of American literary naturalism, one has to be more than a little astonished by his evaluation of *The Man with the Golden Arm*. One wonders, for instance, exactly where in Algren's novel he finds "waifs and strays" exhibiting "tender and beautiful feelings." Moreover, it seems clear that the novel has "little to do" not with any objective reality but, rather, with any reality that Walcutt knows or wants to know.

Walcutt is quite accurate, however, in his perception that "Algren seems to have given up even the pretense that society could be improved or purified," and it is for this heresy that he, like Geismar two years later, condemns the novelist. Yet for Walcutt it is not primarily political concerns that make such a grim assumption unacceptable. Throughout his critical study he asserts that American naturalism, to a significant degree, grew out of the native soil of transcendentalism and thus exhibits an indestructible layer of romantic optimism. Stephen Crane's Maggie is, after all, a delicate flower "that blossomed in a mud puddle," a character who on the inside remains fundamentally and rather inexplicably unaffected by the sordidness of her environment.

In contrast to Algren, Walcutt gladly welcomes Sherwood Anderson into the central canon of American literary naturalism. Written thirty-seven years after the book's appearance, his discussion of *Winesburg, Ohio* remains an especially perceptive analysis of some of the key factors that transform Anderson's characters into grotesques: "*Winesburg, Ohio* is full of insights into the buried life, into the thoughts of the repressed, the inarticulate, the misunderstood. Most frequently frustrated is the desire to establish some degree of intimacy with another person. A tradition of manners would accomplish just this by providing a medium through which acquaintance could ripen into intimacy. Small-town America has wanted such a tradition" (228). Walcutt adds: "[Anderson's] ideas are all in the naturalistic tradition in that they are motivated by the feeling of need for their expression of the 'inner man.' Anderson assumes that this inner man exists and is good and 'should' be permitted to fulfill itself through love and experience. The need is alive and eager; it is the social order that prevents its satisfaction" (229). To Walcutt, then, the inhabitants of Winesburg, Ohio, are clearly naturalistic beings: they are the victims of environmental determinism; they are psychologically and spiritually warped by "the social order." But they are not finally threatening: the "inner man" within them all is "good."

In contrast, the "inner man" in most of Algren's people, especially the males, is as irrevocably warped as the visible being that houses it. It should be said that Algren is, in fact, often guilty of sentimentality in his portrayal of female characters; the *central* female figures in his novels commonly exhibit genuine strength and moral courage. The men they foolishly care about rarely, if ever, manifest such positive qualities. Two prime examples of this male-female dichotomy in Algren's customary approach to characterization are Frankie Machine and Molly-O Novotny of *The Man with the Golden Arm*.

To convey the essence of his male characters (and usually his supporting female figures), Algren perfected a deliberately harsh and mocking rhetoric. He refers to them as "wonders," as "the Republic's crummiest lushes." Moreover, he documents their grotesque behavior in a prevailing mode of Absurdist humor. Like *Winesburg, Ohio*, Algren's work clearly reflects the national mood of the period in which it appeared. *The Man with the Golden Arm*, for instance, exhibits the bitter disillusionment of the years immediately after World War II. Though the novel is usually thought of as an exposé of drug addiction, that theme, which seemed so sensational in 1949, was, in fact, an afterthought on Algren's part. He initially conceived the book as a war novel: "I was going to write a *war* novel. But it turned out to be this 'Golden Arm' thing. I mean, the war kind of slipped away, and those people with the hypos came along . . . and that was it."[7] In fact, the war has not completely "slipped away" in the finished novel; traces of the book Algren originally planned can still be detected. For instance, Frankie Machine's morphine addiction resulted from a war wound; he likes to wear an army combat jacket; and he has a car wreck that injures his wife, Sophie, after drinking several "A-Bomb Specials," a particularly dangerous drink invented by Antek Witwicki at his Tug and Maul bar. The damage done to the American psyche by World War II and "the bomb" is a major subtheme in *The Man with the Golden Arm*.

The novel's grim pessimism also reflects its wide range of literary influences. Algren more than once acknowledged his debt to Crane and Dreiser, but he also expressed his admiration for certain European writers, especially the Russian novelist and short story writer Alexandre Kuprin and the French fictional explorer of human "absurdity," Céline. A line from Kuprin's exposé of prostitution in czarist Russia, *Yama, or the Pit* (1922), appears at the beginning of book 1 of *The Man with the Golden Arm*: "Do you understand, gentlemen, that all the horror is in just this—that there is no horror!"[8] In *Yama* these words are spoken by a journalist named Platonov, who is attempting to make a group of Russian students who frequent brothels understand the specific kind of evil manifested in prostitution. His point is that this form of evil is especially insidious precisely because it has come to seem prosaic to most Russians—an accepted and thus usually ignored fact. The horror of prostitution for Platonov and, one assumes, Kuprin is that no one *is* particularly horrified by such a vicious system of dehumanization—not even the victimized prostitutes themselves. Interestingly, Algren quoted the line from Kuprin in *Man with the Golden Arm*, his only novel that does not treat prostitution in any significant degree. In fact, Kuprin's novel gave Algren a perspective on all forms of social injustice. The exploitation of human beings continued in the United States, Algren believed, because the middle and upper classes, which profited from it, had learned to accept and to ignore it. As in Kuprin's czarist Russia, social injustice in post–World War II America had come to seem prosaic, even a little boring. Ultimately, nothing would so prove Algren to have been correct in this assessment than the reactions of Fiedler and Podhoretz to this work.

At least as great an influence as Kuprin upon Algren's vision of the urban grotesque was Céline, whose work Algren discovered while in the army: "[He] was tremendously impressed by Céline's *Journey to the End of the Night*. When asked who, of his day, was trying to break out of the middle-class world and show the under-world legions of the city, Algren answered in one word, '"Céline."'[9] For Céline human conduct was unfailingly "crummy," and Algren's ideas and his mocking rhetoric reveal the direct influence of the French novelist. In fact, Algren discovered in Céline's *Journey to the End of the Night* (1934) a literary model for retaining an embittered kind of narrative compassion while exploring the full range of human depravity. Céline's writing represents a cruel, but ultimately forgiving, mode of satire; *Journey to the End of the Night* describes the experiences of one of modern literature's most memorable antiheroes, Bardamu, as he serves in World War I and travels to French West Africa, New York City, Detroit, and Paris. Wherever he goes Bardamu finds nothing but misery and suffering and decides that he must communicate the totality of what he has seen and known:

> The biggest defeat in every department of life is to forget, especially the things that have done you in, and to die without realizing how far people can go in the way of crumminess. When the grave lies

open before us, let's not try to be witty, but on the other hand, let's not forget, but make it our business to record the worst of the human viciousness we've seen without changing one word. When that's done, we can curl up our toes and sink into the pit. That's work enough for a lifetime.[10]

This vision of human "crumminess" and "viciousness" constitutes the core of an aesthetic of hatred that dominates *Journey to the End of the Night*.

In *The Man with the Golden Arm* Algren is also committed to detailing the crummy and vicious behavior of his urban wonders. But, like Céline, he proclaims the undeniable humanness of his creations. Algren believed in the necessity of the honest writer's working out of a limited form of compassion. In a 1964 series of interviews he stated a preference for the art of Edward Albee to that of Tennessee Williams: "I prefer Albee's harshness. It's a harsh compassion with him. He's not as vulnerable. . . . He doesn't hold out any hope at all. Williams does, and I think it's not a true hope."[11] Inspired by Céline, Algren was already developing his kind of "harsh compassion" in *The Man with the Golden Arm*. The novel achieves its meaning and effect through a recurrent device of deliberately undercutting extensive documentation of crummy behavior by alienated and often desperate characters with sudden assertions of those same characters' unmistakable humanity. Thus, as perceptive as Vonnegut's evaluation is, it is not quite accurate: Algren insists always that his wonders are, in fact, *not* thoroughly dehumanized. His aesthetic insists that, while their humanness may be distorted to the point of being virtually unrecognizable, it is still there. It must be said that Algren's bitterness is never as total as Céline's and that his work can more accurately be described as illustrative of an aesthetic of despair than one of hatred. Nevertheless, it offers no promise of human redemption; Algren is determined not to "hold out any hope at all" in his fiction.

The shift from a small-town to an inner-city setting, the legacy of World War II, and the influences of Kuprin and Céline meant that there would inevitably be dramatic differences between Algren's crummy wonders and Anderson's innocent grotesques. These differences, which are the key to Walcutt's welcoming Anderson into the canon of American naturalism while rejecting Algren, can be quickly illustrated through a comparison of Wash Williams of *Winesburg* and Blind Pig of *The Man with the Golden Arm*.

Williams, the telegraph operator in Winesburg, deliberately cultivates a grotesque and filthy appearance: "[He] was the ugliest thing in town. His girth was immense, his neck thin, his legs feeble. He was dirty. Everything about him was unclean. Even the whites of his eyes looked soiled."[12] The narrator introduces Williams's story by comparing the character to an orangutan in an urban zoo. Still, as with most of the other characters, Anderson uses Williams's "confession" to George Willard as a means of creating reader sympathy for the telegraph operator. Williams was, it turns out, once married and loved his "tall blonde" wife "with a kind of religious fervor" (125), until his discovery that she was, with three different men, deceiving him. Upon this discovery he left her, only to be summoned back by the woman's mother. When he returns he is eager to forgive his wife and take her back, until the woman's mother pushes her naked into the room where he waits alone. Williams's response to this incident is to hate the mother (significantly not his wife) and to cultivate his veneer of filth and ugliness as a means of protecting himself from ever again being deceived and hurt by a woman.

Algren's Blind Pig is also aggressively filthy in appearance. Ultimately, his "profession" is dirty as well—after Frankie Machine kills Nifty Louie, Blind Pig becomes the principal drug dealer on Division Street. His willed dirtiness is so extreme that it infuriates the other patrons of the Tug and Maul bar to the point that they want to hit him but do not dare to do so. The reader learns virtually nothing about Blind Pig that might ameliorate a sense of revulsion at him. The narrator tells us only that the character is so outraged at his loss of sight that he wants to make everyone around him suffer and that he last remembers seeing a stripper in a burlesque show and, since his loss of sight, continually leers at a nude female figure on a runway that exists only in his mind. Blind Pig has never loved anyone or anything with a "religious fervor," and his cosmic rage at his blindness allows him to replace Nifty Louie as Division Street's dealer with no guilt or hesitation.

The contrast between the ways Wash Williams and Blind Pig react to their visions of a commodified female body is revealing. Anderson's character is outraged by the mother who attempted to transform her daughter's body into an object of enticement and exchange, who attempted to objectify and then "sell" her child. Williams can hate the exploiter without condemning the exploited victim. (It is, of course, true that the mother is a kind of victim as well: she acts out of an acceptance of the inevitable commodification of the female body in a capitalistic society.) In contrast, Blind Pig transforms his absence of sight into a mode of continuous voyeuristic enjoyment of one of the most degrading of all the many forms of commodification of the female body in capitalistic America. In a key respect the image in his mind conforms to the probable perceptions of all the men who leer at the nearly naked woman on the runway—in Blind Pig's memory, as in her actual time of nakedness in the burlesque theater, the woman has been stripped of her humanity as well as her clothes.

The thematic significance of Blind Pig and of his professional mentor, Nifty Louie, is overtly summarized by Frankie Machine's self-pitying wife, Sophie: "It's just the way things would be if that Nifty Louie was God 'n Blind Pig was Jesus Christ."[13] Algren's postwar urban world is indeed a fallen, absurd place.

The way in which his aesthetic of despair communicates his vision of the crumminess of the people who inhabit that world while still insisting on their humanity can be illustrated through a discussion of three key scenes in *The Man with the Golden Arm.* Near the end of the novel Molly Novotny, the "girl with too big a heart," the one character in the novel who has, on the inside, not been touched by the sordid reality in which she is forced to exist, has herself become a stripper in a black nightclub. Like that of the anonymous woman trapped in Blind Pig's mind, Molly-O's fate in this part of the novel allows Algren to image the naked vulnerability of the female in a corrupt capitalistic society.

On another, metaphoric level the description of Molly-O as she enters the stage has a quite different, and even somewhat contradictory, significance. Her entrance, in fact, creates a paradoxical effect:

A brown and white chorus came out one by one, seemingly too indifferent toward each other to come out together, till there were five. Though each wore only slippers and a G string, all seemed overdressed, so studiously had their nakedness been donned. Each pore powdered, each taut pink nipple tinted with fingernail polish and dusted with some mauve talc, the armpits shaven and deodorized, each navel dusted and the hair swept back behind each small catlike ear. (307)

The nudity of the five women seems a crafted disguise, a protective costume. Their disguised, deodorized nakedness functions in Algren's novel as a metaphor for respectable society's desire not to see the urban lumpenproletariat.

In the 1960s Algren began to describe the United States as a "third-person society," and he had already realized the essence of American third-personness in 1949. The middle and upper classes, he believed, exploited those trapped in the inner city while simultaneously denying their humanity and even their existence. Drug traffic, prostitution, and gambling flourished in the ghetto because those outside it wanted and needed such activities. Drugs, prostitution, and other illicit vices, Algren insisted, constitute, in fact, an unacknowledged, but essential, part of the economic structure of the city. Those who survive through urban vice are, of course, an embarrassment to the "respectable" people in the city and the suburbs and thus must be denied and, consequently, to a significant degree dehumanized.

Traditional social protest such as that found in Gold's *Jews without Money* is not central to Algren's novel because his characters live such a subterranean existence that reform could never reach them. Yet the novel does have its political dimension; social outrage, in fact, underscores its every aspect. A passage from the early pages of *The Man with the Golden Arm* describes the symbiotic relationship between God and the ward supervisors: "God loans the super cunning and the super forwards a percentage of the grift on Sunday mornings. The super puts in the fix for all right-thinking hustlers and the Lord, in turn, puts in the fix for the super. For the super's God is a hustler's God; and as wise, in his way, as the God of the priests and the businessmen" (7). It is no wonder, then, that, in postwar Chicago, Nifty Louie appears to be God and Blind Pig appears to be Christ. Neither the cop on the street nor the lone hustler can successfully challenge such an alliance between God and the urban bureaucracy. Only those hustlers who contribute to God *and* to the super can hope to survive. *The Man with the Golden Arm* is an example of a socially engaged but profoundly pessimistic literature that denies itself the consolation of any realistic hope for social reform.

Yet Algren's aesthetic insists upon forcing the middle-class reader to look beneath the "deodorized" nakedness of the lumpenproletariat and recognize this group's obscured, but not fully erased, humanity. Understanding the middle-class need to deny even the existence of the inner city, he understood the difficulty of creating a fiction that would realize such an ambitious goal. Increasingly in his fiction, he used prison and police lineup scenes to challenge the middle-class reader's reluctance to confront sordid and degraded levels of urban reality. Prison scenes were a staple of Algren's work from the beginning of his career. *Somebody in Boots* (1935) describes the boredom and mindless sadism of existence in a west Texas jail, and *Never Come Morning* (1942) and *The Devil's Stocking*, Algren's last novel, published posthumously in the United States in 1983, contain such extended scenes.

Typically, these scenes emphasize the victimization of the prison inmates by brutal and corrupt police officers and guards as well as by one another. In *Man with the Golden Arm*'s opening jail sequence the emphasis is quite different. Here Algren is primarily intent upon presenting to the reader an extended image of the alienation and desperation of his particular fat man, the urban lumpenproletariat.

The narrative strategy in the scene is to focus upon the reactions of the novel's main character, Frankie Machine, professional card dealer and morphine addict, and his constant companion, Sparrow Saltskin, as they observe the wonders imprisoned with them. The inmates, the crummiest lushes of the republic, are all condemned by "the great, secret and special American guilt of owning nothing, nothing at all, in the one land where ownership and virtue were one":

> Guilt that lay crouched behind every billboard which gave each man his commandments; for each man here had failed the billboards all down the line. No Ford in this one's future nor ever any place all his own. Had failed before the radio commercials, by the streetcar plugs and by the standards of every self-respecting magazine. . . .
>
> He had not even been a success in the taverns. Even there he could not afford the liquor that lends distinction nor the beer that gives that special glow of health, leading, often quite suddenly, to startling social success. (17)

Prison, it seems, is the appropriate place for these individuals who have betrayed the "morality" of capitalism and who, consequently, feel the weight of their own worthlessness. At any rate, they have, by disobeying the "commandments" of U.S. capitalism as preached through advertising, forfeited their right to claim the national identity: "All had gone stale for these disinherited. Their very lives gave off a certain jailhouse odor: it trailed down the streets of Skid Row behind them till the city itself seemed some sort of open-roofed jail with walls for all men and laughter for very few. On Skid Row even the native-born no longer felt they had been born in America. They felt they had merely emerged from the wrong side of its billboards" (17). Michael Gold might have endorsed Algren's condemnation of the religion of U.S. materialism, but, as Vonnegut sees, there is a tone of bitter hopelessness in these passages that would dismay any determined social reformer.

In a tone of cold detachment that deliberately approaches condescension, the narrator describes the inevitable fate of these disinherited residents of the inner city:

> These were the luckless living soon to become the luckless dead. The ones who were fished out of river or lake, found crumpled under crumpled papers in the parks, picked up in the horse-and-wagon alleys or slugged for half a bottle of homemade wine, in the rutted tunnels that run between the advertising agencies and the banks.
>
> Some the Demonstrators' Association would invite to attend an autopsy party. For these the cold white dissector's table would be the grave; there wouldn't be enough left to honor with American earth or the simplest sort of cross. Yet some who had been unlucky so long might turn out to be the very luckiest after all: they were to be embalmed through the courtesy of the Balmy-Hour School of Beautification & Sanitary Bloodletting. Not many, of course, could be so lucky; for so few deserved such luck.
>
> Occasionally one of the stiffs, still stubbornly intent on making trouble for everybody, would require one [a pine coffin] longer or broader than he had any real right to at all. Gas and river cases gave the most trouble this way. There were not many giants any more. (18)

As clearly as anything in his work, this passage reveals Algren's debt to Céline. Its emphasis upon the grotesque in describing the ways in which certain forms of suicide and subsequent embalming procedures affect the corpse and its mocking language echo the ways in which the French novelist writes about death in *Journey to the End of the Night* and *Death on the Installment Plan* (1933). For Céline and Algren death is the final obscenity of absurd existence—the last, and conclusive, proof that life is controlled by a pervasive and inescapable anonymity. Any claim to real importance by individuals condemned to such a fate is truly absurd and deserving of ridicule. Still, there is in the Algren prophecy of the future deaths of the prison inmates a note of social as well as cosmic outrage that one does not expect to find in Céline. It is significant that "the rutted tunnels" in which these grotesques live "run between the advertising agencies and the banks," the central temples of the U.S. religion of capitalism. Algren's narrator is implying that death will not be as anonymous or as obscene for the middle and upper classes, who can hire their own embalmers. That this is only true to a degree does not negate the narrator's muted note of protest. The startling sentence, "There were not many giants any more," exemplifies, in itself, the way in which Algren's aesthetic works. Appearing at the end of a paragraph describing the difficulty of finding large enough coffins for especially distorted corpses, it implies that the "giants" of contemporary urban America are merely those individuals more thoroughly corrupted than most by capitalism. For Algren the cruel excesses of his society merited severe condemnation, even if there was little, if any, hope of reforming them.

In addition to Kuprin and Céline, among European writers, Algren admired Dostoevsky, and he occasionally alleviates the pervasive secular despair of his fiction with brief allusions to religion in general and to Christianity in particular. Algren, in these unexpected moments, echoes the Christian existentialism of the author of *Crime and Punishment* (1866) and *The Brothers Karamazov* (1879–80). Frankie Machine, for instance, looks through the bars of his cell to watch most of the other inmates washing at a communal water bucket and sees "the Republic's crummiest lushes lining up to dip their hands gingerly and touch their foreheads, each with a single drop, as if it were holy water and each were on the way to confession instead of twenty dollars or twenty days on the Bridewell floor" (16). For Algren these luckless men, despite their social ostracism, their grotesque appearance, and even the inevitable obscene anonymity of their deaths, merit the compassion and forgiveness that is the legacy of all human beings.

After drawing his cumulative picture of the disinherited, the narrator, through the eyes of Frankie Machine and the Sparrow, focuses upon one especially pathetic, if deliberately disgusting, individual. An "old wino dragging a pair of matted suspenders to the floor" insists that Frankie and Sparrow remember that he used to be the night watchman on the old Wabash railroad. The two merely taunt the old man, however, until he turns

> his behind upon them both deliberately and leaning so far forward he creaked, began a compulsive sort of scratching through the yellowed underwear, the fingers working with a life of their own, starting below the low sagging hill of the fallen thighs and laboring methodically upward as if pursuing the blood like a dog following its fleas; up over the hill and there paused, digging with blunted fingernails but yet without haste and even with something of pleasure.

The description continues for a while even beyond this, thus constituting what must be the longest, most detailed, and least aesthetic behind-scratching scene in American literature.

The "old wino" has, of course, turned his back not only on Frankie and the Sparrow but on the implied middle-class reader as well. Algren's narrative strategy here is to shock and offend his implied reader, who is assumed to be a representative of respectable society. He allows his fictional creation, one of the most deliberately grotesque manifestations of the fat man in American naturalistic urban fiction, an unusual and prolonged expression of contempt for the society that first condemned and then forgot him. Abruptly, however, the old wino makes a very different kind of appeal to Frankie and the Sparrow and to the reader; he straightens up and pleads, "Remember me?" and then sorrowfully concludes, "They don't remember people around here, any more" (19–20). The pathetic character's protest against anonymity, and especially the shared anonymity of death, has universal overtones that no reader can deny.

The *Man with the Golden Arm*'s opening prison episode is thus a revealing illustration of Algren's aesthetic. So is its police lineup scene, which concludes part 1 of the novel. The central figure in this segment of the novel is one of Algren's most complex and fascinating characters, one Record Head Bednar, a world-weary police officer who creates a kind of absurdist theater out of police lineups by carrying on a cynical, mocking dialogue with the "suspects." For years during lineups Bednar listens with bored contempt as the accused seem to be joined in an absurd contest to see which of them can invent the most ridiculous alibi. But on this crucial day, which will change Bednar forever, a "defrocked" minister who has been arrested on a bad-check charge, tells the officer and the rest of his unseen audience that "we are all members of one another" (198). Subsequently, Bednar is so haunted by the preacher's words that he begins to understand that he is guilty of the worst sin of all. He realizes that he has betrayed his fellow mortals by denying the humanity of those whom he has judged: "The captain realized vaguely that the thing he had held secretly in his heart for so long against them all was simply nothing more than a hostility toward men and women as men and women" (297).

Moreover, he cannot even see a way of doing penance for his sin: he feels intensely that "it was time to be stoned" but knows of nowhere to go to plead for redemption and forgiveness. So, "Record Head wept" (298–99). To himself only, and with great anguish, Bednar has acknowledged his own human potential for sin and criminality. By secretly accepting his bond of humanity with the condemned, he has admitted his inner capacity to commit any and all of their crimes. He has, in short, been forced into shocked recognition of something that Sparrow Saltskin will tell him later in the novel: "Everybody's a habitual in his heart. I'm no worse'n anyone else" (276).

For years, without even having to think consciously about it, the captain, through a form of Sartrian bad faith, has shielded himself from the possibility of feeling any identification with the suspects regularly paraded before him: he has wrapped himself tightly in his cloak of authority in order to deny any bond with those in the lineup. He has created an identity as a police officer and not as a human being. But on this day, even before the startling assertion of the preacher, he is troubled by a strange sensation: he feels "the finger of guilt tap his forehead and the need of confession touch his heart like touching a stranger's heart" (197). When the lineup ends he abruptly recognizes the suspects as innocents who disappear "through a green steel doorway into a deepening darkness," while the spectators have been artificially shielded from the threat of any contact with those whom they have come to observe and ridicule. The spectators leave "through a well-lighted door into a clean, well-lighted street" (199). Bednar wants desperately to find a means of confessing that he has played the role of an unofficial and unseen judge who has condemned the innocents. He now knows that he has, for years, functioned as a kind of "grand inquisitor," defining, with the help of an endless set of files in his mind, all those who have been ordered to appear before him as manifestations of the Other. He has been the police captain contemptuously judging the very human "Christs" of the ghetto. Now he wants to confess his humanness, his own inherent capacity for "felonious acts," but, in Algren's secular and fallen world, there is no one to hear his confession. God is, after all, worse than dead: he has been transformed into Nifty Louie and Blind Pig.

There are a number of obvious literary inspirations for this scene. Bednar's grand inquisitor role echoes Dostoevsky's *Crime and Punishment*, while the "defrocked" preacher, as a disgraced and persecuted prophet of human brotherhood, recalls the persona often adopted by Walt Whitman in his poetry as well as John Steinbeck's Jim Casy in *The Grapes of Wrath* (1939). Finally, the description of the "well-lighted" door through which the spectators exit and the well-lighted street in which they find refuge seems to be something of a rhetorical bow to Ernest Hemingway. In fact, Dostoevsky, Whitman, Steinbeck, and Hemingway were all writers for whom Algren, on occasion, expressed admiration. His attempts to claim a kind of literary partnership with Hemingway verged sometimes on the embarrassing—for instance, in his 1965 travel book, *Notes from a Sea Diary: Hemingway All the Way*.

Yet this police lineup episode remains unmistakably Nelson Algren's creation. Like prison scenes, descriptions of lineups are something of an Algren signature motif. There is a memorable one in *Never Come Morning*, and his short story "The Captain Has Bad Dreams," included in the exceptional 1947 collection *The Neon Wilderness*, is essentially an earlier version of the Bednar episode in *Man with the Golden Arm*. Algren seems intuitively to have recognized the unique applicability of the police lineup to his own highly idiosyncratic art. There is a great deal of his absurdist humor in the scene. The suspects' explanations of why they have been arrested do entertain their unseen audience: "For climbin' a telephone pole at t'ree a.m. wit' a peanut machine on my back"; "For makin' anon'mous phone calls to call my wife dirty names"; "Went upstairs with a girl, 'n came down with a cop" (190). But when Bednar is suddenly "impaled" on the spear of his protective arrogance the mood shifts completely.

The lineup becomes a paradigm of Algren's controlling aesthetic in the novel and in most of his fiction. The suspects exhibited beneath the bright lights represent all the grotesque ghetto characters in *The Man with the Golden Arm:* the one-way mirror that shields them from the spectators is a metaphor for the protection normally implicit in the experience of reading fiction (while reading a novel, we see the characters, but they do not see us); the safe spectators represent Algren's implied middle-class readership; and Bednar stands for both the implied author as creator and manipulator of the scene and a hoped-for ideal reader who will also be impaled by the novel's insistence upon the humanity of society's "habituals." Algren's habituals are some of the most memorable embodiments of the ghetto fat man in American naturalistic urban fiction.

In addition to Captain Bednar, four characters step forward and claim special attention in *Golden Arm*'s gallery of grotesques. Frankie Machine is the novel's antihero, an almost legendary card dealer in Chicago's Polish-American ghetto, the claustrophobic setting Algren used here, in *Never Come Morning*, and in several of his best short stories. Frankie is also a guilt-ridden morphine addict. The most important horror that the novel explores is, in fact, not the external sordidness of the inner city but, instead, the dealer's crippling existential anguish. Through a kind of authorial afterthought, Frankie's drug addiction metonymically represents the limited determinism central to much contemporary naturalism. His habit originated in the unbearable pain of a war wound; it was in the midst of this pain that he was introduced to Private McGantic, the "thirty-five-pound monkey" he carries on his back. Frankie, then, is originally a kind of war casualty, but he is unable to shake McGantic—in large part because of his fear of confronting a pervasive internal guilt.

The novel, then, begins with Frankie and his devoted follower, Sparrow Saltskin, in jail. A locally famous dealer in Zero Schwiefka's long-running poker game, the young veteran is familiar with jail. Maxwell Geismar has pointed out that Frankie, like other Algren male characters, welcomes prison as an "iron sanctuary" that temporarily suspends his "fevered and distorted hopes" (187). In truth, the dealer has excellent reasons to seek sanctuary: in addition to his morphine habit, he is trapped in one of the most destructive marriages in American literature. It is necessary to emphasize that Frankie Machine would be a victim if he had never taken morphine. His guilt originates in an indifference to and a fear of life which permeates the core of his being. Frankie, in fact, lives a life of Sartrian bad faith.

The opening jail sequence incorporates a striking metaphor for his fear and his guilt. To kill time he observes the desperation of a cockroach struggling to escape drowning in a water bucket. After promising himself that he will rescue the roach to celebrate his release, he forgets his vow when the time finally arrives and the roach drowns:

> It was too late all right. Too late for roaches or old Skid Row rumdums; it was even getting a little late for cripples and junkies and punks too long on the same old hustle. The water-soaked corpse was only half afloat, the head submerged and the rear end pointing to the ceiling like a sinking sub when the perpetual waters pull it downward and down forever. "I could have saved him," Frankie realized with a faint remorse. "It's all my fault again."

Malcolm Cowley has correctly seen this episode as exemplifying naturalistic writers' fondness for animal and reptilian symbolism.[14] But what is most important about it is Frankie Machine's unnecessary assumption of responsibility for the roach precisely so that he can once more fail and feel guilt. That he can never be saved is foreshadowed in the faintness of his remorse.

Frankie's wife, Sophie, also emerges as a distinctive and memorable character in the novel. The union of these two is, from the first, cemented by a perverted love that must be perpetually fed by guilt. In fact, a careless reading of the novel might lead one to see Sophie as the source of the dealer's problems. Dreading someday being deserted by him, she intuitively plays on his inner guilt, and he has given her a dramatic way of doing so. In a

112

flashback scene the drunken dealer wrecks a car, injuring Sophie. This incident becomes for her "the blessed, cursed, wonderful-terrible God's own accident that had truly married them at last" (66). Physically, the accident does not seriously hurt her, but she does suffer from shock, which leaves her momentarily unable to move her legs. She then convinces herself that she is truly and permanently crippled, and Algren provides a mysteriously reappearing crutch with a cracked handle to symbolize her accelerating paranoia. In the novel's present tense she keeps a scrapbook entitled *My Scrapbook of Fatal Accidence* [*sic*], which is filled with newspaper clippings describing especially grotesque deaths. The way in which Algren handles the concept of chance in the novel's account of the car wreck and its aftermath distinguishes him from the traditional naturalist. It is not completely the result of malevolent or indifferent external forces: Frankie *was* guilty of drunken driving, and Sophie's paranoia makes it have a negative result in gross disproportion to what was necessary.

Moreover, her mental disintegration allows her a horribly correct perception of the reality of postwar urban America. Algren conveys her vision in a memorable passage of sustained ironic lyricism, a common stylistic innovation in his work:

> For the city too was somehow crippled of late. The city too seemed a little insane. Crippled and caught and done for with everyone in it. . . . Nobody was at home to anyone one else any more.
>
> No one moved easily, freely and unafraid any longer, all hurried worriedly to work and anxiously by night returned. . . .
> "God has forgotten us all," Sophie told herself quietly.
>
> The wind was blowing the flies away. God was forgetting his own. (96–99)

Sophie remembers a different kind of world when she recalls her childhood and her courtship by Frankie: "Years when everything was so well arranged. When people who did right were rewarded and those who did wrong were punished. When everyone, in the long run, got exactly what was coming to him, no more or no less. God weighed virtue and sin then to the faction of the ounce, like Majurcek the Grocer weighing sugar" (62). Her memory of this lost Eden is a highly selective one, because even then Frankie treated her with a brutal indifference. When a further "fatal" accident does finally shatter her union with the dealer, Sophie's paranoia is complete. She dreams of being crucified, while alone in her room, by a mad Christ (300–301) and is last seen in a bare, white psychotic ward remembering "the sorrowful name of Frankie Machine" (311–13). A woman who has been transformed into something almost monstrous by her suffering, Sophie seems to haunt the grotesque world of Algren's novel.

The idealized Molly Novotny contrasts sharply with Sophie. In the opening of the novel she lives in an apartment just below the one in which Frankie and Sophie conduct the ongoing warfare of their marriage and is involved with one of Algren's most Céline-like creations, the sadistic alcoholic Drunkie John. She understands that Frankie needs her to attain any kind of salvation and waits for him to realize sufficient strength to free her from a universe of Drunkie Johns. Her capacity for love is underscored early in some dialogue between Frankie and Owner Antek of the Tug and Maul saloon:

ANTEK: She got too big a heart, that girl. . . . A guy can walk into her heart with army boots on.
FRANKIE: There ain't many hearts like that no more. . . ."

(30)

Molly is, in fact, too idealized in the novel, largely because she fulfills a symbolic function. She personifies that almost dead part of Frankie Machine which longs for life and psychological health, while Sophie embodies his guilt, his fear, and his longing to surrender completely to his addiction. While struggling to find the courage to face the horrors of the "cure," Frankie comprehends that, for him in the future, "it would be Molly-O or a quarter-grain fix, he'd never make it alone" (120).

Probably the most unforgettable character in *The Man with the Golden Arm* is Sparrow Saltskin, the focus of much of the novel's absurdist humor and the chief wonder in Algren's gallery of grotesques. The Sparrow is a self-proclaimed "unincapable punk," who is constantly baffled by the unforeseen but inevitable results of his absurd plans and actions. Professionally, he is a "lost dog finder," which means a dognapper, and the principal evidence of success in his vocation is Rumdum, a ludicrous disaster of a dog—a mutt of unfathomable breed who becomes, in the Tug and Maul, a hopeless alcoholic. Sparrow brags about his "scraunching route," which is how he describes the back alleys in which he practices window peeping until he is rescued by the sexually insatiable Violet Koskozka, who lives in a state of constant frustration because of the lack of interest shown in her by

her "Old Husband" Stash. Stash is interested in tearing off the dates on the calendar, leaning out the window to check the temperature on a thermometer that hangs above the fire escape, finding bargains, and in getting a good night's sleep, but never in sex.

The Violet-Sparrow-Stash love triangle culminates in "The Great Sandwich Battle," an extended absurdist scene that ridicules the incompetence of a Chicago cop, or "ace," describes the further humiliation and arrest of Stash, and ends with Sparrow climbing into bed with a sausage string dangling from his mouth. Inevitably, the sausage string tickles Violet, and, when she protests, "Sparrow generously switched the string to the other corner [of his mouth]." Still, she decides to be satisfied, because at least this "is better than no love at all" (140). Algren has written here a love scene in which the ludicrous and sordid take the place of traditional romance. He makes the reader understand that Violet and Sparrow are simply seeking love wherever and however they can find it: a lover with a sausage string hanging out of his mouth is better than no lover at all. With one short sentence Algren affirms the humanness of his two otherwise absurd characters and challenges the reader to acknowledge a momentary identification with them.

Sparrow and Violet's lovemaking is, however, only a brief respite from the absurdity and sordidness of their existence. The Sparrow talks Frankie Machine into attempting petty theft in a department store, and, as a result, the dealer is arrested, and Sparrow is left alone on the city's streets. In desperation he is soon reduced to dispensing morphine for Blind Pig. Ultimately, he betrays Frankie Machine to the relentless Record Head Bednar. In the last half of the novel the element of comedy, with its redemptive power, is withdrawn from the characterizations of Violet and Sparrow.

The centrality of Frankie Machine, Sophie, Molly-O, and the Sparrow to Algren's narrative focus allows them to stand apart from the novel's highly idiosyncratic minor characters, some of whom are, however, unforgettable. For instance, there is the landlord, Schwabatski the Jailer, and his retarded twenty-one-year-old son, Poor Peter, who plants paper daisies in the darkened stairwell; Umbrella Man, who walks the streets with "a battered umbrella strapped to his back" (102); and Meter Reader, the devoted coach of the hopeless sandlot baseball team, "the Endless Belt and Leather Invincibles, an aggregation that hadn't won a game since Meter Reader had taken it over" (102). All these characters congregate at the New Year's Eve "coming out" party for Old Husband (because Old Husband had just come out of jail), which is assumed to be an engagement party for Violet and Sparrow.

Especially unforgettable is Blind Pig, who is Algren's tour de force in human crumminess and perversity.

The aesthetic richness and complexity of *The Man with the Golden Arm* can be illustrated through comparison to Gold's *Jews without Money*. While he does suffer from some guilt, especially in his feelings for his mother, Gold's Michael is shown to be much more the victim of poverty and social injustice than of internal anguish. He can be saved quickly and one assumes completely through his encounter with "the man on an East Side soap-box." No such chance, dramatic encounter could redeem Frankie Machine nor any of the grotesques in Algren's novel: there is no quick, simple cure for their crumminess. Gold produced an ethnic protest novel in which Marxism exists as a deus ex machina to relieve the suffering of his tenement people. In *Native Son* Richard Wright started with the ethnic protest formula but subordinated it to his portrayal of a complex, frightened, and frightening young protagonist. Algren is writing about an exploited ethnic group, Chicago's alienated Polish Americans, and he expresses great outrage at the corruption of U.S. urban politics, but he holds out virtually no hope for social reform. The ethnic protest formula has largely been abandoned in *The Man with the Golden Arm*.

Yet it must be said that Algren, more than once, described himself as belonging to a "radical tradition of American literature," in which he placed Whitman, Crane, Dreiser, and Hemingway. His concept of a native American literary radicalism recalls Sartre's call for "a committed literature," an art that, above all, speaks for the powerless and the voiceless. The writer, he felt, must choose the side of the oppressed in conscious opposition to the oppressor. As his career progressed, and certainly by the time of *The Man with the Golden Arm*, witnessing for the oppressed did not, however, imply that he must write from a reformist emphasis. In his most mature and best work he treated the inner-city lumpenproletariat with a harsh compassion that offered no hope for their ultimate reform or salvation.

Algren did find in the turn-of-the-century naturalists, in Walt Whitman, and, somewhat inexplicably, in Ernest Hemingway, a native tradition of committed literature in which to anchor his own art. But he was at least equally influenced by Kuprin, Dostoevsky, and especially Céline and, as a result, created his own unique and deeply pessimistic fiction. The inner man in his characters is not inherently good and is, in fact, often hard to see at all. For critics such as Walcutt, Algren's brand of absurdist naturalism seemed excessively harsh and foreign in its refusal to affirm an internal benevolence residing within the inner-city grotesques whom it portrayed. What should be understood, however, is that Algren's brand of naturalism represents an evolutionary stage in a literary tradition that extends back to Norris, Crane, London, and Dreiser and forward, then, to Sherwood Anderson. It is, moreover, an evolutionary stage that revitalized American urban naturalism and paved the way for what June Howard, citing the fiction of Hubert Selby specifically, calls a "latter-day naturalism."[15]

Notes

1. Leslie Fiedler, "The Noble Savages of Skid Row," *Reporter* 15 (12 July 1956): 43–44.

2. Norman Podhoretz, "The Man with the Golden Beef," *New Yorker* 32, 2 June 1956, 132, 134, 137–39.

3. There are two important recent exceptions to this general neglect. John W. Aldridge was inspired by Algren's last, and generally ignored, novel, *The Devil's Stocking*, published posthumously in 1983, to consider Algren's entire career in a new and sympathetic light (Aldridge, *Classics and Contemporaries* [Columbia: University of Missouri Press, 1992]). Also, in a pathbreaking new study, *Writing Chicago: Modernism, Ethnography, and the Novel*, Carla Cappetti discusses the influence of "the Chicago school" of sociology on James T. Farrell, Richard Wright, and Algren. Cappetti's book is a persuasive argument for a reaffirmation of the sociological dimension of literature and for a reevaluation of the leftist writers who were largely driven out of the canon in the 1950s (Cappetti, *Writing Chicago* [New York: Columbia University Press, 1993]).

4. Maxwell Geismar, "Nelson Algren: The Iron Sanctuary," *American Moderns: From Rebellion to Conformity* (New York: Hill and Wang, 1958), 191.

5. Kurt Vonnegut, "Introduction" to the Four Walls Eight Windows Press edition of Nelson Algren's *Never Come Morning* (New York, 1987), xix.

6. Charles C. Walcutt, *American Literary Naturalism: A Divided Stream* (Minneapolis: University of Minnesota Press, 1956), 299–300.

7. Alston Anderson and Terry Southern, "Nelson Algren," *Paris Review* 11 (Winter 1955): 39–40.

8. Alexandre Kuprin, *Yama, or the Pit*, trans. Bernard Guilbert Guerney (New York: Modern Library, 1932), 100–101.

9. Bettina Drew, *Nelson Algren: A Life on the Wild Side* (New York: Putnam's, 1989), 172.

10. Louis-Ferdinand Céline, *Journey to the End of the Night*, trans. Ralph Manheim (New York: New Directions, 1983), 18.

11. H. E. F. Donohue, *Conversations with Nelson Algren* (New York: Hill and Wang, 1964), 231–33.

12. Sherwood Anderson, *Winesburg, Ohio* (New York: Penguin, 1976), 121.

13. Nelson Algren, *The Man with the Golden Arm* (New York: Doubleday, 1949), 123.

14. Malcolm Cowley, *The Literary Situation* (New York: Viking, 1958), 89–90.

15. June Howard, *Form and History in American Literary Naturalism* (Chapel Hill: University of North Carolina Press, 1985), 165–66.

Chapter 5

The Game of Mum
as Theme and Narrative Technique
in Hubert Selby's *Last Exit to Brooklyn*

Early in Hubert Selby, Jr.'s *Last Exit to Brooklyn* (1964), the members of a Brooklyn street gang, who constitute a cumulative main character in the novel, play a game of "mum." The rules of the game are brutally simple: one gang member steps to the center while others circle him, punching him in the back and sides until he identifies the author of an individual blow who then replaces him in the center. The game continues in this fashion until boredom ends it. The game of mum in Selby's novel is an act of controlled, even ritualized, violence with different individuals accepting the role of victim until they have the opportunity to victimize others. It is also the central trope of the novel in two ways. *Last Exit to Brooklyn* is a sustained depiction of seemingly random violence that is, in fact, quite codified and which is, in part, a reaction to alienation and pervasive boredom, which are rooted in a self-centered purposelessness. Inner awareness of their powerlessness causes the novel's characters to assault savagely anyone who openly expresses pain and vulnerability. The expression of need for another human being, beyond instant and quickly forgotten sexual gratification, is seen as an open declaration of weakness. Such declarations of weakness must be ridiculed and punished in the novel because they make public the masked and disguised inner needs of all the characters.[1]

The game of mum serves as metaphor for the novel's narrative strategy. *Last Exit to Brooklyn* marks a radical departure in the evolution of the American naturalistic inner-city novel for a more important reason than its relentless violence, its depiction of drag queens, or its linguistic brutality. As discussed earlier, Stephen Crane and Frank Norris, in their pioneering fictional investigations of the inner city, utilized narrative techniques that grant the reader a reassuring distance from the disturbing subject matter of *Maggie: A Girl of the Streets* and *McTeague*. Crane, in *Maggie*, developed a narrative voice that reports the external violence of Rum Alley while attempting, as Alan Trachtenberg has said, "to convey physical landscapes equivalent to his perception of the subjective lives of his characters."[2] Maggie's narrator hopes to reveal the spiritual and psychological violence of the Johnson family by documenting its external manifestations. This narrative strategy is, in fact, not far from Selby's in *Last Exit*. Yet Crane's narrator signals, throughout the novel, his awareness of a distance and *a difference* from the book's characters.

Moreover, there are the moments in *Maggie* when the narrator interrupts the plot to make summary value judgments—most famously, of course, the declaration:

> The girl, Maggie, blossomed in a mud puddle. She grew to be a most rare and wonderful production of a tenement district, a pretty girl.
>
> None of the dirt of Rum Alley seemed to be in her veins. The philosophers up-stairs, down-stairs and on the same floor, puzzled over it. (16)

The philosopher narrating the novel is, in contrast, reassured by it. Crane apparently needed to believe in the possibility of Maggie's purity in order to soften the prevalent grimness of his vision of the Bowery ghetto. In order to preserve this illusion of his central character's innocence, it was necessary for Crane to adopt the unusual narrative strategy of distancing his narrator from her.

By contrast Frank Norris in *McTeague* virtually revels in shock effect. The novel contains, after all, two brutal murders, a deadly hand-to-hand struggle in Death Valley, and repeated acts of sadomasochism. William E. Cain argues that *McTeague* represents a kind of narrative rape: Norris continually assaults his characters, brutally stripping away their privacy.[3] This repeated assault upon the characters creates its own ironic narrative distance. One feels that McTeague, Trina, Marcus, Zerkow, Maria Macapa, and the others are no more than pawns in the hands of an intensely ironic stage manager. Moreover, the narrator repeatedly calls McTeague "stupid," mocks the characters' primitive taste in home furnishings and public entertainment, and intrudes upon the plot in order to deliver such pronouncements as "Trina was a strange woman during these days."[4] Indeed, she is so obviously "strange" that the narrator's overt evaluation of her condition is unnecessary. Finally, the characters in *McTeague* constantly act "without thinking," the tag often appearing to represent the narrator's opinion that they are incapable of thought. June Howard has observed that Norris's characters ultimately seem to be exotics living in some "alien territory," which the reader is exploring in company with the narrator.[5] Explorations end, of course, and the explorer goes home. Norris is, in fact, utilizing his characters as projections of the Other, the dark and recessed parts of the middle-class psyche which may be approached only when fictionalized and thus made safe.

Selby, in *Last Exit to Brooklyn*, does not allow his reader any such reassuring distance. Howard points out that, in *Last Exit*, "the narrator's voice is almost entirely merged with the characters" (165). It is important to qualify Howard's observation: an external narrator does sometimes intrude into *Last Exit*'s plot. She is, nevertheless, accurate in describing what Selby is attempting to do. In a 1981 interview he said: "I've discovered this about myself. I'm a frustrated preacher and a frustrated teacher. I fought for years to get that out of my writing. The most difficult thing for a writer to do is to get himself out of his work, but getting oneself out is absolutely necessary. The ego has no place there."[6] It is especially interesting that this comment comes in response to the interviewer's asking what it means "for a writer to have compassion for a character." Selby, in *Last Exit* and in his other novels, makes a determined effort to repress and disguise his compassion for and identification with his characters. Yet he reveals, in the same interview, a deep underlying compassion for them. He refuses to accept the interviewer's description of them as "psychotic"; instead, he argues that they are "tragic" because they "lack vision" (323). *Tragic* cannot, of course, be understood here in any classical definition of the term. Not only do Selby's characters lack stature, or high social position, they are so immersed in violence and brutality that they often seem caricatures of complex, full-dimensional human beings. They exemplify Don Graham's concept of the characters of "circumscribed consciousness" who dominate much naturalistic fiction.[7]

As two perceptive critics have shown, there is a definite moral, even allegorical, aspect of Selby's fiction. Charles D. Peavy emphasizes that "Selby's microcosm is pictured . . . as a sort of Dantean hell, and the dominant motivation in the collection making up *Last Exit* is Selby's almost obsessive concern with the existence of sin, a symptom perhaps of his deep-rooted Puritanism." Peavy concludes that, in the tradition of Swift, Selby is a moral satirist warning of the wages of the deadly sin of pride.[8] The art of satire works in part on the principles of exaggeration and distortion. A satirist exaggerates human flaws until characters are barely recognizable as human, often to the point of denying, as Swift did in *Gulliver's Travels* (1726), outward human forms. In their unrelenting rage, hatred, and self-loathing, Selby's characters often seem other than human. His art, then, is an art of calculated excess that ultimately negates a traditional mimetic mode.

Richard A. Wertime approaches *Last Exit* as psychological, rather than moral, allegory: he sees the novel's street gang as "psychic avengers" repeatedly enforcing a "primitive" "retributive justice." Wertime is most perceptive in arguing that the street gang is a projection of the internal terrors of Harry, the central character in *Last Exit's* long central section, "Strike." Inwardly, Harry is constantly judging himself and returning a verdict of guilty. His guilt, Wertime observes, originates in a complex internal dread made up of "the terror of being one of an undifferentiated mass; the primacy of conflict and competition in human relationships; the essential fear of sex, of vulnerability and openness. . . ."[9] The street gang, whose members often seem vague and undifferentiated in the novel, does indeed act as punisher of the transgressions and weaknesses of other characters. The unforgivable sin in the internal world of the novel is to appear vulnerable, and the price of the sin is thorough and immediate physical and/or psychological brutalization. To appear vulnerable is to place oneself in the circle of a deadly game of mum.

Selby agrees that the moral and psychological allegory of the novel, in conjunction with a largely absent narrative voice, produces a claustrophobic effect. In discussing his fiction, the novelist has said:

> The walls start closing in. Oh yes, it's very claustrophobic. Because every one of my characters is locked in his own particular prison. There're no open spaces. They're all very self-obsessed people, which is why they're so miserable and unhappy. (O'Brien interview, 325)

As with Bigger Thomas in Wright's *Native Son*, this claustrophobic existence in combination with ever-present reminders of material luxuries denied to them results in paranoia and sociopathic behavior by Selby's characters. As Gerd Hurm says, "Because of their enclosure and impotence, the slum dwellers are hardly able to cope with the cunning strategies in consumer capitalism, with the open and subliminal lures, omnipresent in billboards, ads, and TV commercials. Economically barred from access to commodities of middle-class society, they reject its rules" (284).

The narrative strategy of the novel is to place the reader together, repeatedly, with the vulnerable character inside the game of mum's circle so that the full immediacy of the brutal punishment can be felt. Selby does not assume the same position toward his characters that Frank Norris does toward the inhabitants of Polk Street. Selby's people are not merely projections of the hidden psychic fears of the middle-class reader, which can be revealed and then exorcised. Norris's narrator allows the reader to step back from the sordid violence of Polk Street, but it is more difficult simply to step outside an extended fictional game of mum. Eric Mottram says that "in *Last Exit*, the bourgeois reader is invited to scan dramatizations of carelessness and despair, hopelessness and violence both explosive and continual, without the escapes of summary, implication, suggestion and beliefs in impending possibilities for change."[10] This evaluation is not quite, but almost, true—the moments of narrative summary and suggestion in the novel are so few as to almost leap out at the reader.

On an important level Selby wants the middle-class reader to acknowledge an identity with his fictional creations. He has said that his work constitutes a warning against "choosing evil" and forfeiting "control." Americans in the twentieth century, he believes, have surrendered "responsibility" for the consequences of their actions. Selby seems to equate excessive "pride" with such abdication of ethical responsibility. Thus, despite the ghetto setting of *Last Exit*, he argues that his characters must not be seen as mere victims of socioeconomic oppression. They are, instead, extreme and thus clear examples of the sin of pride in twentieth-century America: "I hope that by the time I'm finished, my body of work will have created a microcosm. I think that I will give you a terrific picture of America" (O'Brien interview, 322).

The world of *Last Exit* is thus a microcosm on two levels—an externalization of the inner terrors of its most vulnerable characters and an exaggerated mirror of modern America. In fact, Selby, who in the years after writing *Last Exit* was himself to undergo a religious conversion, wants his fiction to have something of an evangelical effect. "Frustrated preacher" and "frustrated teacher," he is also a prophet warning of the consequences of the abdication of ethical responsibility in twentieth-century America.[11] The purpose of a jeremiad is precisely to prevent the audience from comfortably walking away and resuming normal activities.

Selby's characters, the brutal avengers as well as the vulnerable victims, are meant, in part, to be extreme projections of the sin of pride infecting all of America, including the middle-class reader. His fat man is deliberately grotesque. In his art of calculated and often surrealistic excess, Selby depicts his slum dwellers as violent, cruel, and even murderous. Then he demands a shock of recognition of shared humanity from his middle-class reader. Hurm offers a perceptive and concise summary of the reformist thrust in *Last Exit to Brooklyn*:

> Annihilation of [Selby's] . . . characters' feelings, minds, and bodies relates to the hollowing out of the American city, once seen by many as the core and apex of culture. Selby discloses the dire results of exploitation and segregation. Trying to reach readers outside the working-class slums, he hoped to rouse indignation and have the privileged in suburbia face reality in the inner city. (289–90)

The surrealistic effect of Selby's claustrophobic vision has caused some critics to deny that he is a naturalist. John T. O'Brien, for instance, writes: "What is incredible to me is that . . . [Selby's style] should be seen as naturalistic. That it is seen as such illustrates where we gain our sense of the naturalistic—not from nature but from art." O'Brien goes on to argue persuasively that Selby's narrative style is adopted from popular fiction and films. In fact, the narrative technique and the language of *Last Exit* reflect the influences of the Dashiell Hammett–Raymond Chandler "hard-boiled" school of detective fiction and the Warner Brothers gangster films of the 1930s and 1940s.[12] Michael Stephens goes farther than O'Brien and asserts that Selby's surrealistic fiction "brought naturalism to its long awaited end—not with a whimper but a gang bang": "Selby printed a first novel which became a best seller because of its naturalistic plot. And secretly the book was the angel of death for that form. *Last Exit* annihilated naturalism and gave poetry to fiction. A great poet chose to give us poetry in the guise of a naturalistic novel."[13] In respectively arguing that *Last Exit* is not naturalistic and is even the end of naturalism, O'Brien and Stephens are working from a shared assumption about a naturalistic style—that naturalistic fiction always exhibits the kind of documentation and detail associated with Dreiser and Norris. The doubtfulness of such an assumption should be obvious to any reader of Stephen Crane. Yet there is a more valid reason for questioning Selby's relationship to the tradition of American literary naturalism. It is, at first glance, difficult to reconcile Selby's assertions that *Last Exit* is a study of the moral consequences of abandoning control and choosing evil with the centrality of determinism in literary naturalism. One function of a jeremiad, after all, is to call attention to the necessity of moral change; it must then posit as an underlying assumption that such change is possible. In this regard Selby says:

> One of the things I find insane is that we seem to believe in this country that if we change the society, then the individual will be changed. That doesn't happen. The transformed individual makes a transformed world. All these people I write about are looking to outside forces to do something for them. Not one of them wants to know what he can do for somebody else. (Interview, 317)

This moral conviction prevents the novelist from accepting the reduction of his characters to passive victims of environmental determinism.

Still, environment is obviously important in a novel that depicts the Brooklyn proletariat and lumpenproletariat in the 1940s and 1950s. In fact, *on a strictly realistic level*, the novel focuses on two distinct environmental classes. Harry, the central figure in "Strike," as well as other minor characters in the first five sections of the novel, and especially in its "coda," entitled "Landsend," represent the exploited working classes of Brooklyn. (That they are exploited by their union officials as well as by the company for which they work is made clear in "Strike.") The street gang members engaged in random theft and other petty crime, Georgette the transvestite "anti-heroine" of "The Queen Is Dead," and the prostitute Tralala are representatives of the lumpenproletariat, the criminal and/or outlaw class existing side by side with the working class.

One of Selby's and John Rechy's central contributions to the American naturalistic novel was to broaden the concept of the lumpenproletariat to include homosexuals, a group thrust out of respectable society because of sexual orientation and thus convicted of moral heresy. A third surrealistic environment emerges in the novel in the interaction of the working-class characters and the lumpenproletariat protagonists. The most important interaction constitutes the psychic punishment meted out by the street gang, Wertime's "psychic avengers," on Harry, a married factory worker who cannot control his homosexual impulses, and on Georgette and Tralala, lumpenproletariat characters who reveal their vulnerability. Harry, Georgette, and Tralala are all punished in especially brutal variations of the game of mum. In fact, all three become vulnerable by not remaining mum, by revealing forbidden needs. In this way Harry, Georgette, and Tralala are markedly different from the hapless soldier who is savagely assaulted by the street gang in the opening section, "Another Day, Another Dollar." The "doggie's" only sin is to invade the territory of the gang. In contrast, Harry, Georgette, and Tralala transgress against codes of conduct ascribed to by one or both of the environments in which they exist (working-class society and the society of the "criminal" lumpenproletariat). In Harry's case the prescribed code of behavior is also internalized, and, as Wertime has suggested, the passages describing his punishment seem especially surrealistic. On one level the assault of the gang metaphorically represents his internal self-condemnation.

Without rejecting Selby's assertion that he is not writing about environmental victims, one can thus see that determinism is central to the novel. Hurm correctly sees Selby's determinism as existing on external as well as internal levels:

> First, there is the powerlessness against outside forces; people in the Brooklyn slum are imprisoned within an affluent society. Second, there is the loss of control over their inner lives. This "lack of power," an impotence no less profound, is internalized; characters are devoid of controlled responsibility or free will. The body, their prime barter in the exchange for money and power, is degraded by its excessive exploitation through drugs, sex, and violence. For lower-class figures, physical decline means defeat. (289)

Selby's characters are circumscribed by the economic and spiritual wastelands in which they exist and which are dominated by a code of morality which denies forgiveness, mocks gentleness and love, and punishes overt expressions of vulnerability. They do lack control, and they do choose evil, but they also exemplify John J. Conder's Hobbesian paradox. In *Naturalism in American Fiction: The Classic Phase* Conder reconciles the dual existence of determinism and free will in much naturalistic fiction through Hobbes's argument that man is free in those ways in which his actions are not naturally proscribed.[14] The characters in *Last Exit* consistently choose badly and self-destructively in part because the environment in which they exist offers them severely limited possibilities from which to choose.

Selby places biblical quotations at the beginning of each section of the novel in part to emphasize its underlying harsh Old Testament morality. Eric Mottram says of the six biblical epigrams:

> Their effect is to frame the [novel's] social criminality within texts from a book, the Old Testament, notorious as a resource for violent

law and vengeful deific authority. . . . In such a context, the violations of *Last Exit* are in danger of being absorbed into the eternal verities of reactionary Christianity: nothing changes under the sun. (358)

The Old Testament epigrams also work ironically and poetically in the way that biblical references do in T. S. Eliot's *The Waste Land*. For instance, "Strike" is introduced by these lines from Proverbs:

> I went by the field of the slothful, and by the vineyard of the man void of understanding;
> And, lo, it was all grown over with thorns, and nettles had covered the face thereof, and the stone wall thereof was broken down.
> (24:30, 31)

And "Landsend," which is set entirely within a housing project, is headed by a passage from Job:

> How much less in them that dwell in houses of clay, whose foundation is in the dust, which are crushed before the moth? They are destroyed from morning to evening: they perish for ever without any regarding it. Doth not their excellency which is in them go away? They die, even without wisdom. (4:19–21)

The novel's setting is depicted then as a spiritual wasteland devoid of love or meaning. The isolated biblical epigrams have a function that, in more conventional fiction, would be the responsibility of an internal narrative voice: they cumulatively posit a transcendent ethical code and pass a judgment of spiritual deprivation upon the novel's characters for violating it. To an even greater degree than Algren's, Selby's characters have become grotesque by surrendering to existential absurdity.

Yet the punishment received by Georgette and Harry involves a crucial irony. They are made to suffer precisely because they overtly express their yearning for love and understanding. Georgette, the transvestite, loves Vinnie, a member of the street gang who prides himself upon a past distinguished by a brief imprisonment for theft. Like most of the flamboyantly "male" characters in Selby's fiction, Vinnie hates and fears women. Jacqueline Hendin correctly points out that "most of Selby's [male] characters hate women so totally that they do not want to get close to them even to destroy them."[15] Women are the enemy for Selby's males largely because the vagina represents, to them, a taunting demand for violation *and* a frightening threat of castration. They are tormented always by an inescapable awareness of their impotence—they are the pawns of a bleak environment, of daily tedium, and of their own vocabulary. Aware always of their social, economic, and temporal insignificance, they release their rage upon women. They talk constantly about sexual intercourse in a language of calculated brutality and engage in it with the purpose of punishing their female partners for their own pervasive sense of emasculation.

Gilbert Sorrentino, defending Selby against the charge of writing pornography, emphasizes the profoundly nonerotic nature of sexual passages in his work. "Sex scenes" in Selby, Sorrentino says, are "horrifying" precisely because they are "totally devoid of love, or 'tenderness.'"[16] In fact, heterosexual intercourse, in Selby, is always a form of rape, an aggressive assault upon a tangible symbol of male impotence. Vinnie can be interested in, and even intrigued by, Georgette's flirtation without feeling a sense of rage largely because, not possessing a vagina, she does not threaten him with emasculation.

Georgette is, in many ways, the most sympathetic character in the novel. She is honest and direct about her sexual preference and appropriated sexual identity:

> Georgette was a hip queer. She (he) didnt try to disguise or conceal it with marriage and mans talk, satisfying her homosexuality with the keeping of a secret scrapbook of pictures of favorite male actors or athletes or by supervising the activities of young boys or visiting turkish baths or mens locker rooms, leering sidely while seeking protection behind a carefully guarded guise of virility . . . but, took a pride in being homosexual by feeling intellectually and esthetically superior to those (especially women) who werent gay[.][17]

She is also one of only two characters in the novel openly seeking love.

She is exceedingly foolish, though, in her determined pursuit of Vinnie. Her choice of the young hoodlum reveals that she, like the other characters in the novel, is a victim of American popular culture. The swaggering hood seems to her the essential romantic outlaw, a youthful John Garfield or Humphrey Bogart. Vinnie's criminality has been, in fact, as prosaic and purposeless as everything else about his life.

This false heroic persona is completely convincing to Georgette, and, in another editorial intrusion, Selby describes the appeal of Georgette's idolatry to Vinnie: "mistaking in his dull, never to be matured mind, her loneliness for respect of his strength and virility . . ." (31). The hoodlum is also attracted to the drag queen on a level of simple biology; lacking a vagina, she does not threaten him with fears of castration. Early in the story, he pats her buttocks and says: "Too bad I didn't haveya upstate. I had a couple of sweet kids but they didnt have chips like this" (30). To Vinnie, Georgette, like the young inmates in prison, offers the temptation of phallic penetration without psychic risk. He is, however, quick to mock effeminate-appearing males as being "queerbait." Charles D. Peavy offers an insightful summary of Vinnie and his gang:

> The sexual aberrations of Georgette and her "girl" friends (Goldie, Lee, Camille) are mirrored by Vinnie and the boys in his gang (Harry, Malfie, Sal), for if they are homosexual transvestites (queens), the latter group of men are bisexuals who, under certain conditions, may be had for the price of liquor and narcotics. Georgette's group prides itself in fake femininity, constant preening, and catty observations about the dress of rival queens. Vinnie's group, on the other hand, revels in an exaggerated maleism which is as perverted as the feminine airs assumed by the transvestites. . . . [Vinnie] is still subscribing to the rigid code of *machismo*, which allows him to be the active partner in pederasty and the passive partner in fellatio and still maintain his status as a "straight," or normal male. The pride of Vinnie's peer group allows them to enjoy homosexual relations without any danger to their male ego, for they always cover up any pleasure they might derive from such acts in the ridicule, hostility, and cruelty they direct toward the overt homosexuals.[18]

In one brief symbolic moment Selby signals that the gang leader embodies the death of "the hip queer's" dreams of love and romance: "Vinnie was 12 the first time he was arrested. He had stolen a hearse" (28).

The story's first game of mum occurs in the street outside the Greeks, the gang's favorite hangout, when another gang member, Harry, pulls a knife from his pocket, first threatens Georgette with castration (sadistically offering to remove the part of her body she both hates and denies) and then flips the knife at her, yelling "think fast." Instinctively, then, the gang enacts a parody of "a grade B western," encircling Georgette and making her dance to avoid the knife, which they take turns throwing at her. Finally, the blade strikes and sticks in the calf of her leg, the only penetration she is to experience in the novel. Afterward Vinnie, her beloved, goes into the Greeks and gets a bottle of iodine, which he empties onto her wound "and laughed, with the others, when Georgette screamed . . ." (32–34).

Brutal as it is, the knife wound is the lesser of two assaults by Vinnie and his companions on the drag queen. The second symbolic game of mum occurs when Georgette and her transvestite friends entertain the gang. The party, an orgy of alcohol and drugs, moves back and forth between two apartments. Imagery of birth and death runs throughout the scene. A pregnant sister (ironically named Mary) of one of the queens intrudes on the party until, about to give birth, she has to be rushed away to a hospital in a cab. Mary's condition occasions mocking from Vinnie and his friends ("Shes going to have a baby—O is she? I thought perhaps it was gas. They roared with laughter" [63]) but produces disgust and anxiety in Georgette and her friends ("O shes bringing me down" [64]). Georgette is jarringly reminded by the woman's pregnancy of the anatomical barriers against her dreamed-of romance with Vinnie. Still, sex is not the true basis of her fantasy: she longs for "a strange romance where love was born of affection, not sex . . ." (53).

Such a concept of romance is totally foreign to the world of *Last Exit to Brooklyn*, in which affection is equated with weakness and vulnerability and thus must be destroyed. Once again Georgette is victimized by her naive faith in popular culture—she associates Vinnie with the sensitive-criminal figures of Hollywood films. She realizes, however, that, even for the most sensitive of petty criminals, sex must be the prelude to romance. Images of love-as-death underscore the scene when Georgette begins to recite Poe's "Raven" to Vinnie while a recording of Charlie "Bird" Parker plays in the background. Briefly, it seems that the young man might succumb to her indirect appeal of romance: "[Vinnie thinks:] Hes a good lookin guy and real great, especially for a queen . . . being honestly moved by Georgettes reading, but even with the bennie stimulating his imagination it was impossible for him to get beyond the weirdness and the kick" (67).

The "weirdness" exists on several levels for Vinnie—the slightly unnerving strangeness of his attraction to a male homosexual; the unreality created by the combination of Poe, Parker, and drugs; and the foreignness of a personal appeal based on affection. Quickly, he retreats from weirdness by helping Harry drag Lee, the most beautiful of the queens, to the bedroom. Once there Vinnie and Harry take turns having anal sex with Lee. Typically, the two young men verbally humiliate the attractive transvestite before having sex with her: "You wanna look like a broad ya gonna get fucked like one" (74). Lee is, in fact, something of a physical ideal for Vinnie and the other hoods: looking like a woman, she becomes an object to be humiliated and possessed; lacking a vagina, she represents no threat of castration. Her fantasy lover's betrayal signals to Georgette, through a drug-induced haze, that her dream is about to be shattered, and, when Vinnie returns, he induces her to perform fellatio on him. Throughout the act and afterward she is tormented by the thought of excrement on his penis—she has tasted the death of her fantasy of "a strange romance where love was born of affection." As in the knife-throwing scene, her open expression of love has made her vulnerable to humiliation; she finds herself once again in the center of a brutal game of mum.

In contrast, Tralala, for most of her story, enforces brutality. Now a rapacious prostitute, she learned early that the world valorized her body. She can, she knows, trade it for money, things, and, most of all, tributes to her power. Inwardly hating herself for being reduced to a commodity, she seeks revenge on those who pay to have sex with her. Her story is perfectly encased by expressions of her entrapment in sheer physicality, beginning with the quick assertion that "Tralala was 15 the first time she was laid" (95) and ending with a one-sentence, several-page-long description of her destruction in a gang rape, which she instigates. For a while she is content with her existence as a commodity: "But she got what she wanted. All she had to do was putout. It was kicks too. Sometimes. If not, so what? It made no difference. Lay on your back. Or bend over a garbage can. Better than working" (96). During the war she especially enjoys stealing from the servicemen who engage her. Being invaders of the neighborhood, and thus the only world she knows, they represent appropriate targets for assault. Her destruction begins when an officer takes her out of her physical environment and offers her not the comforting familiarity of money-for-sex but, rather, the upsetting strangeness of love.

In fact, Tralala's brief affair with the officer constitutes a disorienting spatial, class, and behavioral displacement. She moves temporarily out of the colony of Brooklyn into the controlling culture of downtown Manhattan; she is involved with a representative of the dominant male power structure, and she is thrust abruptly into a world in which sex is not automatically equated with cash. The officer's offer of love is, to her, a foreign communication, and she immediately attempts to reaffirm the only values she understands by frequenting a Times Square bar, where she repeatedly picks up servicemen. When she is told to leave the Times Square bar, she begins a descent through the bars of the city, moving ever downward to the depths of the city and of prostitution. Selby depicts her degradation in a surrealistic manner, which reads like an infinitely more frank and brutal version of Crane's impressionistic account of Maggie's descent into the pit of prostitution:

Time passed—months, maybe years, who knows, and the dress was gone and just a beatup skirt and sweater and the Broadway bars were 8th avenue bars, but soon even these joints with their hustlers, pushers, pimps, queens and wouldbe thugs kicked her out and the inlaid linoleum turned to wood and then was covered with sawdust and she hung over a beer in a dump on the waterfront, snarling and cursing every sonofabitch who fucked herup and left with anyone who looked at her or had a place to flop. (110)

Having been thoroughly debased by her encounter with the full horror of prostitution, she begs finally for a sign of society's continuing valorization of her body by displaying her breasts in Willies, her old, familiar Brooklyn bar: "Tralala pulled her sweater up and bounced her tits on the palms of her hands and grinned and grinned and grinned and Jack and Fred whooped and roared . . . and Tralala slowly turned around bouncing them hard on her hands exhibiting her pride to the bar" (113). This time, though, her flaunting of "her pride" results in a horrific gang rape, which leaves her a broken, discarded thing in an alley. Tralala indeed pays an Old Testament price for her sin of pride. Narrative voice in this section of the novel remains consistently detached, providing few, if any, interpretative comments about Tralala's sordid life and brutal destruction, leaving the reader to experience it with shocking immediacy.

"Strike," the novel's longest section, centers on a character, Harry Black, who is tormented by very real fears of impotence and insignificance. Harry is "the worst lathe operator of the more than 1,000 men working in [a Brooklyn] factory" (128). Aware of his insignificance as a worker, he regularly abuses his position as a union shop steward by attempting to win petty, meaningless victories over management which will pacify his desperate needs for recognition and power. Harry is unmistakably an assembly line man—a faceless cog in a process that results in a product in which he can feel no pride or even meaningful involvement. The detached narrator of "Strike" makes it clear that Harry's sense of insignificance is legitimate: to management he and the other workers are as faceless and interchangeable as the pieces of steel they cut. His humanity denied at work, Harry is tormented by feelings that his manhood has been violated and that it can only be reasserted in little skirmishes with management.

When a strike is called, the steward's importance is briefly and ironically affirmed. While he is given the job of managing strike headquarters and is exhilarated by the illusion of being on the front lines in a climactic war with company management, Selby's detached narrator makes it clear that, for the company, the strike is simply an inconvenience, which it has anticipated and for which it has planned. Still, Harry does attain, during the strike, a limited and ironic importance of which he is never aware. During negotiations the management representatives attempt to make firing him a condition of settlement. Since they are only trying to rid themselves of a nuisance, they ultimately retreat from this position. Thus, the only power Harry ever attains is completely anonymous: he is an unidentified clause in the early stages of management-labor negotiations. His temporary importance, in fact, primarily affirms the superior power of management, which can afford to extend the strike while seeking to swat an annoying fly.

As is usually the case for Selby's male characters, Harry's sense of social and economic insignificance is inextricably linked to unacknowledged fears concerning his sexual identity. Married and the father of an infant son, he hates his wife's body, perceiving her vagina as a smothering, castrating organ. It is hardly surprising that Harry regularly brags about imaginary seductions of women and that he does so in assaultive language. He constantly feels the need to affirm his masculinity to others and, most of all, to himself. Heterosexual intercourse, for Harry, can only be assault; women as personifications of his castration fear must be violated and punished. Moreover, for Harry, as for most of Selby's male characters, language itself has become a trap: he talks so obsessively about intercourse as rape that he can think of it in no other way. Yet it is hardly surprising that the other male characters, and particularly Vinnie and the gang, sense Harry's desperation and laugh at his claims of sexual prowess.

In fact, Harry is suffering a considerable amount of confusion resulting from a growing attraction to, and fascination with, homosexuals, especially gay transvestites. Like other Selby males, he verbally ridicules "fairies" and thus intensifies his inner guilt. His verbal assaults on gays, of course, only add another layer to the trap of language in which he is caught.

Increasingly, however, he is unable to deny his attraction to the homosexual world and begins to frequent gay bars. As he drifts into the homosexual underground, he undergoes a sense of displacement parallel to that experienced by Tralala in Manhattan. Like hers, Harry's journey in not merely spatial; it has class and behavioral overtones as well. (The principal gay bar he patronizes is named Marys, another of Selby's ironic allusions to the Madonna.) In search of a love that would at last bring him peace, he finds himself exploring a world defined by a sexual preference condemned in his Brooklyn working-class environment.

For a while, with a drag queen named Regina, he believes that he has realized his dream of love, but, as Georgette had learned earlier in the novel, Selby's world does not sanction sustaining, healing emotions. In a reversal of Tralala's experience with the army officer, Regina dismisses Harry once the strike is settled and he no longer controls the union's strike fund. Harry then reaches out once more for a relationship with someone "small, soft, and weak" and attempts to have oral sex with a young boy, but Vinnie and the gang intervene and savagely beat Harry, leaving him momentarily impaled by a splinter and hanging to a fence.

The gang's brutal assault of Harry is the climactic game of mum in the novel. In making his homosexual needs overt and in his desperate attempt to seduce the boy, Harry has stepped into the center and become vulnerable to punishment. He is, in fact, in the center throughout the "Strike" section, even when, as during the company officials' attempt to fire him during strike negotiations, he is unaware of it. Harry's profound sense of impotence mandates eventual brutal retribution. Wertime is correct in arguing that the gang's attack on Harry is, on one level, self-inflicted retributive justice carried out by the "psychic avengers" within the shop steward's own consciousness. It is also the novel's most powerful example of the environment's instant and primitive punishment of those who make their vulnerability overt. After their beating of Harry, the gang is momentarily jubilant: "The guys washed up in the Greeks, drying their hands with toilet paper and tossing the wet wads at each other, laughing. . . . The first good rumble since they dumped that doggy" (231). Yet the reader knows that they will soon sink back into the tedium that characterizes their existence between rumbles.

Harry's position impaled on the fence obviously recalls the Crucifixion and constitutes only one of the ironic Christ parallels in the novel. The narrator emphasizes that Harry is thirty-three, but the steward clearly fails as a caretaker of anyone, including himself. Lying broken on the ground, he attempts to yell "GOD YOU SUCK COCK," but the words cannot escape, and "the moon neither noticed nor ignored Harry as he lay at the foot of the billboard, but continued on its unalterable journey" (230–31). In Selby's fiction, as in Crane's, the universe is coldly indifferent to human beings. As Charles D. Peavy points out, there is considerable ambiguity in the words Harry tries unsuccessfully to pronounce:

Harry has always defied authority figures, such as the various company bosses, and it is characteristic that he defy God himself when, in
his pain and humiliation, he hurls his blasphemous and obscene in-
vective toward heaven. Behind this obloquy, however, is not only
Harry's arrogance and pride, but also the necessity for him to believe
that God, too, is a homosexual. Blinded by his own blood, his arms
ripped from their sockets, Harry attempts to raise his battered head
in a gesture of proud defiance.[19]

To a degree the words constitute a cosmic curse, an indictment of God
conceived in the language and values of the novel's environment. They thus
constitute the final evidence of Harry's linguistic and cultural entrapment
and represent a final self-condemnation. It is worth noting that Selby has
said that, for a time after nearly dying of complications arising from tuber-
culosis early in his life, "[he] had a terrible, intense hatred for God" (O'Brien
interview, 333).

The novel's coda, entitled "Landsend," functions as an absurdist foot-
note to the rest of the novel. Set in a housing project, it depicts the sometimes pathetic, more often ridiculous, pretensions of those who live there.
Vinnie, who may or may not be the same Vinnie of the Georgette episode,
is married to a young women inevitably named Mary, and the couple fight
constantly, culminating in a battle inspired by Vinnie's insistence that their
son's hair be cut. Vinnie is demanding that any outward manifestation of
androgyny in his child be aborted. Yet he usually tries to avoid having sexual
intercourse with Mary, and the couple never talk to each other; they only
scream back and forth. Their dialogue is conveyed by Selby solely in capital
letters. "Landsend," then, depicts the incomplete domestication of Vinnie:
he can never attain a meaningful level of maturity. Throughout the novel
Selby blurs his characters' identities so that it is often impossible to separate individual characters from encompassing character types. Georgette,
Tralala, and Harry Black do stand out as distinct individuals. In the shop
steward's case, however, even this demarcation is blurred; the arrogant and
abusive gang member named Harry in the Georgette section is obviously
not Harry Black. In his 1986 short-story collection *Song of the Silent Snow
and Other Stories* Selby uses the name Harry for various incarnations of the
dispossessed urban Everyman.

Selby's deliberate shadowing of the boundaries of identity conveys his
point that the novel's environment is destructive of any complete and sus-

taining sense of identity. In the world of *Last Exit to Brooklyn*, fragile, constantly threatened identities can only be protected if encased in inhuman limitations: to venture outside this protective shell is to enter the center of a game of mum. The reader, abruptly immersed in this world largely without the comforting presence of an identifiable external narrative voice, is placed within this same center of retribution.

In *Last Exit to Brooklyn* Selby takes the concept of socially transgressive fiction to an extreme: the text is meant to assault the middle-class reader's faith in the existence of a safe, civilized reality. Selby's narrative strategy represents, then, a significant departure from Crane and Norris. He merges his narrator's voice with character and setting to evoke an often surrealistic vision of the fat man—the marginalized slum dweller as grotesque and even murderous product of economic oppression, twisted sexuality, and the sin of pride.

It is also worth mentioning that *Last Exit to Brooklyn* falls within Michel Foucault's idea of fiction that attains meaning because it gives voice, through the evocation of violence, to the repressed madness of modern society. In *Madness and Civilization* Foucault writes that

> For Sade as for Goya, unreason continues to watch by night; but in this vigil it joins with fresh powers. The non-being it once was now becomes the power to annihilate. Through Sade and Goya, the Western world received the possibility of transcending its reason in violence, and of recovering tragic experience beyond the promises of dialectic. After Sade and Goya, and since them, unreason has belonged to whatever is decisive, for the modern world, in any work of art: that is, whatever any work of art contains that is both murderous and constraining.[20]

Few novels utilize violence to give voice to unreason more eloquently than *Last Exit to Brooklyn*.

Notes

1. Gerd Hurm identifies the specific economic and historical time of *Last Exit to Brooklyn:*

> The novel is divided into two major sections: the first five stories, loosely arranged around a bar, the "Greeks," are set in the late 194os, while "Landsend," the "Coda" of the novel, takes place in a low-income housing project in the

Red Hook area near the Gowanus Canal in the late 1950s. The two periods signify a transition in the architectural environment of the poor: the Greeks' part describes the conditions of the older street-corner slum of unsanitary tenements; "Landsend" records the results of liberal urban planning and welfare programs in public housing. (Hurm, *Fragmented Urban Images: The American City in Modern Fiction from Stephen Crane to Thomas Pynchon* [New York: Peter Lang, 1991], 288–81).

2. "Stephen Crane's City Sketches," in *American Realism: New Essays*, ed. Eric J. Sundquist (Baltimore: Johns Hopkins University Press, 1982), 144.

3. William E. Cain, "Presence and Power in *McTeague*," in Sundquist, *American Realism*.

4. Frank Norris, *McTeague* (New York: New American Library: Signet Classics Edition, 1981), 239.

5. June Howard, *Form and History in American Literary Naturalism* (Chapel Hill: University of North Carolina Press, 1985), 88.

6. John T. O'Brien, "Interview with Hubert Selby, Jr.," *Review of Contemporary Fiction* 10 (Spring 1981): 318.

7. Don Graham, "Naturalism in American Fiction: A Status Report," *Studies in American Fiction* 10 (Spring 1982): 10.

8. Charles D. Peavy, "Hubert Selby and the Tradition of Moral Satire," *Satire Newsletter* 6 (Spring 1969): 35–39.

9. Richard A. Wertime, "Psychic Vengeance in *Last Exit to Brooklyn*," *Literature and Psychology* 24 (1974): 153–66.

10. Eric Mottram, "Free like the Rest of Us: Violation and Despair in Hubert Selby's Novels," *Review of Contemporary Fiction* 1 (Spring 1981): 354.

11. Paul Metcalf in an article comparing Selby to Herman Melville concludes: "I suppose Selby must be thought of as a Christian novelist. The Wages of Sin, etc." ("Herman and Hubert: The Odd Couple," *Review of Contemporary Fiction* 1 [Spring 1981]: 369).

12. John T. O'Brien, "The Materials of Art in Hubert Selby," *Review of Contemporary Fiction* 1 (Spring 1981): 378.

13. Michael Stephens, "Hubert Selby, Jr.: The Poet of Prose Masters," *Review of Contemporary Fiction* 1 (Spring 1981): 392.

14. John J. Conder, *Naturalism in American Fiction: The Classic Phase* (Lexington: University Press of Kentucky, 1984).

15. Josephine Hendin, *Vulnerable People: A View of American Fiction since 1945* (Oxford: Oxford University Press, 1978), 60.

16. Gilbert Sorrentino, "The Art of Hubert Selby," *Review of Contemporary Fiction* 1 (Spring 1981): 343.

17. Hubert Selby, Jr., *Last Exit to Brooklyn* (New York: Grove Press, 1965), 25.

18. Charles D. Peavy, "The Sin of Pride and Selby's *Last Exit to Brooklyn*," *Critique* 2 (1969): 38.

19. Peavy, "Sin of Pride," 42.

20. Michel Foucault, *Madness and Civilization: A History of Insanity in the Age of Reason*, trans. Richard Howard (New York: Vintage, 1988), 285.

Chapter 6

"Hey, World"
John Rechy's *City of Night*

In the climactic and nightmarish New Orleans section of John Rechy's *City of Night* (1963) a grotesquely dressed drag queen named Chi-Chi is surrounded by a group of tourists who taunt her, while one man demands that she pose for a picture. Chi-Chi is "enormous," "over six feet tall," and always armed with "a foot-long fraily thin silver-beaded cigarette holder."[1] Not surprisingly, the crowd of spectators, who are fascinated by New Orleans during Mardi Gras *and* by the underground gay culture in the United States, treat her as a freak. The would-be photographer and his wife are especially insulting until Chi-Chi in rage and desperation lunges at him "like a grotesque jack-in-the-box," smashing him in the face and knocking him to the ground. Afterward Chi-Chi asks someone to retrieve her cigarette holder, which fell to the ground during the drag queen's assault on the tourist, so that she can resume her customary pose of guarded dignity. She first exhales cigarette smoke at the now shocked crowd and then completes her moment of defiance:

> Gazing savage-eyed at the hectic crowds, she defied the world in a loud, clear voice:
> "*Hey, world!*" she shouted.
> And she punctured the dark air sharply with the beaded cigarette holder. (334)

In this emblematic scene the novel's narrative voice merges with the characterization of Chi-Chi. In *City of Night* Rechy depicts a subculture that personifies the sexual fear of much of heterosexual middle-class America: he creates a graphic image of this culture's suppressed awareness of its own androgny. He then demands recognition of the fundamental humanness of those who inhabit this hated subculture. The grotesque dimension of Rechy's fat man is, then, essentially a reflection of the prejudice and internal fear of middle-class heterosexual America. Like Hubert Selby's *Last Exit to Brooklyn*, *City of Night* can be said to utilize an assaultive narrative technique:

both novels are intended to shock "respectable" readers into awareness that the worlds they describe do, in fact, exist. Rechy's novel appeared in the early 1960s, a period when the United States had not publicly acknowledged the gay subculture that existed primarily within its urban centers. Rechy's personal experience had, moreover, taught him that straight America, which controlled the national political structure and the national media, wished to keep the existence of that subculture submerged in the darkest recesses of the cities of the night. He intended his novel to be, in part, a fist in the face of American heterosexual complacency and self-righteousness. The tourist with the camera whom Chi-Chi attacks becomes a metaphor for the heterosexual, middle-class reader who would deny the humanity and, as long as possible, the very existence of drag queens and homosexual hustlers. Rechy hoped *City of Night* would be such a full and honest picture of the world inhabited by such people that it would forever invalidate any misleading verbal "snapshots" taken by condescending tourists exploring the gay subculture of urban America. Chi-Chi's act of smashing the mocking tourist to the ground is then a metaphor for the novel's narrative strategy.

In retrospect it is not surprising that the initial reception of *City of Night* was entirely different from what Rechy anticipated. He recalls, in a 1990 essay, the critical and popular reactions to the appearance of his first novel: "I had thought *City of Night* would sell modestly and be critically acclaimed. Instead, it became a top best-seller and received vitriolic reviews, with notable exceptions."[2] Rechy then speculates that the negative critical reaction to his novel resulted from resistance to its subject matter (homosexual male hustling, furtive sexual encounters, life in the "nightcities") and hostility toward its publisher, Grove Press. Grove, which would publish Selby's *Last Exit to Brooklyn* in the following year and which had already become the publishing home of William S. Burroughs, was committed to bringing America's underground subcultures to the surface of the nation's consciousness. This commitment was inevitably threatening to the conservative guardians of American literature. Moreover, the determination of Rechy, Selby, and Burroughs to expand the concept of the oppressed lumpenproletariat beyond strictly economic considerations to include homosexuals made the nation's intellectual Left uncomfortable as well. To support his argument that the critical attack on *City of Night* represented, in large part, the critical establishment's opposition to the publishing program of Grove Press, Rechy recalls three 1963 reviews of the novel:

140

And so I believe that many of the attacks on *City of Night* were also attacks on what Grove had come to represent. How else to account for the shrieking review by Alfred Chester in the lofty *New York Review of Books*—and the equally malicious one by Richard Gilman in the *New Republic?* Chester screeched that *City of Night* was "the worst confection yet devised by the masterminds behind the Grove . . . machine." And here's Gilman: ". . . the line I would love to pursue is a theory of how Grove Press, dismayed by the failure of the age to produce enough ugly, outrageous, know-nothing yet *vital* and *talented* writers on its own, has finally been compelled to fashion one in the office." . . . On the other hand, Edmund Wilson was marvelously honest, declaring that I had talent—but that my subject was "too sordid" for him. (139)

In the decade of the 1960s Grove Press won its battle to expand the limits of permissible subject matter for American literature—to a degree, anyway. The works of Rechy, Selby, and Burroughs came to be regarded as "underground classics," fiction of high quality about subjects at least slightly outside the mainstream of American culture. Ironically, the initial popular success of *City of Night* may well have been an unintended result of the attacks by the novel's initial reviewers; it is at least possible that some readers sought out the novel for its rumored shock value. If such a supposition is true, Rechy's assaultive narrative strategy succeeded in a way that he did not anticipate.

As one might anticipate, the few academic critics who have written about *City of Night* in the years since its controversial reception have discovered much more important levels to the novel than the shock value of its surface. Thus far, Ben Satterfield has offered the most incisive reading of not only *City of Night* but also of Rechy's work through his fifth novel, *The Fourth Angel* (1972). Satterfield perceives that Rechy is a "moralist" out to shock American society into an awareness, and a repudiation, of the destructive insensitivity and intolerance that dominates it:

But Rechy is a moralist, not merely a countercultural revolutionary, and his use of "sensational" material is not for the easy purpose of sensation, as those critics who belabor the superficial suggest. Underneath all the ugliness and perversion of his novels is a childlike innocence and remarkable sensitivity. . . . Rechy is outraged at the world,

141

and I contend that he writes "outrageous" books in an effort to jolt society in the groin of its hypocrisy. Like the guileless child in "The Emperor's New Clothes," he sees the truth, but he does not state it quietly; he screams, "Look! See!"[3]

Satterfield further understands the complex nature of Rechy's outrage. In part, it is rage at society for denying the humanity of the homosexual outcast, while, on a deeper level, it is an essentially existential anger at the absurdity of man's entrapment in the material. In the words of Satterfield:

> What makes Rechy's characters different from the "outsider" figure popular in American literature is that Rechy's people are alienated from themselves and nature as well as society; and what makes Rechy's world crueler than, for instance, Dreiser's is its unrelenting hostility. Rechy evokes not just the indifference of society to pain and suffering, but the outright malignancy of the world at large, a world in which death is final, religion is false, and love is seldom found. (78)

Like Nelson Algren and Hubert Selby, Rechy combines the tradition of literary naturalism and the philosophy of existentialism to create a profoundly pessimistic art. The phrase "no substitute for salvation" appears in all of his novels, and he has said that it is the key to the philosophical assumptions underlying his work: "That's one of the major themes of my writing—the search for a substitute for salvation. There isn't one, and that's the existential nightmare."[4]

The gay characters in his fiction are both societal and existential victims. Rejected by the dominant culture, they are also threatened, like everyone, by the absurd nothingness of death. A key early scene in *City of Night* describes the death of the narrator's dog, Winnie, when he is at "that timeless time of [his] boyhood, ages six through eight" (9). The dog is dying during a relentless West Texas dust storm, and the narrator tries desperately to keep her alive by giving her water and watching over her: *"If I keep looking at her, she cant possibly die!"* (10). But, even as he thinks this, a tumbleweed rolls over the dog, and the narrator confronts the fact that he may not be able to save her. He then turns to his Catholic mother for assurance that Winnie's soul, at least, will be saved. But on this occasion his mother is uncharacteristically insensitive: "Dogs dont go to Heaven, they havent got souls. . . . Shes dead, thats all . . . the body disappears, becomes dirt" (11). Afterward the narrator must confront the fact that the dog has indeed died

142

and, with the help of his brother, buries her. After the burial he prays that God will save Winnie, will admit her to heaven. But the grave proves to be too shallow to withstand the relentless wind, and the boy begins to smell her decaying body. He reburies the dog and never again exists in the "time-less time" of innocence: "I had seen the decaying face of death. My mother was right. Soon Winnie will blend into the dirt. There was no soul, the body would rot, and there would be Nothing left of Winnie" (11–12).

Rechy has discussed the autobiographical nature of this scene and its symbolic significance for the rest of his novel:

> This is the narrator's first contact with the existential horror. As long as you can cling to the concept of the soul, there's a meaning to this shit, but when you exclude the soul—when you see the body rotting after death—all there is is death; not only death, but decay—physical decay, like my dog. Symbolically, the boy's innocence is buried when the dog is re-buried, decaying, soulless. (Giles and Giles, "Interview," 27)

After Winnie's death the narrator is, like the rest of the novel's characters, inescapably trapped in time and materiality. For Rechy the "existential hor-ror" is that ultimately nothing except the nothingness of decay and dirt awaits anyone. Thus, Satterfield is correct in his observation that, for Rechy's creations, the "world at large" is "malignant." Since the final absurdity of death and decay exists everywhere, the novelist can hardly posit a pastoral ideal as a realistic counterpoint to the sordid reality of America's cumulative city of night. In his second novel, *Numbers* (1967), Rechy, using his West Texas background, gives an ironic twist to the American myth of a free and open frontier. The central character in *Numbers* is a homosexual hustler from Texas named Johnny Rio, who adopts a mock persona of an old west-ern gunfighter to help him hustle "scores" in Los Angeles.

The pain and alienation of Rechy's gay characters is intensified by the social rejection that they have all experienced either directly or indirectly. Not only are they, like everyone, threatened with ultimate death and decay, but their very right to participate freely and openly in society has been denied. On one level *City of Night* is a work of social protest in the natural-istic tradition of Crane's *Maggie*, Sinclair's *Jungle*, and Steinbeck's *Grapes of Wrath:* Rechy is asserting, with the force of all his anger, that homosexuals should not have to suffer from the contempt of society in addition to the horror of existential Nothingness. Satterfield perceives that the only "substitute for salvation" Rechy can propose as affording at least temporary relief from suffering is love. Yet his characters desire a kind of love that mainstream society has branded as "sinful" and "perverted." Rechy has said that "there's no more alienated figure than the homosexual": "It's the only minority against whose existence there are laws" (Giles and Giles, "Interview," 21). It would be difficult to imagine a determinism more total than that found in Rechy's fiction: his characters face not only existential oblivion but also the fact that they are trapped in a sexual preference that the dominant culture has labeled perverted and ruled illegal. In order to fulfill one of their most fundamental human needs, they are forced underground. Rechy's brand of naturalism combines the environmental determinism common to literary naturalism since Zola with a unique vision of biological entrapment.

As Satterfield points out, in Rechy's work a fundamental and cutting irony underlies the outlaw status of the gay world: in its lovelessness and selfishness the gay subculture depicted in *City of Night* simply mirrors the dominant culture. Throughout the novel characters, including the narrator, retreat from love, which constitutes the only salvation possible in the city of night. Instead of love, they seek impersonal and anonymous sex because, to them, it represents, in Satterfield's words, "a life stimulant" (81–82). An implied theme of Rechy's novel is that the determined retreat from love in the gay world echoes the ugly impersonality and cruelty of mainstream America. The tourist with the camera who mocks Chi-Chi sees in the grotesquely dressed drag queen an image of his own repressed feelings and needs. Chi-Chi is to him and to his wife a frightening image of the Other, and their fear forces them to assault such a terrifying vision of their hidden and denied selves. The rigid conformity and ugly repression that characterized life in the United States in the 1950s were, to Rechy, the inevitable results of a pervasive fear and self-loathing. The "normal" heterosexual, middle-class American male could only feel hatred for anyone with such a fundamentally different lifestyle because such an individual personified his own desperately repressed androgyny.

The most painful and ironic aspect of *City of Night* is the degree to which the novel's characters, the objects of fear and hatred, reflect those same negative values in their determined quest for impersonal and unfeeling sexuality. The novel details both an external and an internal journey. On one level the narrator is taking the implied straight, middle-class reader on a tour of America's urban gay community, and the lasting impression of this world which emerges from the journey is of its fundamental loneliness and alienation: it is as if the inhabitants of the homosexual underground desire only contact of the most superficial kind. The more important journey in the novel is the narrator's internal exploration. By the end he has confronted the full extent of his own deep fear of commitment to another human being and of his capacity for selfish denial of others. The novel's "plot" is essentially a parallel elaboration of these two journeys, or quests. Rechy has said that his novel "began literally as a letter I wrote to a friend" (Giles and Giles, "Interview," 19) and has described it as "a confession" ("one of the last scenes is of the narrator trying to find a confessor, which I tried to do in New Orleans—and I encountered all those bummer priests that weren't about to be awakened" [Giles and Giles, "Interview," 22]). What the narrator finally confesses to a young man named Jeremy is his own fear of lasting emotional involvement with anyone and his capacity for a cruel self-centeredness that mirrors both the dominant heterosexual culture and the gay subculture. It has taken the entire novel for him to come to this epiphany.

In order to depict the intertwined external and internal explorations that constitute his novel, Rechy uses a narrative structure derived from two naturalistic predecessors. *City of Night* alternates chapters focusing on the narrator's journey of self-discovery beginning with a terrifying childhood in El Paso, Texas, and culminating in his experiences as a homosexual hustler in New York City, Chicago, Los Angeles, San Francisco, and New Orleans with chapters depicting his involvement with other characters. With one notable exception each of the second group of chapters possesses sufficient artistic unity to stand alone as an independent short story. This structure recalls both John Dos Passos's *U.S.A.*, with its "subjective" and clearly autobiographical "camera eye" segments interspersed throughout an "objective" plot, and Steinbeck's *Grapes of Wrath*, with its alternating chapters of authorial commentary and those describing the odyssey of the Joads. Rechy's unnamed narrator represents a unique variation on what June Howard has labeled the "spectator" narrative consciousness, which she sees as a recurrent device in American literary naturalism.[5] The unnamed young man repeatedly becomes a sexual partner with other characters, but, until his shattering encounter with a man in San Francisco, keeps his essential self distant from, and untouched by, those with whom he is involved. For most of the novel he sincerely believes that he feels and sometimes even expresses a profound compassion for those whose pain he closely observes, but, after San Francisco, he realizes that his kind of compassion has been so distant as to be virtually meaningless. He has indeed been a spectator of the suffering of others.

Recurrent references to windows, mirrors, and photograph albums constitute a metonymic reference to the novel's thematic emphasis on observation. As a child, the narrator is fascinated by the world outside him and spends hours watching it from behind the window of the house where he lives:

> I liked to sit inside the house and look out the hall-window—beyond the cactus garden in the vacant lot next door. I would sit by that window looking at the people that passed. I felt miraculously separated from the world outside: separated by the pane, the screen, through which, nevertheless—uninvolved—I could see that world.
> I read many books, I saw many, many movies.
> I watched other lives, only through a window. (17–18)

Clearly, the spectator mentality is deeply ingrained in the narrator from as early as he can remember. The emotional turmoil within his house has caused him to look outward for release. His embittered father feels and expresses hatred for everyone and everything and regularly touches the young narrator in a sexual way. In contrast, the boy's mother offers him generous and unqualified love, but a love so intense that it smothers him emotionally. Without rationally comprehending it, the boy feels his very self evaporating as a result of the contrasting emotional advances of his parents. He feels separated, cut off from the world outside his home, and, consequently, observes it with a sense of accelerating desperation.

But it is only when the young boy turns away from windows and becomes fascinated by mirrors that one realizes the totality of the psychological damage he has suffered. The adult narrator vividly remembers this defining moment in his adolescence:

> Yet I was beginning to feel, too, a remoteness toward people—more and more a craving for attention which I could not reciprocate: one-sided, as if the need in me was so hungry that it couldnt share or give back in kind. . . .
> And it was somewhere about that time that the narcissistic pattern of my life began.
> From my father's inexplicable hatred of me and my mother's blind carnivorous love, I fled to the Mirror. I would stand before it, thinking: I have only Me! . . . I became obsessed with age. At 17, I dreaded growing old. Old age is something that must never happen to me.

The image of myself in the mirror must never fade into someone I cant look at. (18)

The narrator never escapes from this mirror stage of development. In fact, what he essentially discovers in his internal exploration is the full extent of his self-absorption. He is never able to reciprocate or share attention and certainly not love, and he ultimately comes to realize that all other people are to him merely mirrors. He seeks in them reflections of his own attractiveness and nothing more.

For him physical attractiveness becomes the supreme virtue because it is the coin by which he earns tribute from others and because it is the visible sign of his youth. He is terrified of age because he believes that it will represent the end of his attractiveness to others and because it will bring him closer to death and Nothingness. The narrator believes that his ultimate fate will be no different than Winnie's. He cannot believe in an eternal human soul any more than he can, after the dog's death and decay, believe that animals have souls. For him the body is all, and the only meaningful sign of its continuing vitality is its external beauty. Moreover, sex is the way in which others signal their recognition and appreciation of that external attractiveness. Thus, he obsessively seeks sexual contacts and preferably with strangers. The willingness of a stranger to pay him for sex is, he feels, the most pure and uncomplicated recognition of his physical attractiveness. The very anonymity of such sexual contacts affirms that his attractiveness is still intact, not yet marred by the inevitable ravages of age. It is essential that he respond to these anonymous sexual advances with a cold and aloof detachment: there must be no confusion; the sexual act must be understood by the partner to be nothing more or less than a tribute to, and an affirmation of, the beauty of the narrator's body. The money exchanged is important to the narrator only as a tangible symbol of the stranger's recognition of his physical attractiveness. The full extent of the psychological damage that the unnamed young man suffered in his childhood is evident in the insatiable nature of his narcissism: there can never be enough recognition from others of his youth and beauty. Thus, his hustling takes on a desperate obsessiveness. In *Numbers* Johnny Rio, who seems an extension of *City of Night*'s narrator, journeys from Laredo, Texas, to Los Angeles simply to see how many anonymous sexual contacts he can crowd into a brief period of time.

The accelerating terror felt by the young narrator in *City of Night* results from his beginning to see more reflected in the "mirrors" to which he reduces other people than mere validation of his own physical attractiveness. Rechy gives the mirror trope a second level of signification. In his commitment to a code of cold detachment the narrator himself mirrors the novel's dominant vision of the urban gay subculture. This world, as depicted by Rechy, values, above all else, instant physical gratification and self-absorption. In it youthful hustlers are depersonalized as nameless "youngmen," and it is understood that, above all, they must show no signs of intelligence or unusual sensitivity. Rechy truly does envision the gay subculture as a cumulative city of night, a world of dark anonymity.

Before he is ready to make his final confession to Jeremy, the narrator must journey across the country and look into the darkest recesses of his self. After leaving Texas, he travels first to New York. Ben Satterfield points out that

> Rechy is not meticulous in his descriptions of real cities. . . . he refers to New York City as "a Cage," and a mere thirteen pages later this "Cage" becomes an "islandcity" which is "like an electric, magnetic animal"—and fifty pages later it's a "jungle." Making a consistent image out of the tropes is impossible, but it is easy to perceive the feeling, which is unmistakably negative. (81)

This analysis is not inaccurate, but it is somewhat oversimplified. For Rechy urban America, especially at night, is, on the surface, dynamic and exciting, and of no city is this more true than New York. Here is his description of Broadway and 42d Street:

> And the world of that street bursts like a rocket into a shattered phosphorescent world. Giant signs—Bigger! Than! Life!—blink off and on. And a great hungry sign groping luridly at the darkness screams: F * A * S * C * I * N * A * T * I * O * N[.] (30)

The city at night may be "lurid," but it is also intensely "fascinating," "bigger than life." Beneath the brilliant lights and within the darkness Rechy's narrator will discover a world of cold despair and death. Thus, the most common images of urban America in *City of Night* have associations of death and entrapment.

The narrator soon discovers that, at its core, New York City is an island cage of isolated souls. In the tradition of Stephen Crane, Rechy utilizes a mode of lyrical narration, rather than the detailed documentation favored by Dreiser, Norris, and other naturalists, to communicate his mixed and emotional reaction to urban America.

In New York the narrator is initially introduced to the urban gay subculture and quickly learns the acceptable behavior for a hustler:

> I learned that there are a variety of roles to play if you're hustling: youngmanoutofajob butlooking; dontgiveadamnyoungman drifting; perrenialhustler easytomakeout; youngmanlostinthebigcity pleasehelpmesir. There was, too, the pose learned quickly from the others along the street: the stance, the jivetalk—a mixture of jazz, joint, junk sounds—the almost-disdainful, disinterested, but, at the same time, inviting look; the casual way of dress.
> And I learned too that to hustle the streets you had to play it almost-illiterate. (32)

But it is when he meets a man named Ed King that his education about the gay world *and* his process of self-discovery really begin. King, "a grayhaired middle-aged man," issues a deliberately cold and unfeeling invitation to the narrator as he stands waiting outside a movie theater on 42nd Street: "I'll give you ten, and I dont give a damn for you" (23). King's invitation succinctly expresses the accepted code for relationships between scores and hustlers in the gay subculture: they should remain strictly cash transactions void of any emotional or even personal overtones.

Ironically, it is King who begins to violate the code of anonymity, initially by advising the narrator to go home before he is swallowed by the street. The Ed King characterization also has an important structural function in the novel; Rechy uses his advice to the narrator to foreshadow the rest of the novel:

> Go on back Home and marry your girlfriend . . . and raise lots of snottynosed little bastards, and I'll tell you what: Keepem away from New York—all those fuckin cities—are you from L.A.? No? Keepem away from there too . . . I was there once, L.A.—too many creeps for me, though: like a nuthouse. . . . That Pershing Square!—it's a loony asylum! . . . 42nd Street, thats the lowest though. All those lights, sure you think theyre Pretty—Im tellinya, listena-me, they aint: It's bullshit—got the same fuckin lights in New Orleans—are you really from the South? New Orleans maybe—no, you wouldnt be so nervous if you were—12 years old there and youd know Everything: hell,

I know a 12-year-old boy there, hustles. But all this shit aint worth knowing, like I say. It was Chicago for me. . . . (25–26)

Los Angeles—and, specifically, Pershing Square—New Orleans, and Chicago will all be important stops for the narrator in his journey to self-enlightenment. King's emphasis upon the degradation and sophistication of New Orleans will be painfully confirmed for the narrator. It is significant that King does not mention San Francisco, the city in which the narrator comes to realize the full extent of his own capacity for selfish cruelty. In this early section of the novel the narrator could not anticipate that his education would involve such a shattering epiphany.

King's most serious violation of the hustler-score code occurs when he grudgingly acknowledges some genuine feeling for the narrator while proposing that they meet again, this time between the statues of the two lions in front of the New York Public Library:

I—uh—kinda—like you. . . . But dont get no ideas . . . theres dozens just like you—all of you even get to look alike—pictures in a fuckedup album. What the hell, I dont give a damn for you or all the others like you. . . . If youre there to meet me, okay. If not, theres someone else around the corner—just as good, maybe better. . . . But be there, punk—between the two lions. (28)

The narrator has been a better student than King anticipated, however, and even this highly qualified expression of affection causes him to flee from any further contact with the older man.

King's reference to pictures in an album introduces the novel's third metaphor for a limited, spectator relationship between people and foreshadows the narrator's other significant experience in New York. A bedridden Professor pays the young man for sex but, more important, to listen to his endless monologues about the nature of God and his past experiences with attractive young hustlers, whom he calls "angels." The Professor's comments about God exemplify the existential consciousness that informs Rechy's novel—for example, "Ah, life—that vast plain of—what? . . . Like a cold card dealer, God deals out our destinies" (61).

The references to a "vast plain" of nothing and to God as an unfeeling force that determines human destiny impersonally and arbitrarily echo both T. S. Eliot's vision of the twentieth century as a spiritual wasteland and the secular existential vision of the absurdity that controls human life. The Professor's solution for dealing with this universal spiritual alienation is, on an abstract level, the same as Rechy's: "Love, dear child, which is, indeed, God!" (60). But, like the narrator and most of the other characters in the novel, the Professor dooms his quest for love by the way he searches for it. As his obsessive monologues indicate, he is always at the center of his own consciousness.

Yet, his self-centeredness does not prevent the monologues from often expressing valid and important ideas; indeed, one often feels that the Professor is speaking for Rechy:

> "The only immorality is 'morality'—which has restricted us, shoved into the dark the most beautiful things that should glow in the light. . . . Yet this unreasoning world ignores the true obscenities of our time: poverty, repression, the blindness to beauty and sensitivity—*vide*, the sneaky machinations of our own storm troopers—the vice squad!" (70)

> "Alas! the Ice Age of the heart has not left us. Here and there, a flicker of compassion arises courageously to thaw out the icy blanket—but it is just that: a valiant flicker, soon snuffed out by the very ice it sought to melt! . . . "(73)

Despite such insights, his search for love is always superficial. He keeps a photograph album full of snapshots of the young men, the angels whom he has paid for sex. The photographs are the Professor's mirror, into which he peers for signs of his attractiveness. He can pretend to forget that the young men only went with him for the money.

Inwardly, he knows that such a pretense cannot last and, in one of his early monologues, foresees both the inevitability of his death and his real cause: "people—die—when they see life— at last—without —Illusions—" (70). This unbearable epiphany comes abruptly to him during his last meeting with the narrator. Once again the Professor is showing his beloved album to the young man when he suddenly is unable to deny the truth about his beloved angels any longer: "The angels! The voracious angels! . . . The ones who drained me—who never know *Me!*—never respected Me. Love? Bought! . . ." (79). He is correct in his assessment that his angels never cared for, or respected, him. What he dies without confronting is the fact that, except as snapshots in his album, he never cared for them either. A powerful irony underlying the Professor's story is the contempt and suspicion with which he treats his male nurse, Larry, who truly does care for him: "Larry is not an angel. . . . I distrust him sometimes. Do you suppose . . . that Larry is a misplaced agent for the FBI—in the *wrong* cell?" (72). For the Professor, as for most of the inhabitants of the city of night, expressions of genuine affection for someone else constitute evidence of an unforgivable weakness.

Rechy will continue the trope of the angels throughout the novel. His angels are usually young men whose physical attractiveness only serves to transform them into sexual objects, to bind them even more strongly to this world and, thus, to mortality. The Professor describes them as Satan's children, created specifically as an act of rebellion against, and defiance of, God, and the world in which they exist is certainly a fallen one in which spiritual redemption is not to be found. The novel's ironic religious symbolism reaches its climax in the New Orleans section, in which, again in a manner reminiscent of T. S. Eliot, it is combined with allusions to other forms of spiritualism and the supernatural to depict, in a poetic way, a bleak and godless world. In one important scene a female Gypsy fortune-teller followed by an "urchin-boy" accosts the narrator to warn him against remaining in New Orleans without the kind of supernatural protection she can provide him: "New Orleans is Evil, boy. . . . I got Powers. They can protect you." The urchin-boy then acts as a kind of chorus, echoing the Gypsy's woman's warning: "Evil city, boy." One, of course, remembers Eliot's famous description of London as the "Unreal city." Despite the narrator's efforts to escape from her, the Gypsy woman does complete her prophecy, "almost as if it were a curse aimed directly at [the narrator]:

"Mardi Gras aint just any old carnival. Them others got it all wrong. Im gonna tell you The Real Truth: People wear masks three hundred and sixty-four days a year. Mardi Gras, they wear their own faces! What you think is masks is really—. . . *Themselves!*" . . . "Witches!" . . . "Devils! Cannibals! Vampires! Clowns—lots of em. . . . And some— . . . just some, mind you: some— . . . *angels!* . . . " (289–91)

The few angels, those people genuinely seeking a redemptive love, in the "evil city" of contemporary urban America are inevitably devoured by those transformed into grotesques by their cruel selfishness. The New Orleans section of Rechy's novel is richly evocative, echoing not only Eliot but also, in its emphasis upon masks and evil, the Poe of "The Cask of Amontillado" and "The Masque of the Red Death." The narrator is unable to escape hearing the Gypsy woman's prophecy because it is in New Orleans that he fully confronts his capacity for selfish cruelty, which has transformed him into a grotesque fundamentally no different than the other lost and lonely people trapped in the darkness of the urban subculture.

For the New Orleans section of the novel to be meaningful, it had to be preceded by the crucial and defining California chapters. After his experience with the Professor, the narrator flees New York City, in part, one suspects, to escape the realization that he too has been reduced to a snapshot in a dead man's album of angels. He first returns briefly to El Paso and then journeys to California. Ultimately, California will bring him an almost unbearable glimpse into his own tortured soul, and, as with New York City, Rechy's impressionistic description of California is dominated by images of death and entrapment; for instance, he introduces the Los Angeles section of the novel with this passage:

> Southern California, which is shaped somewhat like a coffin, is a giant sanatorium with flowers where people come to be cured of life itself in whatever way. . . . This is the last stop before the sun gives up and sinks into the black, black ocean, and night—usually starless here—comes down.
>
> *You can rot here without feeling it.* (87)

Yet the first Los Angeles chapter, "Miss Destiny: The Fabulous Wedding," offers the only comic relief in the entire novel. Miss Destiny is a deliberately outrageous drag queen who dreams of someday having a "fabulous" Hollywood wedding: "*Me!* . . . Me . . . in virgin-white . . . coming down a winding staircase . . . carrying a white bouquet! . . . and my family will be crying for joy. . . . And there will be champagne! cake! a real priest to puhfawm the Ceremony!—" (98). Miss Destiny, like many of the novel's other characters, has clearly been brainwashed by American popular culture: her dream of the fabulous wedding comes straight out of *Gone with the Wind* and the American romance novel. Scarlett O'Hara is a special heroine to most of the novel's drag queens. Miss Destiny's desire to be seen as a virgin is especially comic since she, like the narrator and the others to whom she regularly recites her dream, haunts Pershing Square constantly looking for scores. Rechy concludes her story with a delightful comic twist: she disappears, and a rumor begins to circulate through Pershing Square that her psychiatrist has cured her, has in fact turned her into a "*stud,*" and, as a result, she is getting married "*to a real woman*" (119).

153

Even in this comic chapter there are echoes of the novel's quite serious themes. At one point Miss Destiny tells of the terrifying vision she sometimes has while on drugs:

Sometimes when Im very high . . . I imagine that an angel suddenly appears and stands on the balcony where the band is going—or maybe Im on Main Street or in Pershing Square—and the angel says, "All right, boys and girls, this is it, the world is ending, and Heaven or Hell will be to spend eternity just as you are now, in the same place among the same people—*Forever!*" (115)

Miss Destiny's angel, in contrast to those captured in the Professor's album, is a messenger of destruction. Yet Miss Destiny and the Professor's angels are all equally doomed. The drag queen's vision clearly recalls Sartre's *No Exit* (1944), in which people are sentenced to a hell of tedium and loss of privacy because of the selfish choices they have made and the bad faith they have shown during their lifetimes.

Miss Destiny does not calmly accept her inevitable doom and likes to fantasize about confronting the "joker" god who has sentenced human beings to the final absurdity of death. In describing her fantasy, she first points to all the people surrounding her and says: "*Trapped!*" and describes the way in which she would confront such a cynical and unfeeling god: "But one day, in the most lavish drag youve evuh seen—heels! and gown! and beads! and spangled earrings—Im going to storm heaven and protest! *Here I am !!!!!* I'll yell—and I'll shake my beads at Him. . . . And God will cringe!" Miss Destiny's fantasy is essentially an extreme and outrageous version of the existential protest against death and Nothingness. It is interesting that the germ of *City of Night* was a short story entitled "The Fabulous Wedding of Miss Destiny" and that "Storm Heaven and Protest" was an early title of the novel (Rechy, "On Being," 137–38). Clearly, while the concept of his novel grew darker as Rechy wrote it, existential rebellion against absurdity was a central theme in it from the first.

After the story of Miss Destiny, the Los Angeles chapters of the novel become progressively darker in tone and mood. One of the novel's most memorable, and most painful, chapters is entitled "SOMEONE: People Dont Have Wings"; it recounts the narrator's brief involvement with a young man from Santa Monica who is married and has a son but who finds himself irresistibly drawn to homosexuality. At the end of the chapter he tries to convince the narrator, but more important himself, that he will never surrender to his ever intensifying obsession and thereby destroy his marriage and lose his wife and child. But, as both men inwardly recognize, this desperate denial will prove to be false. His inevitable capitulation to the gay subculture has, in fact, been foreshadowed by an early brief, evocative scene. Along with the narrator the man from Santa Monica watches a bird fly down from the sky and almost crash into the ocean. When, at the last moment, the bird spreads "its wings gloriously and [escapes] into the blue of the welcoming sky," he poignantly says: "It's sad—isn't it?—that people dont have wings too." At that precise moment he becomes aware of a young boy quite near him tossing a beach ball with his father and suggests to the narrator that they leave the beach (229).

The poignancy of "Someone's" crisis, of course, does not rest upon any moral condemnation of homosexuality by Rechy. It results from his being torn between conflicting sexual urges and his awareness that the conventional side of his life must inevitably be destroyed. He cares about his wife and his child but knows that he will have to surrender them to his homosexual needs. Someone is ultimately a victim of the kind of biological determinism central to literary naturalism (he cannot resist the urges of his body) as well as of existential entrapment of the soul in the body (people, in fact, do not have wings and cannot, at the last moment, soar free of the ocean of materiality). His pain affects the narrator, who now leaves Los Angeles for San Francisco, where he will discover not a sanctuary but, instead, the final shattering awareness of his own repressed urges.

In San Francisco he meets the novel's most troubling and pathetic character. Neil is an older man who is obsessed with sadomasochism. He even has eerily lifelike mannequins made which he enjoys placing in various sadomasochistic poses, and he collects costumes associated with dominance and submission to dress them in. Much more ominously, he preaches about the necessary creation of a new order based on pain:

> There are the weak and there are the strong. Pain is the natural inclination: The inflicting of pain—. . . I have to show The Way of Strength—so that the Movement will continue. Masochists—sadists . . . theyll bring new converts to create that Glorious Army . . . of which *I* will be: The Leader! Then—and only then—can I assume my Natural Role! (259–60)

Initially, the narrator allows himself—for a price, of course—to be used by Neil in his grotesque charades of dominance and submission. He permits Neil to dress him in his costumes and pose him in attitudes of dominance.

The narrator increasingly begins to feel uneasy about these activities and senses something truly dangerous in his involvement with Neil: "I was becoming aware of perhaps the most elaborate of seductions—or, rather, I would become aware of it in retrospect: a seduction through ego and vanity, of the very soul" (264). Without realizing it, Neil offers him the most irresistible of temptations: "But I can transform you—if you Let Yourself Go! . . . Let me!—and I'll open the door—Wide!—for you. Youll exist in My Eyes! I'll be a mirror!" (264–65). The older man seems to be offering the narrator what he has sought since childhood—another human being willing to exist only to reflect his physical beauty. Yet the offer is ultimately an illusion. Neil would select the costumes for the narrator to wear and thus would control and define the younger man's attractiveness.

Yet the narrator succumbs to the temptation and soon finds himself in an even more deadly one, one that truly represents the death of the soul. Abruptly, one late afternoon, Neil demands that the charade become real and begs the narrator to inflict actual physical pain on him. When the narrator succumbs to this grotesque appeal and grinds his foot, enclosed in a heavy boot, into the older man's groin, he realizes instantly that he has most of all damaged his own spirituality:

> it was *I* who was being seduced by *him*—seduced into violence: that using the sensed narcissism in me . . . he had played with all my hungry needs . . . had twisted them in order to use them for his purposes, by unfettering the submerged cravings, carried to that inevitable extreme—and disassociating myself from all feelings of pity and compassion . . . that at this moment I could prove irrevocably to the hatefully initiating world that I could join its rot, its cruelty—[.] (267)

In his later works, *The Sexual Outlaw: A Documentary* (1977) and the novel *Rushes* (1979), Rechy makes it clear that his objections to sadomasochism are not based on any conventional morality but, rather, on the opinion that such activity mirrors the dominant society's treatment of the gay subculture. Even in a charade the dominant person is expressing contempt for and asserting the right to inflict pain, whether it is pretended or not, on the submissive partner. Having been brought face to face with his own capacity for cruelty and having realized that in its self-centered denial of others his narcissism had always been a form of cruelty, the narrator leaves San Francisco and California in despair. Neil thus reflects not only the middle-class heterosexual image of the grotesque and sordid gay subculture but the narrator's deepest fears about his inner self as well.

He goes first to Chicago, where he finally comes to an awareness that gives him at least momentary relief from the pain of his experience with Neil: "It's possible to hate the filthy world and still love it with an abstract pitying love" (280). For the rest of the novel he will struggle toward the realization of a comparable, painfully limited form of self-love. Yet it is at this point that he decides to go to New Orleans, a city devoted to cruel charades and deceitful masks.

Unable to bear the awareness of all the pain surrounding him, the narrator, at the peak of Mardi Gras, plunges into an orgy of anonymous homosexual contacts during which he sees Someone from Santa Monica deliberately debasing himself. Afterward, when he wakes up from the extended orgy, he finds himself in bed with Jeremy between white sheets. Through ruthlessly probing questions, Jeremy directs his long delayed "confession." At last the narrator repudiates his hatred for his father but still clings to his image of self-sufficiency:

> Suddenly I heard myself saying: "If I ever felt that I had begun to need anyone, I would—. . ." I stopped.
> "Run away," he finished.
> I stood up, walked to the window. (351)

He then acknowledges that the most he can feel for anyone is an abstract compassion: "Faces of strangers return like ghosts out of the graveyard of my mind. I had a sudden feeling of having played a game of charades." After this admission his heart began "to listen—to something. For something" (354). What he ultimately hears from his heart is truly painful: "I have merely breezed through other lives (like an emotionally uninvolved tourist!). . . . *My God but Im lonely!*" (361–62). Now he knows that, in his need to have others offer constant tribute to his physical attractiveness, he has exploited them, just as have the heterosexual tourists who come to explore the gay subculture.

Yet, having gone this far in his confession, he still rejects the one thing that might be a legitimate "substitute for salvation":

> the world is flaunting before me what could, if tested and found false, be its most deadly myth . . . love . . . implying hope of a miracle in

a world so sadly devoid of miracles. Surrender to a myth constantly belied (a myth which could lull you again falsely in order to seduce you—like that belief in God—into a trap—away from the only thing which made sense—rebellion—no matter how futilely rendered by the fact of decay, of death. (366)

Rejecting the "myth" of love, the narrator leaves Jeremy and returns to the streets. This act constitutes a last and defining failure of faith. Back on the streets he addresses the reader directly ("like you I tried to find a substitute for Salvation" [372]), thus making the novel's previously implied theme that the gay subculture is a mirror of the dominant heterosexual culture overt.

In the still ongoing chaos of Mardi Gras he is suddenly assaulted by a figure dressed as Satan:

Suddenly the devil leapt toward me!
   In red, with long black horns! He opens his arms to embrace me in His batwinged cape! And I lunge toward Him anxious to be claimed, and He encloses the flapping wings about me. . . .
   Freed of his embrace, I look at the ghostly steeples of the Cathedral. *I'll climb to that nonexistent Heaven!* . . . (373)

Having momentarily rejected the devil, the narrator makes a last attempt to find salvation and begins desperately calling priests. But none will see him ("we're closed now"), though one does acknowledge a comprehension of his pain and desperation (*"I know," he said. "Yes, I know"* [378–79]).

After this failed attempt to "climb to that nonexistent heaven," he returns to El Paso, and the novel has come full circle. He hopes that the city of his childhood will be a sanctuary but soon realizes that he cannot escape the wind, which years ago uncovered Winnie's grave ("You always know it's there. Waiting" [379]). All that is left for him is that "abstract pitying love" for "the filthy world" and for himself which he first realized in Chicago. *City of Night* gives a voice to two previously suppressed fat men: the urban gay subculture, which a complacent mainstream America had long denied, and the terror and the void at the center of the narrator's soul. Like Algren and Selby, Rechy creates a deliberately disturbing art designed to shock safe, middle-class readers into awareness that the truly grotesque people are those who repudiate love and compassion and that most Americans fall into this category.

Notes

1. John Rechy, *City of Night* (New York: Grove Press, 1963), 325.
2. John Rechy, "On Being a 'Grove Press Author,'" *Review of Contemporary Fiction* 10 (Fall 1990): 138.
3. Ben Satterfield, "John Rechy's Tormented World," *Southwest Review* 67 (Winter 1982): 79.
4. James R. and Wanda H. Giles, "An Interview with John Rechy," *Chicago Review* 25 (1973): 20.
5. June Howard, *Form and History in American Literary Naturalism* (Chapel Hill: University of North Carolina Press, 1985).

Chapter 7

"Miss Oates" and
the Naturalistic Imagination
Joyce Carol Oates's *them*

Approximately three-fourths of the way through her 1969 novel, *them*, Joyce Carol Oates interrupts the work's detached third-person narration in order to quote from some letters supposedly written by the fictional character Maureen Wendall to her former college English teacher, "Miss Oates." In the letters the now twenty-six-year-old Maureen coldly outlines her plan to escape the ghetto life that she and her family have always known. She will make her belated escape by marrying an already married university instructor: "I am going to fall in love. Tomorrow night I'll see the man I have picked out to love. He is already married; he has three children. I want him. I want him to marry me. I am going to make this happen and begin my life."[1] For the reader who has known Maureen Wendall for over three hundred pages, the calculated deliberateness of this plan is more than a little surprising. During the first twenty-five years of her life Maureen has been, like other of Oates's female characters, passive almost to the point of seeming to lack a real identity. She has been overwhelmed by external forces—poverty, the violence and degradation of life in the ghetto, and the constant invasions of her essential self by her family. In fact, before she reappears in the novel to write her letters to Miss Oates, the reader has last seen Maureen being savagely beaten by Pat Furlong, her stepfather. As a result of this beating, she exists for thirteen months in an almost lifeless state.

Her letters to her former teacher represent, then, her determination to reject the passivity that has characterized her previous life and to create an identity with which she can truly and for the first time *live*. In this way she anticipates Elena Howe, the central figure in Oates's 1973 novel *Do with Me What You Will*. Elena also finally repudiates a life of almost zombielike passivity and acts in a way that will, for the first time, give her a valid inner being. That the self-creations of both Maureen and Elena are dramatized in their conscious pursuits of relatively weak and undistinguished men has caused Oates some problems with feminist critics. Yet it seems clear that Maureen has chosen to escape the limitations of the ghetto and of her earlier life through one of the very few avenues society has left open for her—a distinctly middle-class marriage.[2] Her isolation is, in fact, emphasized in her writing such self-revealing letters to Miss Oates, her instructor in a night class two years earlier. She, in fact, assumes that Miss Oates will not remember her: "Years ago I was a student of yours, you don't remember me. I am writing this letter knowing you won't remember me" (308). Since Miss Oates "failed her" in the class, there is every reason to assume that she won't remember Maureen. Yet Maureen has no one else with whom she can share her plan for re-creating her life. In fact, the very distance of Miss Oates from her life is a central reason that Maureen writes to her. The night-class instructor, who is also a successful writer, lives a life that, to Maureen, from such a great distance, appears to be distinguished by the very safety and order for which she so desperately yearns. Maureen's repeated assertion that Miss Oates failed her takes on a second level of meaning: the secure and prominent instructor failed to "hear" the desperation of the lonely and vulnerable student. Thus, the real novelist Joyce Carol Oates uses the character Miss Oates in part as a device to advance plot and refine characterization.

Yet this most obvious function of the "Maureen Wendall" correspondence is not the most important role it plays in *them*. By interjecting these letters ostensibly written by a fictional character to a persona so obviously based on her real self into an otherwise naturalistic novel, Oates adds a metafictional dimension to her work. In the author's note that introduces the novel Oates makes it seem that the letters were, in fact, real:

> And so the novel *them*, which is truly about a specific "them" and not just a literary technique pointing to us all, is based mainly upon Maureen's numerous recollections. . . . For Maureen, this "confession" had the effect of a kind of psychological therapy, of probably temporary benefit; for me, as a witness, so much material had the effect of temporarily blocking out my own reality, my personal life, and substituting for it the various nightmare adventures of the Wendalls. Their lives pressed upon mine eerily, so that I began to dream about them instead of about myself, dreaming and redreaming their lives. (6–7)

At first glance the author's note seems to imply that a real student of Oates (who, in fact, did teach English at the University of Detroit during the 1960s) wrote letters to her which were much more extensive than the material quoted in the novel and which outlined the grim and sordid lives of the student and her family as well. By enclosing the supposedly real student's name in quotation marks in the author's note, Oates further implies that she has changed the young woman's name in order to protect her privacy as well as the privacy of her family. Moreover, the novelist provides us with one significant piece of information about the fate of Maureen Wendall subsequent to the events portrayed in *them:* "Maureen is now a housewife in Dearborn, Michigan" (7). This fresh detail is meant to signal to the reader that Maureen's plan to escape the ghetto has succeeded and that details about her life prior to the escape could only damage her newly acquired middle-class status.

But, as several critics have pointed out, the sophisticated prose and the depth of philosophical insight in the Maureen Wendall letters make it extremely difficult to accept them as the creations of a real student, especially one who failed the course. Joanne V. Creighton, in fact, writes that Oates, in an interview, confirmed that "the [author's] note and the letters are totally fictitious, merely the trappings of a pseudonaturalistic report; and that one should not confuse the narrator with the author."[3] One, of course, should rarely, if ever, be guilty of this particular kind of confusion, but Oates draws enough parallels between her public self and Miss Oates to make it an especially easy trap to fall into. Not surprisingly, Oates critics have engaged in a lively debate about the significance of the Maureen Wendall letters.

Joanne Creighton sees them primarily as a coded warning to the reader that *them* is a "parody of naturalism" rather than a conventional naturalistic novel. A few critics relate them to what they see as a central, if relatively hidden, concern in the novel with the relationship between fiction and "reality." Eileen T. Bender argues that the novel's characters are perpetually involved in a process of self-creation, in which they seek models of form and order in various kinds of literature and art. Their desire to create themselves anew, she believes, originates in their felt desperation, an inevitable product of the violence and chaos of their lives. Maureen's letters to her former teacher, Bender asserts, defiantly announce her decision to surrender to a distinctly inferior popular "art": "[Maureen] takes control of her own real future by plotting a pulp fiction escape: to fall in love, win security, assume a new identity, and gain even a measure of sly revenge on Oates in particular and academics in general by seducing her current English teacher, Jim Randolph. She plans to rewrite her life as a banal college novel."[4] Bender subsequently refers to Maureen as having "stepped into another equally restrictive, formulaic drama *not* of her own making—a 'Harlequin' romance" (45).

It is true that Maureen has chosen the kind of happy ending commonly endorsed in popular romances—a secure middle-class marriage.

The most perceptive interpretation of the art-reality theme in *them* comes from Robert H. Fossum. Fossum argues that the recurring need of most Oates characters is for order and that her fiction is often concerned with the historic and accidental events that subvert the possibility for an orderly existence, thus her fascination with the Great Depression and with a violence that usually explodes out of frustration at the absence of order and control. The Maureen Wendall letters, he believes, represent a challenge, which is instantly answered, to a traditional academic belief in the inherent form and order of literature:

> The similarity between Maureen and Oates, which they both sense, lies in their comparative perception of chaos. Oates's easy assertion that literature provides it is obviously wrong, as Maureen recognizes; all literature can do is discover the figure in the carpet. And if the carpet has no figure, literature can only mirror the chaos or provide a form not inherent in its raw materials. Maureen's compositions do the former. Oates's novel mirrors the chaos, discovers the emotional patterns to her characters' lives, and creates a work of art having its own formal pattern.[5]

There is, indeed, a complex rage in Maureen Wendall's letters. In part the failed student's rage is directed at what she considers the lies about artistic form which she had heard from Miss Oates: "You said, 'Literature gives form to life,' I remember you saying that very clearly. What is form? Why is it better than the way life happens, by itself? I hate all that, so many lies, so many words in all those books. What I like to read in this library is newspapers. I want to know. . . . But I remember you saying that about form. *Form*. I don't know what that word means" (318). Before the savage assault by Furlong which left her in a coma for thirteen months, Maureen had believed that literature possessed an inherent form and that its presence made literature superior to "life," or reality:

> All around me [in the library in which she writes her letters] there are shelves with books on them and none of those books are worth anything, not the books by Jane Austen I used to love or the book about Madame Bovary you liked so much. Those things didn't happen and won't happen. None of them ever happened. In my life some-

thing happened and I have to keep thinking about it, over and over. (313)

On a literal level Maureen is, of course, right: none of Austen's characters or Madame Bovary ever really existed. It was, in fact, precisely their unreality to which Maureen was drawn.

It is significant that she responded to Jane Austen, while Miss Oates preferred Flaubert. Prior to the savage beating that reduced her for thirteen months to a state of virtual catatonia, Maureen had valued literature most of all for its unreality. Her response to Austen had been a highly superficial one, in which she attempted to withdraw from the sordid world of the ghetto by submerging herself in the British novelist's subtle depictions of the code of manners in aristocratic British society. In comparison, Flaubert's pessimistic realism had seemed too threatening. Maureen had been able to maintain her illusion of the existence in art and literature of a world safe from brutal reality even while engaging in prostitution. During the actual act of intercourse she had been able to abstract her essential self from the men who paid to penetrate her body, and afterward she had hidden the money in an anthology of poetry entitled *Poets of the New World*. But Pat Furlong had violently penetrated her ideal world and had, thus, shown her that any lasting escape from reality is a pure fiction.

It is significant that, after this assault, Maureen prefers newspapers to literature: she believes that, if reality cannot be escaped, it can and must be known and, as far as it is possible, controlled. After a last challenge to Miss Oates, the spokeswoman for the artificial "form" and "order" of literature, she is prepared to leave the sanctuary of the library in order to take control of Jim Randolph by seducing him.[6] One critic sees Maureen's rejection of the comforting illusions of art and literature as a triumph:

> Maureen only begins to exercise some power over her fate, as morally questionable and precarious as that power is, when she refuses to persist in fictionalizing her life. . . . By respecting and rooting herself in her own experiences, she shows that she has learned the most important lesson art has to teach. If, at the end of the book, Maureen's life is not as firmly grounded as she would like to think it is, nor her calculated stealing of another woman's husband in her pursuit of the suburban dream as elevated either in motive or goal as we would like, she is at least not being swept along by the tide of events.[7]

164

Actually, as the novel's last scene indicates, Maureen is not "grounded" very firmly at all even after she succeeds in "taking" Jim Randolph. Her continuing vulnerability is not surprising given the depth and complexity of the rage that she expressed to Miss Oates. Her anger is not directed solely at her former instructor for "lying" to her about artistic form. She is, of course, justly furious at Pat Furlong for assaulting her and at all the men whom she sees as controlling, to the degree that anyone can, the ugly world in which she lives. Her anger extends to the men whom she allowed to violate her body for money (she understands that money is the most visible symbol of power in U.S. society); it extends to all men except her brother Jules. In the United States, she understands, men have created a brutal and oppressive society that denies to women the possibility of real self-fulfillment. Moreover, in the urban ghetto form and order are constantly threatened with extinction by violence: the only constant in this world is the ever-present threat of sudden and senseless outbreaks of violence. Thus, she feels morally vindicated in trying to escape it in any way she can, even by taking another woman's husband, whom she will learn to love later.

The full depth of Maureen's rage and desperation are expressed in a question that she abruptly directs to Miss Oates: "How can I live my life if the world is like this? The world can't be lived, no one can live it right. It is out of control, crazy" (310). Mary Kathryn Grant believes that all of Oates's fiction is an attempt to answer precisely this question (120). This is a valid point, as is Robert H. Fossum's assertion that the crucial difference between Maureen Wendall's letters and Joyce Carol Oates's narration of the story of Maureen and the rest of "them" is the novelist's understanding that, to be meaningful to a reading public, literature cannot simply copy the chaos of reality but also must impose an order on that chaos. The most important function of the Maureen Wendall letters is to allow Oates to interrupt her novel in order to explore briefly the interrelationship between art, reality, and the imagination and to confront directly the traditional questions concerning the viability of naturalistic fiction.

It is important to remember that in her author's note Oates is deliberately vague about how extensive the "recollections" of her former student were. She does say that they were powerful enough to "block out" her own reality and thereby transform her "personal life" into the "nightmare adventures of the Wendalls." This author's note is not the last time that Oates has used the metaphor of the writer of fiction as being a virtually passive receiver and transcriber of the intense feelings of another "writer." Her

1975 short story collection, *The Poisoned Kiss and Other Stories from the Portuguese*, is also introduced by an author's note:

> The tales in this collection are translated from an imaginary work, *Azulejos*, by an imaginary author, Fernandes de Briao. To the best of my knowledge he has no existence and has never existed, though without his very real guidance I would not have had access to the mystical "Portugal" of the stories—nor would I have been compelled to recognize the authority of a world-view quite antithetical to my own.[8]

Of course, Maureen Wendall also "has no existence and has never existed" except in the imagination of Joyce Carol Oates. Oates's vision of the artistic process is hardly revolutionary or even new, but it is interesting for a writer who is, at least to some degree, a literary naturalist. The hidden implication of the author's note in *them* is that the novelist initially feels the force of some facet of reality which, for whatever reason, carries "the authority of a world-view" and, then, through the power of the imagination, extends and amplifies it into "literature." This concept is similar to the views of a good many romantic writers, who often devise a formula for the creative process based upon an interaction of nature and the imagination. For the Oates of *them* nature has been replaced by an ugly and chaotic urban reality that is "antithetical" to the experience of the middle-class writer. Nevertheless, this brutal urban reality inevitably intrudes upon the consciousness of even an academic novelist in a number of ways, but especially through the modern news and entertainment media. In the modern United States even the most sheltered of writers can hardly help but be regularly "invaded" by newspapers, television, and other avenues of information. Norman Mailer, a writer whom Oates admires, has explored the ways in which so much "information" results in no true knowledge and even amplifies chaos. In her letters to Miss Oates a brutalized and embittered Maureen Wendall embraces modern reality in all its chaos, but Joyce Carol Oates knows that, in order to communicate to an audience, the artist must, through the magic of the imagination, impose some order on such chaos. One should remember that *them* is a novel written in and about the 1960s, the years when life in urban America came to seem completely and irredeemably chaotic to many people and the time when the perverse effects of the omnipresent media became dramatically evident. This was, of course, the decade that inspired Mailer's *Armies of the Night* (1968). Oates would explore the surrealistic nature of the 1960s again in the novel that immediately followed *them, Wonderland* (1971).

Oates is speculating about the necessary relationship between the oppressed urban subjects on which contemporary urban naturalism is based and an implied middle-class readership in other ways as well. She thus focuses on the problem that so troubled Richard Wright while he was writing *Native Son.* To a Maureen Wendall or a Bigger Thomas urban reality in the United States is so chaotic that any literary attempt to order it immediately distorts it. Had they the vocabulary, they would say that any honest attempt to document or duplicate it in the mode of traditional naturalism could produce only a catalog of unrelated and inherently meaningless phenomena. Oates does not dispute this but believes that, for it to be artistically comprehensible to a middle-class readership, the catalog must be enclosed within some artificially imposed form, or order. That such an imposition would inevitably make the catalog seem a lie to the real subjects on which it is based is, she believes, simply an unavoidable complication. The realm of the artistic imagination is defined by an inherently subjective "rage for order." In her author's note Oates somewhat playfully hints at the need for making external reality artistically real by distorting it.

In addition to asserting that the novel "is truly about a specific 'them' and not just a literary technique of pointing to us all," she says that Jules Wendall, Maureen's rebel brother, will, at some point, "probably be writing his own version of this novel, to which he will not give the rather disdainful and timorous title *them*" (7). There has been no little critical debate concerning the identity of this "specific 'them.'" Elizabeth Dalton, for instance, seems to equate the adjective with the urban lower classes: "The assumption here is that people like 'them,' the Wendalls of the world, do not respond to misfortune as you or I or the author would, that it is as natural to them as the air they breathe."[9] In contrast, Anthony Decurtis believes that it has a deliberately ambiguous antecedent: "But the specificity of the referent for 'them' seems to shift as the psychological and the social intermingle, and every individual and social group projects their problems, obsessions, and terrors onto a certain 'them'" (127). Robert H. Fossum also sees the word as referring to a shifting projection of the Other: "To Grandma Wendall 'them' means Loretta, the mayor, the governor. To Loretta it means Grandma, blacks, foreigners. To the children it means their parents. Finally, near the end of the novel, the attitudes of the Wendalls find their middle-class variants in the hostility of young revolutionaries toward all authority" (54). At times in the novel Oates's use of *them* seems an imaginative variation on the concept of the Other. Decurtis and Fossum are correct in interpreting it as referring to those individuals or groups whom the powerless perceive as having power. In this sense *them* constitutes an ever-present, if elusive, oppressor.

Still, Dalton's interpretation seems valid as well. At times in the novel *them* refers only to the urban proletariat, and it is this application of the word that demands the use of the lower-case *t*. In the eyes of the middle class the urban lower classes are inferior, dehumanized, without identity. In addition to its prominence in the author's note, the novel proper refers to "them" in two important scenes. In the first Jules Wendall is with an aristocratic young woman named Vera, who voluntarily joins him in the Detroit ghetto only to be cruelly and cynically exploited by him. Vera asks Jules if he is one of the "poor people" and is bewildered after he answers in the affirmative: "But you're not black. Are you very poor?" (438). Soon, however, she implies that the urban poor are not completely foreign to her: "'I think I've been down here, lost, for a long time. I have this feeling that I've been down here, with you or someone like you, and with *them*.' She glanced sideways, hatefully, at people in the street, Negroes mainly, who were passing her and Jules without paying much attention to them" (440). Vera embodies Oates's vision of the self-hating upper-class children of the 1960s who sought to change their identities by rejecting the privileged social position into which they were born. She has believed that the urban poor are profoundly different from her, that they are all black. Thus, it is both a relief and a nightmare to discover that they are often not visibly different from her at all. Her attempt to reject privilege by joining them is doomed, in part, by the fact that "they" are, to a large degree, personifications of her class- and self-hatred.

In this scene *them* refers both to the urban poor and to the Other, to those beings whom upper- and middle-class people dehumanize by projecting onto them their own darkest instincts and needs. This second application of the word echoes, of course, a theme common to urban naturalism since Frank Norris and Jack London. Oates's treatment of the urban poor as the Other differs from her naturalistic predecessors most significantly in its ironic self-consciousness. She is aware and goes to some trouble to inform the reader that Jules Wendall, a product of the urban ghetto, will assuredly not give his fictional account of it such "a disdainful and timorous title." When and if Jules writes his book, he will do so from a perspective similar to Nelson Algren's and Hubert Selby's.

The second important appearance of the word *them* appears in the novel's complex concluding scene. For a close examination of it to be meaningful, other important matters must be discussed. There is, for instance, the question of Joyce Carol Oates's specific relationship to the tradition of literary naturalism. Commentary on this subject by critics and by Oates herself has not truly resolved this matter. As mentioned, Joanne Creighton argues that, because Jules and other characters in the novel ultimately triumph over the external forces that attempt to control them, the novel is truly a "parody of naturalism." Greg Johnson asserts that, "for all its adherence to social history, *them* is no more a purely naturalistic work than any of Oates's other novels." The story of the Wendalls, he clarifies, "follows a conscious and somewhat allegorical design."[10] Sanford Pinsker takes a comparable position, arguing that the "vision of the urban apocalypse" underlying *them* is more "personal" than traditionally naturalistic: "In bookish terms, the influences are less Dreiser than Lawrence, more Yeats' "The Second Coming" than Crane's *Maggie*."[11] Eileen Bender does place Oates's work in the tradition of literary naturalism and perceptively compares it to Dreiser's *American Tragedy* (42–43). In contrast, G. F. Waller contrasts it with Dreiser's *Sister Carrie*, emphasizing that *them* lacks the external "moralistic" commentary that is so obtrusive in the story of Carrie Meeber: "[In Oates's work], we are in a world of intensity, not a world of moral decision."[12] Finally, Donald Pizer places the novel clearly in the American naturalistic tradition: "*them* is probably the best example in contemporary American fiction of the conscious effort by a major writer to recover and renew the themes and fictional conventions of American literary naturalism."[13] A critical consensus seems to emerge that Oates's novel is at least highly reminiscent of American literary naturalism, even though it does not perfectly conform to the tradition. Two critics have, with some genuine success, sought to resolve this seeming paradox.

Steven Barza divides literary naturalism into "two distinctive genres: the Naturalistic tragedy and the Naturalistic success story." In the first category he places *L'Assommoir, An American Tragedy, Maggie, McTeague, and Native Son*, arguing that in these works the protagonists are all crushed by external pressures. His examples of the "Naturalistic success story" are *Nana, Sister Carrie*, and Dreiser's Cowperwood trilogy; in these novels the protagonists seem to transcend the limitations of their environments, but, since they are still "narrowed, twisted, *mis*-shaped, by the drive for upward mobility, the case for the environment is still powerfully made."[14] Barza places *them* in this second group of naturalistic novels. He further emphasizes that in the late twentieth century writers can hardly believe in the kind of "scientific determinism" which underlies the fiction of the turn-of-the-century naturalists. Oates then, he argues, represents a new kind of "contemporary" naturalism in which the external forces shaping the characters' lives are "unnamed, unknown, inscrutable." Above all, Oates has introduced "the Uncertainty Principle" into naturalism (142). The dominant feature of this new naturalism is the tendency of fictional characters to respond in totally inappropriate ways to external stimuli: "The reader [of Oates's kind of contemporary naturalism] is, in fact, always inferring one thing or another. Oates's use of the deviant response involves him as a participant in the creative endeavor. He must deduce, establish causative links himself, find the hidden twists in the path of the psyche, Ellipses, mysteries, riddles, here are the touchstones of contemporary art" (146). Barza's argument for Oates as the creator of a new writerly naturalism is perceptive. None of her characters would ever discover in themselves an inherited tendency toward alcoholism and immediately turn into sadistic drunks, but most of them are driven and molded by vague external forces that the reader must attempt to identify.

Building on his concept of the personal nature of the underlying vision in *them*, Sanford Pinsker develops a comparable argument. While Oates's early novels are distinguished by an unmistakably naturalistic feeling, she should not, he believes, be treated as "merely an extension of Naturalism."[15] Like Barza, Pinsker points out the impossibility of a contemporary writer approaching determinism in the old simplistic manner of Dreiser and Norris:

> In a world closer to the willy-nilly than the firm, determinism's assault on the individual will has been replaced by amorphous threats and a shifting enemy.
>
> For contemporary novelists, the individual (crushed by larger forces, but still shaking his fist against a hostile universe) is less important than the ill-defined THEY who manipulate power and turn paranoid protagonists into clear-thinking, victimized heroes. (59–60)

In this second sentence Pinsker has Heller's Yossarian and virtually all of the creations of Thomas Pynchon in mind. Thus, he believes, Oates and writers as diverse as Heller and Pynchon can legitimately be discussed as having "affinities" with literary naturalism. The fact that the characters in *them* are struggling against powerful external forces and the novel's sordid setting, he argues, makes it "thoroughly naturalistic" (61); even though the complexity and ambiguity of Oates's concept of these forces means that she cannot be labeled as a traditional naturalist. Pinsker is essentially arguing that a modern, more sophisticated naturalism is emerging and that Oates is central to its development.

Oates's most important discussion of her relationship to the naturalistic tradition is found in a critical essay praising Harriette Arnow's novel *The Dollmaker* (1954). She especially values Arnow's naturalistic honesty in portraying the way individuals in the lower classes are crushed by urban capitalism: "Sunk helplessly in flesh, as in the turbulent uncontrollable mystery of the 'economy,' the human being with spiritual yearnings becomes tragic when these yearnings are defeated or mocked or, as in *The Dollmaker*, by Harriette Arnow, brutally transformed into a part of the social machine."[16] Oates adds that "*The Dollmaker* traces the ways in which the spiritual must succumb to the material in a society whose basic principle is competition" (100). The defeat of the spiritual is especially inevitable, Oates emphasizes, in "the brutal city of Detroit," which contains all the most destructive aspects of the entire nation. In her emphasis upon the inevitable destruction of individual spirituality by urban capitalism, she exhibits a naturalistic sensibility with which Stephen Crane and Frank Norris would have been compatible.

But it is not sufficient, Oates believes, for art merely to document this destruction. It must demonstrate that something worthwhile—specifically, human spirituality—has been destroyed. She concludes her praise of Arnow by favorably contrasting her work with "the frantic naturalism" of Selby's *Last Exit to Brooklyn*, which "would give us, probably, a more truthful vision of Detroit, then and now; but such naturalism, totally absorbed in an analysis of bodily existence, is . . . unfaithful to the spiritual and imaginative demands that some people, at least, still make" (110). Selby's fiction, which depicts human beings so completely trapped in materiality as to seem almost lacking in a spiritual dimension, Oates grants, is a useful tool for accurately documenting a contemporary urban America. Still, she rejects this kind of extreme naturalism because it distorts the most important level of the human personality—indeed, the very level that defines one as being human.

There are obvious limitations to this argument as an analysis of *Last Exit to Brooklyn*, but it is still important for what it says about Oates's vision of what fiction should be. She must respond positively to the romantic overtones of Stephen Crane's *Maggie*, for instance. Maggie's beloved and doomed lambrequin is, after all, a metaphor for her inner spirituality. Similarly, the characters in *them*, above all Jules Wendall, fight to save their spiritual selves while living in an urban environment that attempts to repress everything except the sordid, the completely physical. Children are, to Oates, the most tragic victims of the industrial city, and she admires Arnow's powerful portrayal of their victimization: "The children of *The Dollmaker* are stunted, doomed adults, destroyed either literally by the admonition 'Adjust!' or destroyed emotionally, turned into citizens of a demonic factory-world" (105). In different ways Maureen and Jules, like Carrie Meeber, struggle not to "adjust" to their environment.

It must be said that Oates does not accept the label of naturalism for her work. In an afterword to *The Poisoned Kiss* she writes that she treats "the density of existential life" in her fiction and that she believes "that writing should re-create a world, sanctifying the real world by honoring its complexities" (187–88). She has elsewhere referred to poetry as "a sacred rite" that "transcends the personality of the poet and communicates its vision."[17] Yet, she clarifies, a valid art cannot become so mystical as to separate itself from the reality that nourishes it: "One of the little-understood responsibilities of the artist is to bear witness—in almost a religious sense—to certain things. The experience of the concentration camps . . . the experience of suffering, the humiliation of any form of persecution" (278). Literature, she believes, must not only depict the brutality and chaos of the contemporary world accurately, but it also must make that world sacred by giving it a comprehensible form, or order. All of this, of course, does not mean that Oates, or at least the Oates of the first ten novels, cannot be called a naturalist. It merely means that she is, as Barza and Pinsker have said, a new kind of naturalist who responds to social chaos and to existential absurdity. What primarily distinguishes her from Wright, Algren, Selby, and Rechy is her insistence upon the spiritual dimension of contemporary life.

For all five of these writers two subjects of special fascination are the modern U.S. city and the violence that erupts so often and so shockingly in urban America. Some of the most perceptive critical commentary on Oates's *them* focuses upon the role of Detroit in the novel. Certainly, in *them* the city is a "demonic factory-world" and a microcosm of urban America. G. F. Waller even sees it as constituting a metaphor for the determinism against which the Wendalls must struggle throughout the novel: "Detroit represents the deterministic limit of the dark corruption through which the Wendalls must seek transcendence" (139). Yet Oates's treatment of the city is not completely negative: it comes to stand for a dark urban romance, which is especially attractive to Jules Wendall. Greg Johnson provides an interesting discussion of Oates's ambivalent response to "the Motor City":

Some of the violent material of Oates's fiction was originally culled from Detroit newspaper stories, and while her work shows a taut awareness of the city's turbulence, she has also called Detroit "a place of romance." Its very bleakness and unpredictability, as well as its vitality, have evidently symbolized for Oates some of the basic conditions of twentieth-century America, an "imperishable reality" that she finds inspiring, compelling. (72)

Eileen Bender argues that, for Loretta Wendall, the city undergoes a metamorphosis: "To the Loretta of the opening scene, the city is a magical realm, its streets a 'carnival' of wonders. By the novel's conclusion, the city has become a nightmarish 'carnival' of race riot and pillage" (41). It is Jules Wendall, however, who is most significantly identified with Detroit. Mary Kathryn Grant emphasizes the novel's association of the city with violence but argues that this recurrent external violence mirrors the internal rage of the Wendalls: "The city teeming with unhappy, unfulfilled human beings is the ambiance of Oates's fiction. Yet social violence often only mirrors personal violence; the 1967 Detroit riots in *them* merely reflect on a wider scale and scope the turbulent lives of the Wendall family" (18). Perhaps from the moment of his conception, violence follows Jules Wendall: he is shot and almost killed by his lover, and he finds a personal catharsis in the act of killing a policeman during the riots. Jules is the romantic figure in the novel, a representative of the rebel characters that, according to Ihab Hassan, dominate much of post–World War II American fiction: "A dark impulse of *resistance* permeates contemporary letters. . . . [American novelists] agree that the contemporary world presents a continued affront to man, and that his response must therefore be the response of the rebel or victim, living under the shadow of death."[18] In the course of the novel Jules is both "rebel" and "victim," but most of the time he is a young man determined to realize in his life the American dream. The city is, for him, a place of seemingly limitless possibility and adventure, until he is struck down by its senseless and irrational violence. Jules, in fact, responds to Detroit in much the same way that the narrator in John Rechy's *City of Night* responds to New York: the two young men initially perceive their urban surroundings as a place of fascinating possibilities, only to discover the dark corruption behind the bright neon lights.

As Robert H. Fossum points out, violence functions throughout Oates's fiction as an irrational force inevitably destructive of the characters' rage for order. Moreover, they often respond to their environment's destruction of any reassuring and sustaining order with another act of violence. Thus, violence becomes cyclical in Oates: it is frequently stimulus *and* response. Both G. F. Waller and Mary Kathryn Grant discuss the frequency with which frustration over their profound impotence, their inability to resist environmental pressures, causes Oates's characters to lash out at something, anything, around them. In the city, especially, sudden and irrational outbursts of violence are a common means of giving expression to their sense of hopelessness and futility. Violence for Oates assumes the function of scientific determinism in traditional naturalism. Through its very irrationality and unpredictability it controls the lives of the characters in her work. It seems to be a force that exists at the core of the urban environment, which suddenly invades the life of a character, changing it forever. Grant is correct in her idea that external violence in Oates is a reflection of the chaos within her characters. This does not mean, however, that it can be predicted or controlled by these characters.

One of the most important contributions of *them* to American literature is its depiction of violence as the inescapable fact of life in contemporary urban America. It is what inspires Maureen Wendall's crucial question to Miss Oates: "How can I live my life if the world is like this?" Oates's novel would not provide Maureen with any reassuring answers to this question. The fate of Maureen's mother exemplifies the frightening suddenness and irrationality with which urban violence can forever change the life of one of "them."[19] At the beginning of the novel Loretta is a sixteen-year-old girl fascinated by her own youth and attractiveness: "Behind her good clear skin was a universe of skin, all of it healthy. She loved this, she was in love with the fact of girls like her having come into existence, though she could not have expressed her feelings exactly" (10). She also enjoys the attentions of a young tough named Bernie Malin, who puts "her in mind—she didn't know why—of the feature-paper heroes of only the other day, Baby Face Nelson and Dillinger, who were dead now but still very important" (26). Like other young girls, Loretta is entranced by an illusion of male dangerousness. Yet she is aware that she is playing a game with herself because what makes possible Bernie's appeal to her is the certainty that he is not really dangerous at all: "Bernie was all right. He lost his temper and knocked people around and then the next day he was sorry, and he had a job, and whatever it was that kept people from falling through the bottom of the world" (12).

Ironically, Loretta is about to discover that a very real dangerousness exists quite close to her and that, in the wonderland of urban America, absolutely nothing can prevent anyone "from falling through the bottom of the world." She brings Bernie home with her, has intercourse with him, and falls asleep, only to wake up to an awareness that the young man has been murdered by her paranoid brother, Brock. Then she is "rescued" by a young policeman named Howard Wendall, who rapes her. She knows instantly that "it was over, finished, that was the end of her youth," and the next chapter opens with a description of Loretta "pregnant and married" to Wendall (42). She has been forcibly thrust into a treacherous adult world with the suddenness of a lightning bolt, and she will never truly know peace again. She accepts the fact that, since Bernie Malin is dead, she has experienced love for the last time.

For the rest of her life Loretta will be victimized by forces and events that she cannot truly understand, let alone control. Howard Wendall takes her away from the "fair-sized city on a Midwestern canal" (22) in which she had always lived and away from even the illusion of any control over her life. He first loses his job on the police force and leans forward into "a future of pure gravity" (53). Loretta never has any illusions that Howard is safe from falling "through the bottom of the world" and taking her with him. After a period of living in the country and under the domineering thumb of Howard's mother while he is in the service, she makes one attempt to take control of her life by moving to Detroit. But, like John Dos Passos's Bud Korpenning in New York, she cannot find "any center" to the city (71–72) and is quickly arrested on a charge of prostitution. For the rest of her life Loretta leans more and more into an existence controlled by "pure gravity." Howard is killed in an industrial accident; she marries Furlong, who almost kills her daughter; and her brother Brock, who first plunged her into chaos by murdering Bernie Malin as he lay sleeping beside her, comes to live with her.

Several critics have discussed the emphasis in Oates's fiction on insanity; for instance, one insane act by Loretta's brother dooms her to a life spent as a victim of social injustice and oppression. In *them* Oates ties the madness theme to the 1960s. Her vision seems to be that U.S. society perennially seeks without finding a middle ground between a stifling order and an irrational Dionysian freedom. The 1960s were the decade when a youthful obsession with freedom and experimentation veered into a madness from which we have yet to recover fully. Loretta comes to distrust any quest for freedom which might result in a loss of control. Having known nothing but chaos since that day when she was sixteen and her life changed abruptly forever, she yearns for order. Anthony Decurtis discusses the way in which Loretta as well as Maureen become believers in the "traditional American values" of "home" and "family" (123). The fact that they are so completely locked away from it makes mother and daughter yearn for the myth so widely and effectively perpetuated by the media of the stable middle-class life. A still young Maureen simply decides to obtain middle-class stability by marrying Jim Randolph, but Loretta, now transformed into an aging, no longer attractive woman, can only become an advocate of "middle-class values."

Elsewhere I discussed Loretta in the context of Oates's short story "Problems of Adjustment in Survivors of Natural/Unnatural Disasters" (1972). This story is developed around the concept of "psychic suicide" by victims of oppression, which establishes that such victims often adopt the value system of their oppressors in order to survive; in her story Oates specifically refers to this phenomenon as occurring among the survivors of totalitarian concentration camps. I argued that Loretta commits psychic suicide by becoming a spokeswoman for the supposed values of a middle class that she can never join.[20]

Mary Kathryn Grant argues that it is nevertheless important to remember that Loretta is always a survivor. She may be perennially overwhelmed by events, but is never destroyed by them. Grant believes that, while most of Oates's female characters are in fact survivors, Loretta is more admirable than the others: "Her achievement is not only that she survives, but that she also grows stronger and tougher through the experience" (25). This interpretation seems to be correct, but it is also important to note that Loretta has been "stunted," deformed, by her life. The sixteen-year-old girl luxuriating in her youthful prettiness seems an entirely different character than the adult wife and mother. Without quite knowing when or how, Loretta has obeyed her society's command to adjust. Oates does, however, give her one last defiant speech:

> . . . I wasn't meant to be like this—I mean, stuck here. Really I wasn't. I don't look like this. I mean, my hair, and I'm too fat. I don't really look like *this*, I look a different way. . . . You [Loretta's children] think you're all special, all people who are born think they're special, but you're no more special than me. I know who I am—I got a lot of things to do and places to see and this isn't all there is in the world! Not this! Not for me!

Tragically, this is indeed all there is for Loretta: she will never do the things she has to do or see the places she has to see.

Her son, Jules, struggles hard against the pressure to adjust and does and sees a great deal, in fact more than Loretta could ever comprehend. As mentioned, he is the very prototype of Hassan's "*alazon*," the "imposter, compulsive rebel, or outsider" (114). Oates hints that Jules's biological father may be Bernie Malin,[21] and he seems to exist in a dimension outside the rest of the Wendall family. From his childhood he exhibits a dualism of character which separates him from the harsh realities of his environment. He cares for and tries to protect his family, especially Maureen, yet he cannot escape violence and destruction. In a doctor's waiting room he reads a magazine story about a Hindu mystic named Vinoba Bhave, who preaches that "we are all members of a single human family" and says: "My object is to transform the whole of society. Fire merely burns. . . . Fire burns and does its duty. It is for others to do theirs" (95). The mystic's phrase "Fire burns and does its duty" seems to Jules a sacred pronouncement—at least, he never forgets the idea that the old must be burned away before the new can be erected in its place. He, in fact, vows that he will become a kind of secular saint: "He had not liked Jesus. . . . He would be a better man, or at least a cleverer man—why not all the kingdoms of the earth? Why not? The kingdoms of the earth would only go to someone else; that was history" (96).

Ellen G. Friedman describes "the initial Jules" as an intensely romantic character: "[He] never allows his romantic aspirations to be qualified by his experience with the real world. . . . He is the only character in the novel whose vision rises above facticity, who has a sense that life is 'backed by music.'"[22] Actually, Jules is always a curious mixture of romantic idealist and cynical adventurer. At the age of fifteen he is already

> spending his adolescence in the faint shadows of actual gangsters, or the friends of gangsters; something in him yearned for the doomed, derelict, glamorous style of their living. He took some of his language from them or from their imitators or from movies, and his clothes and even his walk had a slightly retarded, lounging, lethargic, contemptuous, self-conscious air about them, a pimp's style; he was very pleased with all this. (90)

Before the novel is over Jules will actually fit all the roles, including pimp, which, at fifteen, he merely emulates. But now he is a believer in the ongoing possibilities for change: "*I will change my life in the end*, he thought.

He would go to California" (94). At the end of the novel a very different Jules Wendall is, in fact, preparing to go to California.

First, however, he revises his concept of travel and learns to think in terms of a journey up the social ladder instead of across the continent. He is introduced to the idea of social mobility by Bernard Geffen, a strange man who presents himself as having close ties to the mob but turns out to be, quite simply, mad. Through Geffen, Jules also meets Nadine Greene, a wealthy young woman from Grosse Pointe whom he transforms into a vision of everything he will ever want or need again. In describing Jules's love affair with Nadine, Oates's writing often becomes intensely romantic, for instance: "He kissed her lightly, wanting to put her to sleep with his kisses, comfort her, his mouth light against hers like the petals of roses or the fluttering wings of moths, nothing substantial. It was all so airy, even this embrace. . . . How he wanted that intoxication" (263). In fact, the romantic side of Jules's nature has simply been waiting for something or someone to idealize intensely and completely. Initially, he believed that wealth and social power would suffice as the goals of his romantic quest, but such abstractions proved inadequate for the full intensity of his passion. From the moment that he can identify Nadine as the personification of all that he has ever wanted, he need seek no longer for his own special holy grail.

In fact, Nadine is a dangerously neurotic and selfish young woman who is not worthy of being the object of anyone's idealistic passion. Jules manages, however, not to see the real young woman. He knows only his romantic conception of her. For Oates, Nadine's shallowness does not diminish the significance of Jules's devotion to her. What she once wrote in an essay about Shakespeare's Troilus and Cressida is applicable to Jules and Nadine: "Nothing is ever equivalent to the energy or eloquence or love lavished upon it. Man's goals are fated to be less than his ideals would have them, and when he realizes this truth he is 'enlightened' in the special sense in which tragedy enlightens men—a flash of bitter knowledge that immediately precedes death."[23] Jules is determined not to be so "enlightened" even after a humiliating trip to Texas with Nadine in which she deserts him when he is penniless, and he subsequently finds himself serving as a human guinea pig for governmental medical experiments. The western frontier functions in Oates's novel much as it does in Rechy's City of Night, as an exploited and degraded illusion of freedom.

Almost as soon as he is able to return to Detroit, he seeks out Nadine, and this time he *may* receive that "flash of bitter knowledge" which "precedes death." The empty, terrified young woman shoots him, and Oates writes that "the spirit of the Lord departed from Jules" (380). The abrupt appearance of this seemingly theological phrase in an overwhelmingly secular novel creates no little ambiguity. Ellen G. Friedman sees it as signaling the inevitable death of the young romantic Jules and his necessary entrance into the realm of the ordinary: "Hamlet has yielded to Horatio" (92–93). In his next manifestation, though, Jules can hardly be described as living an ordinary existence. He reappears in the final section of the novel, subtitled "Come, My Soul That Hath Long Languished . . . ," existing in a lonely and emotionless state in the ghetto: "Impressions flowed through him. Nothing caught hold. He was safe from his own past, kicked free of his own past. . . . Jules had disappeared" (419). He becomes a pimp for the wealthy girl, Vera, and beats her with "a twisted coat hanger" (451). He is adopted by the campus radicals at the University of Detroit and decides to use them, feeling only contempt for them.

Things change abruptly for Jules when the ghetto explodes in the 1967 race riots. Initially, he is merely caught up in the chaos, responding to it with the same emotionless passivity that he has shown for everything since being shot by Nadine. But, when the city begins to explode in flames, he remembers the formula for change he learned so long ago: "Fire burns and does its duty"; "Let everything burn! Why not? The city was coming to life in fire, and he, Jules, was sitting in it, warming to it, the flames dancing along his arteries and behind his seared eyes" (460). In the chaos of the riot he shoots and kills a policeman, and yet another Jules Wendall is born: "Having done this he had done everything. It was over. His blood ran wild, he was not to blame for anything, why should he stop? He aimed the rifle into the man's face and pulled the trigger" (468). He is next seen as a guest on a postriot television program repeating the slogan that "Fire burns and does its duty" and announcing that the old society is being burned away so that a new one can be born.

Oates brilliantly narrates Jules's television program through the eyes of Loretta, who is watching her son and hearing his words with horror. The psychic suicide does not want to hear prophecies of the end of the old American society that has so exploited her, and she especially does not want to hear them from her own son. Moreover, Jules makes a concluding statement about the nature and role of violence in U.S. society that disturbs her even more than the rest of what he has said:

Violence can't be singled out from an ordinary day! . . . Everyone must live through it again and again, there's no end to it, no land to get to, no clearing in the midst of the cities—who wants parks in the midst of the cities!—parks won't burn!

The rapist and his victim rise up from rubble, eventually, at dawn, and brush themselves off and go down the street to a diner. Believe me, passion can't endure. It will come back again and again but it can't endure. (473–74)

Sanford Pinkser reads this speech as being indicative of the fact that "Jules is a mystical—as opposed to a 'political'—animal, a man both embracing and embraced by an apocalyptic vision" ("The Blue Collar Apocalypse" [44]).

    Jules next appears in the novel's last scene. He has come to tell Maureen, his beloved sister, good-bye. She is now married to Jim Randolph, having thus achieved the safe, middle-class life she set out to gain. Thus, she is not glad to see her brother, who has been identified as one of the leaders of the riot and as a Communist. Jules assures her that he is not, in fact, a Communist: "I'm not anything. I'm just trying to get along" (477). In fact, he is doing more than just getting along: he informs Maureen that he is about to leave for California and a position in a federal antipoverty program. Before leaving, he wants to remind Maureen that her new life is much more fragile than she wants to believe: "Don't forget that this place here can burn down too. Men can come back in your life, Maureen, they can beat you up again and force your knees apart, why not? There's so much of it in the world, so much semen, so many men! Can't it happen? Won't it happen? Wouldn't you really want it to happen?" In reminding Maureen of who she really is, Jules makes the novel's third and last crucial reference to "them": "Honey, aren't you one of them yourself?" (478). Here Jules seems to be referring specifically to the urban proletariat and reminding his sister of her lower-class origins.

    I have previously described this last Jules as being "a calculating nihilist."[24] This is not the view held by most critics, and it has been refuted especially well by Greg Johnson: "A nihilist Jules would probably stay in Detroit and live in a state of bitter cynicism [but] . . . Jules has rejected passivity and suffering, having allowed his spirit to assert itself in a criminal but purgative act and thus [preserved] his own idealism, his belief in himself and the future" (88). The idea that Jules achieves a form of spiritual rebirth by killing the policeman is, in fact, the most common critical view. G. F. Waller emphasizes this idea through a contrast between Jules and Maureen:

JOYCE CAROL OATES'S *THEM*

Unlike his sister, who attempts to escape poverty, bigotry, and exploitation only to end in the safe haven of domesticity, Jules persists in his more dangerous search for the authentic. Oates may seen to be sentimentalizing him, but she wants him to stand for an affirmation of hope in the midst of determinism, a buoyant romantic affirmation alongside the despairing passivity of the rest of his family. (140)

It is probably simplistic to describe the Jules Wendall whom we last see as either a nihilist or as a young man who has achieved spiritual transcendence through an act of violence. One should remember the duality of character which has always defined him. When he found an object that *he* believed worthy of his adoration, Jules was transformed into a romantic idealist. Before Nadine Greene he was merely a cynical young hoodlum, not a great deal different, in fact, from Bernie Malin, who may be his biological father, and, after Nadine shot him and "the spirit of the Lord" left him, he existed as a cruel zombielike creature who exploited and tortured a foolish young woman. At the end of the novel Jules seems to be caught in a temporary waiting pattern, hoping that he will once again find someone or something worthy of the full intensity of his passion. He even says that he will return one day from California and marry Nadine Greene. The reader comprehends, however, the true nature of Nadine, even if Jules does not, and it is at least a possibility that he will never find an acceptable object for his idealism. If so, one suspects that he will survive quite well in California, functioning much as he did before meeting the shallow young woman from Grosse Pointe. This time the federal government may be his Bernard Geffen.

Much more than Loretta or Maureen, certainly, Jules struggles to resist adjusting to society. But he cannot avoid being controlled and, at least to some degree, stunted by it. If violence is Oates's substitute for scientific determinism, it is no accident that Jules is always touched by it. He personifies the startling suddenness with which violence in urban America can invade and transform permanently the lives of "them."

In Oates's novel the narrative point of view returns to the position outside and above the inner city. She seems to be viewing the urban ghetto from the same vantage point as Riis, Crane, Norris, and London. But, of course, she isn't. The narrative self-consciousness exhibited in the author's note, the Maureen Wendall letters, and Jules's comments to Maureen in the novel's last scene are Oates's way of acknowledging her inevitable separation from the subject matter of her novel. She is not one of "them" and can never be (ironically, Oates grew up among the rural working classes and, thus, had more direct experience of childhood poverty than either Stephen Crane or Frank Norris). More important, she knows that, by giving her novel order and a form, she is inevitably falsifying the reality on which it is based. Loretta, Maureen, and Jules would probably reject "them," but, one hopes, the middle-class reader and the academic critic will not. While artistic form distorts external reality, it is essential to any meaningful communication between writer and reader. Oates's assertion in her prefatory note that "Jules Wendall will probably be writing his own version of this novel" seems playful unless he is to undergo a final transformation into a literary artist. As Robert H. Fossum points out, "In [Oates's world], the only order is that of art, the only one in control [is] the artist herself" (59).

In the contemporary literary landscape, *them* would seem to illustrate that narrative position in the inner-city novel can never again be as detached and simplistic as it is in *Maggie: A Girl of the Streets, McTeague,* or *The People of the Abyss.* As Steven Barza and Sanford Pinsker have shown, Joyce Carol Oates is a force for the creation of a new kind of naturalism.

Notes

1. Joyce Carol Oates, *them* (Greenwich, Conn.: Fawcett, 1970), 315–16.

2. It should be said that some critics have viewed Oates as a writer sympathetic to women's liberation. See, for instance, Joseph Petite, "'Out of the Machine': Joyce Carol Oates and the Liberation of Woman," *Kansas Quarterly* 9 (1974): 218–26.

3. Joanne V. Creighton, *Joyce Carol Oates* (Boston: Twayne, 1979), 65.

4. Eileen Teper Bender, *Joyce Carol Oates, Artist in Residence* (Bloomington: Indiana University Press, 1987), 44–45.

5. Robert H. Fossum, "Only Control: The Novels of Joyce Carol Oates," in *Critical Essays on Joyce Carol Oates,* ed. Linda W. Wagner (Boston: G. K. Hall, 1979), 56.

6. Mary Kathryn Grant points out that the library has been Maureen's dominant symbol of order, just as cars are for her brother Jules (Grant, *The Tragic Vision of Joyce Carol Oates* [Durham, N.C.: Duke University Press, 1978], 107–8).

7. Anthony Decurtis, "The Process of Fictionalization in Joyce Carol Oates's *them,*" *International Fiction Review* 6 (1979): 126–27.

8. Fernandes/Joyce Carol Oates, *The Poisoned Kiss and Other Stories from the Portuguese* (New York: Vanguard, 1975).

9. Elizabeth Dalton, "Joyce Carol Oates: Violence in the Head," *Commentary* 49 (June 1970): 76.

10. Greg Johnson, *Understanding Joyce Carol Oates* (Columbia: University of South Carolina Press, 1987), 73–74.

11. Sanford Pinsker, "The Blue Collar Apocalypse, or Detroit Bridge's Falling Down: Joyce Carol Oates' *them*," *Descant* 23 (1979): 36.

12. G. F. Waller, *Dreaming America: Obsession and Transcendence in the Fiction of Joyce Carol Oates* (Baton Rouge: Louisiana State University Press, 1979), 130–31.

13. Donald Pizer, "Contemporary American Literary Naturalism," *The Theory and Practice of American Literary Naturalism: Selected Essays and Reviews* (Carbondale: Southern Illinois University Press, 1993), 171.

14. Steven Barza, "Joyce Carol Oates: Naturalism and the Aberrant Response," *Studies in American Fiction* 7 (1979): 141–42.

15. Sanford Pinsker, "Joyce Carol Oates and the New Naturalism," *Southern Review* 15 (1979): 62.

16. Joyce Carol Oates, "The Nightmare of Naturalism: Harriette Arnow's 'The Dollmaker,'" *New Heaven, New Earth: The Visionary Experience in Literature* (New York: Vanguard, 1974), 99.

17. Leif Sjoberg, "An Interview with Joyce Carol Oates," *Contemporary Literature* 23 (Summer 1982): 270.

18. Ihab Hassan, *Radical Innocence: The Contemporary American Novel* (Princeton, N.J.: Princeton University Press, 1961), 4–5.

19. Leonard J. Leff relates the violence in *them* and in all of Oates's fiction to what he perceives as her treatment of the female as a destructive force: "From the center of woman proceeds the destruction of 'man's power to live meaningfully'" (Leff, "The Center of Violence in Joyce Carol Oates's Fiction," *Notes on Modern American Literature* 2 [1977]: item 9).

20. James R. Giles, "Suffering, Transcendence, and Artistic 'Form': Joyce Carol Oates's *them*," *Arizona Quarterly* 32 (Autumn 1976): 219–20.

21. Eileen Teper Bender flatly asserts that Bernie Malin is Jules's biological father (Oates, *Artist in Residence*, 46).

22. Ellen G. Friedman, *Joyce Carol Oates* (New York: Frederick Ungar, 1980), 86–87.

23. Joyce Carol Oates, *The Edge of Impossibility: Tragic Forms in Literature* (New York: Vanguard, 1972), 27–30.

24. In Giles, "Suffering, Transcendence, and Artistic 'Form,'" 225.

Conclusion
The Fat Man Revealed

Stephen Crane, Frank Norris, and Jack London were in the privileged position of being able to view the American slum as a new and exotic phenomenon. It was obviously an economically deprived environment and thus something to be avoided, and its pervasive suffering inspired highly personal reactions in two of these writers. Frank Norris saw his parents divorce in 1894, the year he entered Harvard to study writing under Professor Lewis Gates. The divorce and his father's subsequent remarriage threatened the advantaged socioeconomic position he had always enjoyed. Apparently, fear of descent into the urban lower classes inspired a kind of subtext in much of his work and perhaps explains the curiously desperate tone of *Vandover and the Brute*. In *McTeague, Vandover,* and even those sections of *The Octopus* which chronicle the disintegration of the Hooven family, Norris obsessively explores the horrors of social and economic collapse for individuals trapped in the U.S. city. Jack London used his descent into London's East End, in part, as a kind of purging process. He needed to confront extreme economic suffering in a foreign environment in order to come to peace with his personal experience as a member of the Oakland and San Francisco lumpenproletariat. Writing *The People of the Abyss* seems to have psychologically liberated him and allowed him to create his classic myth of primitive freedom, *The Call of the Wild*. June Howard perceptively argues that a fear of "proletarianization" is an underlying, and unacknowledged, motif in much turn-of-the-century American literary naturalism.[1]

Still, Norris, London, and Crane viewed the ghettos of the new city in part as exotic internal colonies. For Norris, in *McTeague*, San Francisco's Polk Street constituted a neat division between two quite distinctive "territories"—the familiar and safe home of the lower middle classes and the exotic and dangerous world of the proletariat. In much of Norris's work the strange and forbidden parts of San Francisco function like India in the writings of Kipling, an exotic and erotic subculture that tempts the civilized Anglo-Saxon into yielding to atavistic reversals, a temptation that must ultimately be controlled and denied. London's narrator in *The People of the Abyss* views his voluntary descent into the worst of England's urban poverty as a kind of deep-sea diving in which he deliberately submerges himself in a dangerous world in order to view at close hand a "new race" of beings. Less consciously, he is also embarking on an exploration of the recessed areas of his own psyche. Almost certainly inspired by Riis's *How the Other Half Lives* and the pamphlets of certain religious reformers of the period, possibly including his father, Crane, writing *Maggie* at Syracuse with little firsthand knowledge of the tenement world of New York City, created an idealized portrait of a beautiful girl of the slums whose internal innocence and purity is not destroyed even by her descent into a life of prostitution. In order to preserve her purity, he had to keep an extreme narrative distance from her. In addition the fat man is exiled from the second version of his novel. He thereby generally managed to sustain his chosen—and, one assumes, comforting—illusion that such a pure flower as Maggie could "blossom" in the "mud-puddle" of the Bowery.

That London and Crane were working from the kind of reformist emphasis one finds in the Zola of *Germinal* did not prevent them from conceptualizing the inhabitants of the inner city as personifications of the primitive Other, in much the way that, according to Toni Morrison, white Americans have always thought of African Americans. The residents of the ghetto for them do, at least in part, embody the "evil," "rebellious," "fearful," and yet "desirable" "features of the self."[2] In *McTeague* Norris was not concerned with calling for reform and was thus even more free to view his characters as exotic primitives. The early explorations of these three writers can be described as a stage of innocence in the history of American naturalistic ghetto fiction. In order to establish a sense of identification with the middle-class reader, their narrators primarily assumed a privileged position outside and above the created environments from which to view the slum dweller. Even London's narrator made certain that he had a means of quickly ascending from the lower depths of the East End before diving into them.

In the 1930s American naturalistic fiction about the inner city entered a new and distinctly political phase. In *Jews without Money* and *Native Son*, respectively, Michael Gold and Richard Wright wedded the ethnic novel with the naturalistic protest novel; both were writing from an overtly acknowledged Marxist perspective. While Gold remained comfortable with a political thrust throughout his novel, Wright's Marxist emphasis was complicated and compromised by other concerns. He gave the novel a black nationalist subtext that potentially collided with any fictional appeal to a universal proletariat and also added an existential emphasis that, in fact, increasingly came to dominate the last half of the book. Moreover, in the original (and more satisfying) version of *Native Son* he overtly explored the largely repressed and potentially explosive sexuality of Bigger Thomas. These added concerns confused the art of *Native Son* to a noticeable degree, but they also transformed the book into something more complex and satisfying than the traditional ethnic protest novel. Primarily for this reason, *Native Son* has remained in the forefront of literary attention longer than *Jews without Money* or any number of other naturalistic ethnic protest novels, including, for instance, William Attaway's *Blood on the Forge* (published the year after *Native Son*), Chester Himes's *If He Hollers Let Him Go* (1945), and Willard Motley's *Knock on Any Door* (1947). A feminist subtext gives Ann Petry's 1946 novel, *The Street*, a kind of thematic complexity that is comparable to Wright's book.

The narrators in these novels assume a position somewhere between the middle-class WASP reader and the exploited ethnic characters. Their narrative strategy is to inform the privileged reader of the sufferings of their ethnic characters, and even to shock the reader if necessary, while rejecting a similar stance of privilege. Embracing the reformist emphasis, they attempt to convey the need for social change. At first glance Nelson Algren's *The Man with the Golden Arm* appears to use a parallel narrative strategy. Its narrator also seems to locate himself between the middle-class reader and the novel's economically exploited characters, and Algren clearly desires to shock the privileged reader. His purpose, however, is not political. As Walcutt perceived, he has renounced the usual consolation of social protest fiction: he does not believe that the fallen, post–World War II inner city can, in fact, be saved. He desires only to shock the middle-class reader into an awareness of the humanness of his urban grotesques, to convince this reader of the fallacy of assuming any sense of superiority to these distorted and even ugly beings, to convey the message that inwardly everyone is a "habitual," a "suspect."

Normally, he reinforces this point only after mocking his characters, through a deliberately ridiculing rhetoric and extended scenes of absurdist humor. In reality, his narrator distances himself from reader *and* character in order to assault, in different ways and to different degrees, both. *The Man with the Golden Arm* represented a third, sophisticated stage in the development of naturalistic American inner-city fiction. Influenced by such disparate European masters as Kuprin, Dostoevsky, and Céline as well as by Whitman, Drieser, and Crane, it has usually seemed a strangely foreign kind of art to most U.S. critics.

Last Exit to Brooklyn and *City of Night* are, in different ways, variations of the sophisticated stage of inner-city naturalism. Selby's narrator merges his voice with the raging and psychotic men and women who inhabit Selby's working-class Brooklyn. The novel's narrative strategy places the assumed privileged middle-class reader in the center of a relentless game of mum in order to strip him or her of any and all middle-class defenses. Even more reminiscent of Céline than *The Man with the Golden Arm*, *Last Exit*'s purpose is to assault the reader with graphic examples of the human potential for cruelty and depravity. Like Algren's work, it is also not essentially political. Selby created a jeremiad with which to warn of the dangers and distortions of a postwar world in which neither God nor love can exist, in which the female is hated, brutalized, and commodified.

In contrast, John Rechy's goal in *City of Night* is distinctly political, and the narrative strategy of his novel is not completely unlike that of Crane, Norris, and London. His narrator takes the middle-class, heterosexual reader on a tour of the hidden, nighttime world of the homosexual hustler, and the reformist emphasis in the novel is unmistakable. Rechy wants to convince the reader of the vulnerable humanity of the gay male and of the wrongness of discrimination against gays. But his narrator wants also to explore the roots and the full implications of his narcissism. This "youngman" is intent upon a full exploration of all the avenues of gay existence, largely as a means of exploring all the recesses of his own psyche. Consequently, the narrator's quest for self-awareness transcends the novel's reformist emphasis. It should be said that one contribution of both Selby and Rechy is to extend the concept of the exploited urban lumpenproletariat to include homosexuals, to define the lumpenproletariat in other than merely economic terms.

Joyce Carol Oates's *them* brings the sophisticated phase of naturalistic American inner-city fiction to its full maturity. Oates deliberately assumes the outsider narrative perspective of Crane, Norris, and London for the purpose of undercutting it through the "letters of Maureen Wendall." She uses these fictional letters of a fictional student as a device to expose the naïveté of the innocent stage of inner-city naturalism. She creates an assumed author, "Joyce Carol Oates," solely in order to shatter "Miss Oates's" smug assumption of middle-class privilege over "them," the poor-white inhabitants of Detroit's inner city. In adopting this metafictional approach, she "confesses" her inability to convey the "truth" about the lives of the

187

Wendalls and thus liberates herself to romanticize Jules Wendall. There is very little reformist emphasis in *them:* lives that cannot be accurately described by outsiders can hardly be saved through social reform. Of course, just as Oates hoped, after reading her novel, one does feel as familiar with the Wendalls as with Maggie, McTeague, and the inhabitants of London's East End.

During the past twenty-five years inner-city naturalism has not been a dominant motif in American fiction. The eclipse of this kind of fiction has resulted, in large part, from two factors: a retreat from mimesis in the American novels of the 1960s and 1970s as well as a conservative impulse that rejected identification with the economically dispossessed.

A representative example of American urban fiction during the 1960s and 1970s is Thomas Pynchon's *The Crying of Lot 49* (1966). Certainly, this fascinating work is based upon an assumed, and quite complex, brand of determinism; still, it can hardly be labeled naturalistic. For instance, there is the matter of names. Pynchon echoes, in a satiric manner, the modernist technique, as seen in such writers as Henry James and F. Scott Fitzgerald, of giving his characters symbolic names. One readily understands the metaphoric significance of Major Monarch and Dick Diver. In contrast, Pynchon's names—Oedipa Maas, Mucho Maas, Dr. Hilarius, Mike Fallopian, Genghis Cohen, Stanley Koteks—constitute an elaborate system of near-metaphors, false clues, and bawdy jokes which ultimately leads, like the novel's California freeways, nowhere in particular. Such metafictional play is inconsistent with, and would in fact undercut, the reformist thrust of naturalism.

The names are simply one aspect of Pynchon's retreat from mimesis. Ultimately, the reader cannot be certain what, if much of anything, truly happens in *The Crying of Lot 49.* For example, there are few more brilliant and frightening passages in modern American literature than the one detailing Oedipa's journey through a subterranean San Francisco, where she *believes* that she sees the acronym W.A.S.T.E. and the Tristero muted horn everywhere. But Oedipa herself struggles against the awareness that, in choosing to "project a world" in order to protect herself against the threat of madness,[3] she, in fact, may have imagined everything and seen nothing. The "world" she projects may be much of the novel itself. In contrast, while Selby's setting often becomes surrealistic in its excessive verbal and physical violence, the reader still accepts the suffering of Georgette, Tralala, and Harry Black as being based in fictional "reality."

Moreover, the source of the determinism in *The Crying of Lot 49* remains ambiguous literally until and beyond the novel's ending. It, in fact, may not be a conventional determinism at all but only an elaborate joke played by a *possibly* dead man. It certainly lacks a clear socioeconomic dimension. Pynchon's focus in not on the inner city but, rather, on the endlessly sprawling suburbia of southern California.

Some recent writers do remain committed to something of a naturalistic focus when writing about the city. For instance, James Baldwin, in his first novel, *Go Tell It on the Mountain*, and in such later works as *If Beale Street Could Talk* (1974) writes out of the same kind of reformist perspective as does Rechy in *City of Night*. In *Requiem for a Dream* (1978) Selby, utilizing a more conventional narrative mode than *Last Exit to Brooklyn*, graphically depicts the horrors of two kinds of addiction which destroy his lower-class characters. After experimenting with such metaphysical perspectives as the mock Gothic romance, Oates has returned, in recent works, to her early existential naturalism in *Because It Is Bitter, and Because It Is My Heart* (1990), a story of interracial attraction between two teenagers, and in *Foxfire* (1993), a fictional depiction of an urban female street gang.

Finally, and most impressively, there is William Kennedy, who, in *Ironweed* (1983), brings his own combination of naturalism, existentialism, and richly evocative prose to the story of Francis Phelan, who accidentally kills his infant son, Gerald, and then spends the rest of his life "on the bum," futilely attempting to flee his propensity to violence. The scenes in Kennedy's book of Francis and his beloved Helen struggling to survive, while homeless, the winter in Albany, New York, and of Francis and his dying friend Rudy Newton fleeing a vigilante attack on a hobo jungle recall the proletarian writing of Steinbeck and Algren. Still, Francis's worst enemy is his own internal self-hatred. *Ironweed* and, to a lesser degree, the subsequent volumes in Kennedy's "Albany cycle" represent a welcome return in the American novel to a mimetic exploration of the economically exploited in U.S. urban society.

An especially interesting phenomenon in recent American literature is the depiction by Native American writers of the reservation as a kind of inner city transposed to small town and even rural surroundings. Economic injustice, isolation, self-hatred, and the virtual destruction of their true culture haunt the characters in James Welch's *Winter in the Blood* (1974) and in Louise Erdrich's novels exploring the multigenerational interaction of the Morrissey and Kashpaw families, *Love Medicine* (1984, rev. 1993), *The Beet Queen* (1986), *Tracks* (1988), and *The Bingo Palace* (1994). It must be said, though, that Erdrich does not always use a traditionally mimetic mode and, especially in *Tracks*, has the unforgettable character Fleur Pillager embody the mysterious and even supernatural legacy of Native American culture.

My focus in this study has been on six earlier works that cumulatively reveal Stephen Crane's suppressed fat man, his nightmare projection and simultaneous dehumanization of the residents of the inner city, to be the very real and very human inhabitants of America's urban ghettos. They also reveal Crane's envisioned "monster" to be a projection of the Other, those repressed levels of the civilized, middle-class psyche which frighten and disturb through glimpses of imagined evil, criminality, and sexual depravity, while also tantalizing with images of freedom from social and sexual restraint.

Notes

1. June Howard, *Form and History in American Literary Naturalism* (Chapel Hill: University of North Carolina Press, 1985), 95–96.

2. Toni Morrison, *Playing in the Dark: Whiteness and the Literary Imagination* (Cambridge: Harvard University Press, 1992), 59.

3. Thomas Pynchon, *The Crying of Lot 49* (New York: Harper and Row Perennial Library, 1986), 82.

Bibliography

Aaron, Daniel. *Writers on the Left*. New York: Harcourt, Brace, and World, 1961.

Aldridge, John W. *Classics and Contemporaries*. Columbia: University of Missouri Press, 1992.

Algren, Nelson. *The Man with the Golden Arm*. New York: Doubleday, 1949.

Anderson, Alston, and Terry Southern. "Nelson Algren." *Paris Review* 11 (Winter 1955): 39–40.

Anderson, Sherwood. *Winesburg, Ohio*. New York: Penguin, 1976.

Barza, Steven. "Joyce Carol Oates: Naturalism and the Aberrant Response." *Studies in American Fiction* 7 (1979): 141–42.

Bell, Michael Davitt. *The Problem of American Realism: Studies in the Cultural History of a Literary Idea*. Chicago: University of Chicago Press, 1993.

Bender, Eileen Teper. *Joyce Carol Oates, Artist in Residence*. Bloomington: Indiana University Press, 1987.

Benfey, Christopher. *The Double Life of Stephen Crane*. New York: Knopf, 1992.

Brennan, Joseph X. "Ironic and Symbolic Structure in Crane's Maggie." In *Stephen Crane, Maggie: A Girl of the Streets*. Edited by Thomas A. Gullason, 173–84. New York: Norton, 1979.

Bryant, Jerry H. "The Violence of *Native Son*." *Southern Review* 17 (Spring 1981): 303–19.

Butler, Robert James. "The Function of Violence in Richard Wright's *Native Son*." *Black American Literature Forum* 20 (1986): 9–25.

———. "Wright's *Native Son* and Two Novels by Zola: A Comparative Study." *Black American Literature Forum* 18 (1984): 100–105.

Cady, Edwin. *Stephen Crane*. Boston: Twayne, 1962.

Cain, William E. "Presence and Power in *McTeague*." In *American Realism: New Essays*, edited by Eric Sundquist, 199–214. Baltimore: Johns Hopkins University Press, 1982.

Cappetti, Carla. *Writing Chicago: Modernism, Ethnography, and the Novel*. New York: Columbia University Press, 1993.

Céline, Louis-Ferdinand. *Journey to the End of the Night*. New York: New Directions, 1983.

Conder, John J. *Naturalism in American Fiction: The Classic Phase*. Lexington: University Press of Kentucky, 1984.

Cowley, Malcolm. *The Literary Situation*. New York: Viking, 1958.

Crane, Stephen. *Maggie: A Girl of the Streets* and *George's Mother*. New York: Fawcett, 1960.

———. *Maggie: A Girl of the Streets*. Edited by Thomas A. Gullason. New York: Norton, 1979.

Creighton, Joanne V. *Joyce Carol Oates*. Boston: Twayne, 1979.

Cunliffe, Marcus. "Stephen Crane and the American Background of *Maggie*." In *Stephen Crane, Maggie: A Girl of the Streets*. Edited by Thomas A. Gullason, 94–103. New York: Norton, 1979.

Dalton, Elizabeth. "Joyce Carol Oates: Violence in the Head." *Commentary* 49 (June 1970): 75–77.

Decurtis, Anthony. "The Process of Fictionalization in Joyce Carol Oates's *them*." *International Fiction Review* 6 (1979): 121–28.

Dillingham, William B. *Frank Norris: Instinct and Art*. Boston: Houghton Mifflin, 1969.

Donohue, H. E. F. *Conversations with Nelson Algren*. New York: Hill and Wang, 1964.

Drew, Bettina. *Nelson Algren: A Life on the Wild Side*. New York: Putnam's, 1989.

Du Bois, W. E. B. "Fifty Years After." *The Souls of Black Folk*. Greenwich, Conn: Fawcett, 1961.

Fabre, Michel. *The Unfinished Quest of Richard Wright*. New York: Morrow, 1973.

Fiedler, Leslie. "The Noble Savages of Skid Row." *Reporter* 15 (12 July 1956): 43–44.

———. *To the Gentiles*. New York: Stein and Day, 1972.

Folsom, Michael Brewster. "The Education of Michael Gold." In *Proletarian Writers of the Thirties*, edited by David Madden. Carbondale: Southern Illinois University Press, 1968.

Fossum, Robert H. "Only Control: The Novels of Joyce Carol Oates." In *Critical Essays on Joyce Carol Oates*, edited by Linda W. Wagner, 49–60. Boston: G. K. Hall, 1979.

Foucault, Michel. *Madness and Civilization: A History of Insanity in the Age of Reason*. Trans. Richard Howard. New York: Random House Vintage, 1988.

France, Alan W. "Misogyny and Appropriation in Wright's *Native Son*." *Modern Fiction Studies* 34 (Autumn 1988): 413–23.

French, Warren. *Frank Norris*. New Haven, Conn.: College and University Press, 1950.

Friedman, Ellen G. *Joyce Carol Oates*. New York: Frederick Ungar, 1980.

Gallagher, Kathleen. "Bigger's Great Leap to the Figurative." *CLA Journal* 27 (March 1984): 293–314.

Geismar, Maxwell. "Nelson Algren: The Iron Sanctuary." *American Moderns:*

Bibliography

From Rebellion to Conformity, 187–94. New York: Hill and Wang, 1958.

Gelfant, Blanche H. *The American City Novel*. Norman: University of Oklahoma Press, 1954.

Gibson, Donald B. *The Fiction of Stephen Crane*. Carbondale: Southern Illinois University Press, 1968.

Giles, James R. "Jack London 'Down and Out' in England: The Relevance of the Sociological Study *People of the Abyss* to London's Fiction." *Jack London Newsletter* 2 (September–December 1969): 79–83.

———. "Suffering, Transcendence, and Artistic Form." *Arizona Quarterly* 32 (Autumn 1976): 213–26.

Giles, James R., and Wanda H. Giles. "An Interview with John Rechy." *Chicago Review* 25 (1973): 19–31.

Gold, Michael. *Jews without Money*. New York: Carroll and Graf, 1984.

Graham, Don. *The Fiction of Frank Norris: The Aesthetic Context*. Columbia: University of Missouri Press, 1978.

———. "Naturalism in American Fiction: A Status Report." *Studies in the Novel* 10 (Spring 1982): 1–16.

Grant, Mary Kathryn. *The Tragic Vision of Joyce Carol Oates*. Durham, N.C.: Duke University Press, 1978.

Grmela, Joseph. "Some Problems of the Critical Reception of Stephen Crane's *Maggie: A Girl of the Streets*." *Brno Studies in English* 19 (1991): 149–55.

Gullason, Thomas A. "The Sources of Stephen Crane's *Maggie*." *Philological Quarterly* 38 (October 1959): 497–502.

Guttmann, Allen. *The Jewish Writer in America: Assimilation and the Crisis of Identity*. New York: Oxford University Press, 1971.

Hassan Ihab. *Radical Innocence: The Comtemporary American Novel*. Princeton, N.J.: Princeton University Press, 1961.

Hendin, Josephine. *Vulnerable People: A View of American Fiction since 1945*. Oxford: Oxford University Press, 1978.

Howard, June. *Form and History in American Literary Naturalism*. Chapel Hill: University of North Carolina Press, 1985.

Howe, Irving. "Black Boys and Native Sons." *A World More Attractive*, 98–122. New York: Horizon, 1963.

Hurm, Gerd. *Fragmented Urban Images: The American City in Modern Fiction from Stephen Crane to Thomas Pynchon*. New York: Peter Lang, 1991.

Johnson, Barbara. "The Re(a)d and the Black." In *Richard Wright's 'Native Son': Modern Critical Interpretations*, edited by Harold Bloom. New York: Chelsea House, 1988.

Johnson, Greg. *Understanding Joyce Carol Oates*. Columbia: University of South Carolina Press, 1987.

Joyce, Joyce Ann. "Style and Meaning in Richard Wright's *Native Son*." *Black American Literature Forum* 16 (Fall 1982): 112–15.

Katz, Joseph. "[Art and Compromise: The 1893 and 1896 *Maggie.*]" In *Stephen Crane, Maggie: A Girl of the Streets.* Edited by Thomas A. Gullason. New York: Norton, 1979.

Kennedy, James G. "The Content and Form of *Native Son.*" *College English* 34 (1972): 269–83.

Kingman, Russ. *A Pictorial Life of Jack London.* New York: Crown, 1979.

Kinnamon, Keneth. "*Native Son*: The Personal, Social, and Political Background." In *Critical Essays on Richard Wright,* edited by Yoshinobu Hakutani, 120–27. Boston: G. K. Hall, 1982.

Klein, Marcus. *Foreigners: The Making of American Literature, 1900–1940.* Chicago: University of Chicago Press, 1981.

Kuprin, Alexandre. *Yama, or the Pit.* New York: Modern Library, 1932.

Labor, Earle. *Jack London.* Boston: Twayne, 1974.

Lehan, Richard. "American Literary Naturalism: The French Connection." *Nineteenth-Century Fiction* 38 (March 1984): 529–57.

Leff, Leonard. "The Center of Violence in Joyce Carol Oates's *them.*" *Notes on Modern American Literature* 2 (1977): item 9.

Levenberg, Diane. "Three Jewish Writers and the Spirit of the Thirties: Michael Gold, Anzia Yezierska, and Henry Roth." *Book Forum* 6 (1982): 233–44.

London, Jack. *The People of the Abyss.* London: Arco Publications, Fitzroy Edition, 1963.

McElrath, Joseph R., Jr. *Frank Norris Revisited.* New York: Twayne, 1992.

Madison, Charles A. "Preface." In Jacob A. Riis, *How the Other Half Lives.* New York: Dover, 1971.

Magistrale, Tony. "From St. Petersburg to Chicago: Wright's Crime and Punishment." *Comparative Literature Studies* 23 (Spring 1986): 59–70.

Mellard, James M. *The Exploded Form: The Modernist Novel in America.* Urbana: University of Illinois Press, 1980.

Metcalf, Paul. "Herman and Hubert: The Odd Couple." *Review of Contemporary Fiction* 1 (Spring 1981): 364–69.

Michaels, Walter Benn. *The Gold Standard and the Logic of Naturalism.* Berkeley: University of California Press, 1987.

Mitchell, Lee Clark. *Determined Fictions: American Naturalism.* New York: Columbia University Press, 1989.

Morrison, Toni. *Playing in the Dark: Whiteness and the Literary Imagination.* Cambridge: Harvard University Press, 1992.

Mottram, Eric. "Free like the Rest of Us: Violation and Despair in Hubert Selby's Novels." *Review of Contemporary Fiction* 1 (Spring 1981): 353–63.

Nagel, James. "Images of 'Vision' in *Native Son.*" In *Critical Essays on Richard Wright,* edited by Yoshinobu Hakutani, 151–58. Boston: G. K. Hall, 1982.

Nilsen, Helge Norman. "The Evils of Poverty: Mike Gold's *Jews without Money.*" *Anglo-American Studies* 4 (April 1984): 45–50.

Norris, Frank. *McTeague*. New York: Holt, Rinehart, and Winston, 1950.

———. "Zola as a Romantic Writer." In *The Literary Criticism of Frank Norris*, edited by Donald Pizer. Austin: University of Texas Press, 1964.

Oates, Joyce Carol. *The Edge of Impossibility: Tragic Forms in Literature*. New York: Vanguard, 1972.

———. "The Nightmare of Naturalism: Harriette Arnow's 'The Dollmaker.'" *New Heaven, New Earth: The Visionary Experience in Literature*, 97–110. New York: Vanguard, 1974.

———. *them*. Greenwich, Conn.: Fawcett, 1970.

O'Brien, John T. "Interview with Hubert Selby, Jr." *Review of Contemporary Fiction* 10 (Spring 1981): 315–35.

———. "The Materials of Art in Hubert Selby." *Review of Contemporary Fiction* 10 (Spring 1981): 376–79.

Panttaja, Elisabeth. "Interpreting *Maggie*." Paper presented at the 1989 Modern Language Association national convention, Washington, D.C., December 1989.

Parker, Hershel, and Brian Higgins. "Maggie's 'Last Night': Authorial Design and Editorial Patching." In *Stephen Crane, Maggie: A Girl of the Streets*. Edited by Thomas A. Gullason, 234–45. New York: Norton, 1979.

Peavy, Charles D. "The Sin of Pride and Selby's *Last Exit to Brooklyn*." *Critique* 2 (1969): 35–39.

Petite, Joseph. "'Out of the Machine': Joyce Carol Oates and the Liberation of Woman." *Kansas Quarterly* 9 (1974): 218–26.

Pinsker, Sanford. "The Blue Collar Apocalypse, or Detroit Bridge's Falling Down: Joyce Carol Oates's *them*." *Descant* 23 (1979): 35–47.

———. "Joyce Carol Oates and the New Naturalism." *Southern Review* 15 (1979): 52–63.

Pizer, Donald. "Contemporary Literary Naturalism." *The Theory and Practice of American Literary Naturalism: Selected Essays and Reviews*, 167–86. Carbondale: Southern Illinois University Press, 1993.

———. "Frank Norris's Definition of Naturalism." *Realism and Naturalism in Nineteenth-Century American Literature*, 107–11. Carbondale: Southern Illinois University Press, 1984.

———. "Late Nineteenth-Century American Naturalism." *Realism and Naturalism in Nineteenth-Century American Literature*, 9–30. Carbondale: Southern Illinois University Press, 1984.

———. "Stephen Crane's *Maggie* and American Naturalism." *Criticism* 7 (Spring 1965): 168–75.

———. *Twentieth-Century American Literary Naturalism: An Interpretation*. Carbondale: Southern Illinois University Press, 1982.

Podhoretz, Norman. "The Man with the Golden Beef." *New Yorker* 32, 2 June 1956, 132, 134, 137–39.

Thomas Pynchon. *The Crying of Lot 49.* New York: Harper and Row Perennial Edition, 1986.

Rechy, John. *City of Night.* New York: Grove Press, 1963.

———. "On Being a Grove Press Author." *Review of Contemporary Fiction* 10 (Fall 1990): 137–42.

Reilly, John M. "Criticism of Ethnic Literature: Seeing the Whole Story." *MELUS* 5 (1978): 2–13.

———. "Giving Bigger a Voice: The Politics of Narrative in *Native Son.*" In *New Essays on Richard Wright*, edited by Keneth Kinnamon, 35–62. Cambridge: Cambridge University Press, 1990.

Rideout, Walter B. *The Radical Novel in the United States, 1900–1954.* Cambridge: Harvard University Press, 1956.

Riis, Jacob A. *How the Other Half Lives.* New York: Dover, 1971.

Rubin, Steven J. "Richard Wright and Albert Camus: The Literature of Revolt." *International Fiction Review* 8 (Winter 1981): 12–16.

Satterfield, Ben. "John Rechy's Tormented World." *Southwest Review* 67 (Winter 1982): 78–85.

Scott, Nathan A., Jr. "The Dark and Haunted Tower of Richard Wright." In *Richard Wright: A Collection of Critical Essays*, edited by Richard Macksey and Frank E. Moorer, 149–62. Englewood Cliffs, N.J.: Doubleday, 1984.

Selby, Hubert, Jr. *Last Exit to Brooklyn.* New York: Grove Press, 1965.

Sherman, Bernard. *The Invention of the Jew: Jewish-American Education Novels (1916–1964).* New York: Thomas Yoseloff, 1969.

Sjoberg, Leif. "An Interview with Joyce Carol Oates." *Contemporary Literature* 23 (Summer 1982): 267–84.

Sorrentino, Gilbert. "The Art of Hubert Selby." *Review of Contemporary Fiction* 1 (Spring 1981): 335–46.

Stallman, R. W. *Stephen Crane: A Biography.* New York: George Braziller, 1968.

Stephens, Michael. "Hubert Selby, Jr.: The Poet of Prose Masters." *Review of Contemporary Fiction* 1 (Spring 1981): 389–97.

Swados, Harvey, ed. *Years of Conscience: The Muckrakers.* Cleveland: World, 1962.

Tanner, Laura E. "Uncovering the Magical Discourse of Language: The Narrative Presence in Richard Wright's *Native Son.*" *Texas Studies in Language and Literature* 29 (Winter 1987): 412–31.

Trachtenberg, Alan. "Experiments in Another Country: Stephen Crane's City Sketches." In *American Realism: New Essays*, edited by Eric J. Sundquist, 138–54. Baltimore: Johns Hopkins University Press, 1982.

Tremaine, Louis. "The Dissociated Sensibility of Bigger Thomas in Wright's *Native Son.*" *Studies in American Fiction* 14 (Spring 1986): 62–86.

Tuerk, Richard. "*Jews without Money* as a Work of Art." *Studies in American Jewish Literature* 7 (Spring 1988): 67–79.

Vonnegut, Kurt, Jr. "Introduction." In *Nelson Algren, Never Come Morning*, xvii–xx.

New York: Four Walls Eight Windows Press, 1987.

Walcutt, Charles Child. *American Literary Naturalism: A Divided Stream.* Minneapolis: University of Minnesota Press, 1956.

Waller, G. F. *Dreaming America: Obsession and Transcendence in the Fiction of Joyce Carol Oates.* Baton Rouge: Louisiana State University Press, 1979.

Wertime, Richard A. "Psychic Vengeance in *Last Exit to Brooklyn.*" *Literature and Psychology* 24 (1974): 153–66.

Wixson, Douglas. *Worker-Writer in America: Jack Conroy and the Tradition of Midwestern Literary Radicalism, 1898–1990.* Urbana: University of Illinois Press, 1994.

Wright, Richard. *Native Son.* New York: Harper and Row Perennial Edition, 1987.

———. *Native Son.* In *Richard Wright, Early Works.* Edited by Arnold Rampersad. New York: Library of America, 1991.

Index